a life in
loose strides

Also by Colin Hogg

Living with Summer (1983)

Angel Gear: On the Road with Sam Hunt (1989)

Is That an Affair on Your Mind or Are You Just Glad to See Me? (1997)

The Awful Truth: An Unauthorised Autobiography (1998)

a life in loose strides

THE STORY OF

BARRY CRUMP

COLIN HOGG

Hodder Moa Beckett

For Philippa and Michelle

ISBN 1-86958-822-3
© 2000 In the original text — Colin Hogg

© 2000 Design and format – Hodder Moa Beckett Publishers Limited

Published by Hodder Moa Beckett Publishers Limited
[a member of the Hodder Headline Group],
4 Whetu Place, Mairangi Bay, Auckland, New Zealand

Produced and designed by Hodder Moa Beckett Publishers Limited

Cover photograph — courtesy of Ray Richards

Printed by Publishing Press, Auckland, New Zealand
Film by Microdot, Auckland, New Zealand

contents

acknowledgements

The genesis of this biography goes back to the late 1980s when, after completing a book about the poet Sam Hunt, I was leaned on by my then publisher, Andrew Campbell, to write one about Barry Crump. Working with Sam had been a life-altering experience and I had a feeling at the time that Crump would just about finish me off.

So I demurred, making excuses about not wanting to do two major blokes in a row, and went off to reconnect with my feminine side.

Then in the early 1990s, some years before Crump's death, I travelled down the country to meet and interview him at his home in Central Otago for what turned out to be a lengthy article for a magazine I was editing at the time. Taking advantage of the fact that Crump seemed a little short of the readies, I also persuaded him to write a monthly column for the same magazine. I left the magazine a few years later and Crump left too.

After he died, my magazine article was used as an introductory piece in a book published by Hodder Moa Beckett called *A Tribute to Crumpy*. Then in 1998, I was asked by Hodders to write the text for *Back Down the Track*, a collection of Crump's rustic photographs. Shortly after, I started work helping shape and write a television documentary for Greenstone Pictures called *Crump*, which screened in 1999.

So when the idea of a biography came up again, I felt fairly fully armed with Crump. Spilling over, in fact. I'd moved from the slightly awestruck tone of that magazine article to the bleaker approach of the documentary. Along the way I've interviewed quite a crowd of people, among them Tina Lester, Martin Crump, Shirley Tucker, George Johnston, Fleur Adcock, Peter Crump, Jack Lasenby, Alan Seay, Robin Lee Robinson, Ray Richards, Alex Fry, Craig Howan, Maggie Crump, Kevin Ireland, Mike Bennett, Alex and Lorna King, Jean Watson, Sam Hunt, Lyall Crump and Vanda Lyndon.

There are other stories of Barry Crump that can be traced through newspaper and magazine articles and television interviews. And through letters. And through his own evasive, friendless autobiography, *The Life and Times of a Good Keen Man*.

And there's a story of Barry Crump in his books, which represent a kind of living as he may have wanted it. Those are the ingredients. The rest just involved stirring.

introduction

Barry Crump's life, to my mind, is like one of those old cautionary folk songs. This book is just my version. It's not everything. I'm not sure anyone could track down the everything of the life of Crump.

This book is based on interviews, overheard conversations, overhead guidance, underworld connections and various underhand methods. Crump wouldn't have approved of anyone writing a book about him, but he might have approved of the methods.

His life was the best story Crump ever wrote and he instinctively knew that from his first book, the legendary *A Good Keen Man*. With a twist of circumstance, Crump could have been a cult leader, a killer, a faith-healer or a politician. But instead he wrote stories and, for a while back there, he entranced a whole country and helped make it possible for Fred Dagg and Billy T James and Alan Duff and anyone else who ever dared to talk to us in our own voice.

I hope this book helps to remind us that Barry Crump's greatest, most lasting legacy are his books, leaping straight out of his life, some of them still ringing down the years, vivid with the detail and rough humour of another time, some of them rendered a little more recumbent by the passing years and some never that good in the first place. But he wrote so many of them, that's hardly surprising. And he sold more than a million copies of his books, often to the sorts of people who never previously have bothered much with reading. His lifestyle challenged the likes of William Burroughs and Keith Richards for excess and waywardness. He was a bastard and he was some sort of saint.

Colin Hogg

'...there's only one story.

Everyone's only got one yarn really,

but you can put so many

slants and angles on it...'

Barry Crump

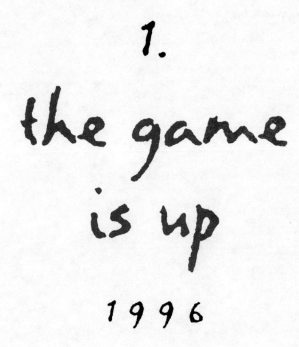

1.

the game
is up

1996

He fences. Every day he hauls his aching bones out of bed, pulls on his strides and his Swanndri and goes out and fences like his life depends on it, like he's trying to catch a taste of his own past, when he fenced like a Viking. But he's past 60 now and, Christ, he aches like he's never ached before. When he breathes, sometimes it's like pulling air through tar and there are terrible, unpredictable stabs of pain to his heart.

But he rolls a fag and he gets out there on the side of that hill. And he works while he waits for redemption…

He's longing to shoot through again. And this time there's only one place left to shoot through to.

He's travelled thousands of miles trying to slip his skin, but of course he never can. Everyone in his tiny country knows him. At most, they want a piece of him, something to remember, something to blow up and boast about. At least, they watch him while they make up their silent minds. It sometimes gets to where he can't stand it.

Everything is everything it always was, only less so. There's a new pub to sit in, a bit like the old pubs. The usual bullshit. But the game is up. Truth is, it was up almost as soon as it began.

§

2.
a ghost
who walks
1935

They call him Barry John Crump at his birth, on 15 May 1935, in his grandmother's bedroom in Papatoetoe, South Auckland. Barry John is the second son of Wally and Lily-of-the-Valley Crump. Bill is the oldest and other children will follow — Colin, Shirley, Carol and Peter. It's a shit of a life to be born into.

'How did you come to meet up with the old man, Mum?' us kids asked her one day. She told us, "I was walking along a lane where we were living and he cantered along on a mare he was breaking in and scooped me up and rode off with me." And knowing our father, that'd be about right.'

Wally Crump doesn't take no for an answer. In fact he doesn't care for answers at all. He has an anger that leaps into his big hands like lightning and he takes no responsibility for it. Why should he? He works hard and those hands that hold a team of horses can as easily break bones, splash his wife's blood across the hallway or take a child to the edge of death.

The best times are when Wally is away. He's a dedicated gambler — especially the horses — and he shoots through, sometimes for a few days, to attend race meetings. The long Easter weekends are sacred for reasons other than being a religious holiday. It is their special time when the old man is away chasing the horses. They can relax. They can briefly be themselves with just Mum telling her stories and the kids getting up to all sorts of stuff they shouldn't. Life takes on a whole new meaning for a few days. They feel so free, so full of joy it seems like a sin, having a few days where they know no one is going to be trapped in the old man's big hands and beaten, not having to worry about Mum. These are moments to be treasured. Bubbles of bright air in a dark, fathomless sea.

No one can explain Wally, least of all Wally himself. They don't know why he hates them the way he does, but he'll hate them as naturally as he looks to the sky every morning. It's in his heart to hate them and resent them and he seems to hate and resent sweet-faced little Barry most of all. Barry stands out from the others — a special little boy, a dreamer with something of his mother's gentle nature. Lily's mother, Alice Hendery, was an artist who was brought up in England and her education continued well into her twenties. She fell in love with with an academic, 'a dux of Edinburgh University' in science and mathematics. Two more ill-equipped people to decide to come out and be pioneers in New Zealand would be hard to find. But they did cross the world to the edge of civilisation and they probably shouldn't have.

They didn't have what it takes to travel to a wild new faraway place and break in the land and turn it into a good life. Life was very hard for them. There were six in the family and they lost some children. But the genetic mix of her creative talent and his academic abilities created some unusual people among the children who did manage to survive. There were some who could do things very readily with their hands and there were the ones who were particularly bright academically. There were the arty types and the ones who loved to read and write.

They were deeply, slightly crazily, religious too. Barry's grandmother speaks in tongues, in church and round the house. She paints, specialising in portraits of Jesus Christ. The eyes look like they're alive to her grandchildren.

But Wally is the other side of the equation to the sweet, God-fearing Lily. His father was an Australian bushman and Wally worked a lot with horses. It is his forte. He trained trotting horses at one point, and was a blacksmith, a farrier. His family are loveable enough, apparently, church-going Methodists. But the Lord drives a dark spike into Wally when he makes him. Lily is living in Ararimu when he comes by on his horse. He's a good-looking young man and she is a lovely young woman, full of promise. But the promise is thrown on hard, unforgiving soil. She marries Wally swiftly and the babies start coming.

Lily likes to write. She makes up poetry off the top of her head and the kids sit enthralled. She's a fine sewer and works hard to make sure her children are dressed well with the limited means at her disposal. Later, she goes out to work, which is unusual for a married woman in these times, to buy the few extras she's allowed.

They are of the generation of hard New Zealanders, caught between brutal old colonial ways and something newer and even harder. The country has been scorched dry by the Great Depression and country folk like the Crumps who don't own land have a hard time of it. Lily does all the washing for her ever-growing, ever-dirty family by hand, boiling it in a copper. She works her hands to the bone and she sometimes wonders why the Lord has brought her children into this awful life and to this dreadful distant, moody, abusive husband.

Lily has a soft, forgiving nature, loves her children dearly and does her best to protect them. She is a very religious woman and this is her weakness. She prays that things will be different, but she does nothing, tells no one, suffers in silence. She's well-versed in the Bible and God looms large in her life, excusing, helping her to paint over the terrible cracks with prayers.

Wally is Jekyll and Hyde. He can be sociable enough. He'll help a neighbour. He's strong and fit and he's a good shot with a rifle. He can even be quite the entertainer and plays the piano, but at heart he's a hard man. He doesn't believe much in possessions and he has never been interested in owning a place. The family always rents. At one point, Lily works and saves up half the deposit needed to buy the State house they're living in by then and puts it to Wally. 'I've saved up half, why don't you put in the other half and we'll buy the house.' But Wally's not interested. He doesn't want to have to paint the place and worry about the upkeep.

He's a big man, tall and with those huge hands. If he gets hold of you, he's got a powerful grip. And once he's got you, there's worse to come. And when you're on the ground, he'll kick you, that angry gumboot of his smashing its rubbery smell and its ugly memory into Barry's head.

There is another sort of violence. He doesn't call any of his children by their given names. No one ever hears him call Barry anything other than 'Dopey', unless there are visitors, and there aren't often visitors. All the children have their labels. The Wally who seems a hard worker, a good enough man to his neighbours, wears another face when he takes his family inside and closes the door.

Now he's a man who labels one of his daughters 'Bitch'. Now he's the sort of father who knocks Barry to the floor and stands on his neck until he stops breathing. When Wally finally relents, lifts his great stinking foot and Barry gets his breath back, there is a sock print left, livid, on his neck.

It seems that, to Wally, the children have no worth, barely deserve to live. Barry is begrudged the very air he breathes. The only life lesson his father teaches him is that he should have no sense of self-worth whatsoever. Wally teaches him from day one that he is useless … dopey, worthless. There is never an occasion when his father offers him a word of comfort or encouragement, tells him he's done a good job.

Wally sometimes seems to be trying to kill his kids. When he is about eight, Barry is sent into a paddock by his father to break up two bulls that are fighting. They're big brutes, one has lost its horn and there's blood everywhere. The animals are out of their minds, totally enraged and Wally sends little Barry in with a stick to separate them, knowing full well that they might kill the boy. But, already made fearless through fear of the old man, Barry manages to get them apart.

And because he has been taught so callously and constantly that he is useless, Barry learns to take risks with his life. Though, because he feels that he has no worth, they aren't risks to him. And Wally is a powerful teacher. His attitude is a constant. He's not a drinker, so there's none of that usual stuff to blame his behaviour on. He just plain hates his children and, perhaps because of the spark Barry has, Wally hates his second son the most.

Barry is beaten unmercifully, even when there doesn't seem to be a reason. There are times Barry is beaten to the very edge of his existence — literally flogged by his father until he can no longer move. Wally walks away and leaves Barry lying there. Then, some time during the night, Barry drags himself under the house where sister Shirley finds him. For three or four days she takes him food until he's strong enough to come out and rejoin the family like nothing had ever happened. And wait and watch out for the next time. It was always round the corner.

Once, when the family is having a meal at the table, Barry reaches across and accidentally knocks the teapot over, burning sister Carol. Wally leaps to his feet, grabs Barry with those huge hands and drags the boy to the bathroom where he holds his head under the hot tap. The children live in total fear. They never come home from school and open the door feeling sure about what they'll find. No one escapes. Once, there is so much blood down the hall and into one of the rooms, they think this time he's killed Lily.

Wally's vile temper extends to the livestock as well. He'll throw buckets of boiling water over the backs of cows that have done something to annoy him in the cowshed during milking. Once Barry is gently coaxing a calf to take milk from a bucket, feeding it drops from his finger and then trying to lower its head into the bucket. But it isn't learning fast enough for Wally who gives it a terrible boot in the head and its lower jaw slides, broken, out from under the top jaw. Then he gives it a whack on the head with a hammer and throws its twitching corpse away. He is unbelievable.

Of course, some of the wider family have a fair idea about what's going on and the neighbours must know bits and pieces of the life being lived next door. But people mind their own business, the Crumps are always moving house and their houses are often out of eye and earshot of the nearest neighbour and there's no telephone. There are few books or toys and a lot of hand-me-downs. In the early days, the Crump kids are reasonable achievers at school, but as they grow older the responsibilities of more learning, more studying and having to have a uniform make it hopeless.

They never have the right gear. Barry goes to school and is caned for not having the right uniform or is in trouble for not having done his homework. But the Crump kids never have what they need to do homework, especially when their father straight-out forbids them to do it. Wally won't let them waste power by having a light on to do their school work on winter nights. And they're always moving. Barry goes to more than a dozen schools. But he is a reader when he can lay his hands on a book. All the Crump kids love books, though they don't have many of them.

But the Crump kids always have each other, even if they don't talk about it. Many times, one takes one of the old man's floggings for someone else if they think the other has copped too much of a beating already. And they always worry about their mother's safety. The three oldest boys even hatch a plot to kill Wally ... to lure him outside and put a bullet through him. But it comes to nothing.

Wally will haunt Barry for the rest of his life — a ghost who will even walk in his writing.

Years ago, during the Depression, when I was only six years old, my father got a job as coalminer and we went to live in a remote mining settlement on the West Coast.

The owner of the mine was a great bully of a man called Big Nudd. He was huge and powerful and he had the whole district in a state of confusion and fear. He rode up and down the muddy bush roads on a big flat-decked dray which was drawn by two nervous, ill-treated horses. We soon learned that Big Nudd would give a man a job and a house to live in, and then visit his wife and family while he was down in the mine. I don't think he actually got up to any real physical mischief, but he seemed to enjoy terrorising the defenceless women and children. The approach of the big dray, rumbling along the road on its iron wheels, would send everyone scurrying apprehensively for cover inside their houses.

Many of the women were too afraid for their husbands, themselves, or just the jobs, to tell their husbands what was going on while they were underground. But such conditions cannot be kept secret for long. Husbands became suspicious. Homes broke up. Occasionally a desperate father or husband would try to fight Big Nudd, but they always ended up injured and jobless for their pains, while their wives and families would have to find somewhere to live and something to eat for themselves until they'd recovered.

For some reason Big Nudd never bothered my mother or me, and I remember Mother saying once that Father must have had some kind of arrangement with him.

But my father would refuse to discuss it whenever she introduced the subject.

This was the situation in the settlement for several months after we arrived there. Father seemed content enough to simply have sufficient money coming in to keep us going until the Depression ended. None of us could afford to move on to another place, and Big Nudd, in his brutish way, took advantage of the situation at every opportunity. I think he must have enjoyed the hold he had over the people who were forced by circumstances to work for him.

Life went on in the little settlement with a strange atmosphere of waiting; waiting for some relief from the financial rigours of the Depression, from the constant striving to keep enough food in the houses to feed the people, and from the persecutions of Big Nudd. Then relief from one of those things came in a most unexpected way.

The people of the settlement had organised a dance to celebrate the wedding of a popular young man who was bringing his bride back from one of the large towns on the Coast. Straight after the service he was to put his bride on the bus and return with her to the settlement, where he had a job and a house to live in. About five miles from the village was a hall, where they were to stop for the usual celebration. The bus would then go into the settlement to collect all those who didn't have cars and return with them to the hall. The bus would collect them from the hall at midnight and take them back to the village.

All these arrangements were made as discreetly as possible, for fear that Big Nudd would come to hear of the function, which he would have taken great delight in crashing in on and breaking up, either by getting drunk and smashing things or by simply being there.

We drove to the hall in our car and arrived early to help with the supper and the organising of things. By the time the bus with the rest of the people arrived and had greeted and toasted the newly-weds, it was getting dark. At eight o'clock I was put to bed on the back seat of the car, wrapped warmly in blankets, as I usually was on these occasions.

I used to enjoy sleeping in the car at parties and things. I could either sit up peeping at the people and lights, or lie there listening to the singing and voices until I went to sleep. It was very exciting and my parents were always close by so I was never afraid.

On this night I knelt up in my blankets with my chin on the ledge of the car door, watching the funny shadows of the people as they passed through the band of light coming from the hall doorway, which cut across the stony area in front of the building, slicing cars and trees right in half.

It must have been about half past nine in the evening and the people were all inside the hall, dancing and laughing and drinking toasts, when Big Nudd's dray came trundling up out of the darkness, its iron-shod wheels crackling on the stones as it passed through my patch of light, making a huge shadow across the ground and parked cars, with Big Nudd hunched like a great motionless bear with the reins slack in the lumpy silhouette of his hands. The strange contraption passed through the light and stopped with a growl on the far side. I could just see the end of the dray and one big spoked wheel at the edge of the light. I remember wondering if the horses could see me from out there in the dark if they looked.

Big Nudd scraped and creaked off the dray and clumped in his big boots into the light towards the hall doorway, almost shutting off the light completely for a moment as he passed through the door and disappeared inside. The noisy laughter stopped suddenly, and then slowly picked up again with a lower, slower sound to it.

Then I heard a voice, raised indignantly, shout, 'Private function!' A roar from Big Nudd and then a bump and a shriek of screams from the women that faded quickly to indignant murmuring.

After a while the music started up again in a half-hearted kind of way, and there was nothing much to see for a long time. Once my mother came out to see if I was all right, and, as usual, I ducked into my sleeping position and pretended to be asleep. When she had gone I lay there listening. I heard some men walk out past the car towards the grass and didn't look because I was a young lady. I heard one of them say,

'...just walked in and blew his nose on her veil.'

And another said:

'There'll be trouble here tonight, you mark my words. I'm going to round up my wife and kids and get off home before he gets any more of that wine and beer under his belt.'

'What about the rest of us?' asked another. 'Most of us have to wait for the bus.'

'Someone'll kill him one of these days,' said another man.

The men then went back into the hall, taking their voices with them.

I slept a little after that and only half-woke every now and again when an uproar started in the hall, or when my mother or father came out to see if I was all right. Then I heard something I didn't recognise, but it woke me instantly. I rose up to peek carefully over the car door.

The hunched figure of Big Nudd wavered drunkenly along the wall to one side of the hall doorway, his monstrous black shadow sliding back and forth in and out of the darkness. As I watched he took a jerky step forward and put one arm out to lean on the wall. Then he turned towards me and raised one hand to wipe his mouth as though he was going to eat it like a big toffee apple. He began to stumble and grope his way towards the car, grunting and spitting.

I was terrified, but I kept watching as he came right up to the car. Just as he was about to crash the whole car, with me in it, to pieces, he veered past. I heard the faint rasp of his hand on the bodywork and felt the car sway ever so slightly as he leaned on it in passing. The sound of his boots, scuffling erratically on the gravel, stopped, and then scuffled on into the darkness.

a ghost who walks

Suddenly I heard the raised voice of my mother and saw the people crowded silently in the doorway of the hall. This silence was what had awakened me. There was a slight commotion as my mother was bustled protesting into the hall, attended by several comforting women.

Big Nudd appeared, stumbling weakly along at the edge of the light towards the dray. He found it and crawled on to the tray, for all the world like a big pup trying to climb steps. He crawled along the dray until only his legs and one arm could be seen in the light. Then he lay still and in a few seconds he began to snore huge snores.

Somebody at the hall doorway said in a loud voice:

'It's all right now, he's out cold. I've seen him like this before. He won't wake up for hours.'

'Not surprising, with all he's drunk. It's a wonder he doesn't kill himself,' said someone else.

'It's a *pity* he doesn't kill himself,' said a woman.

'Okay now, back to the party everybody,' called somebody importantly.

And people began to drift back into the hall. My mother and father both hurried out towards the car and I ducked under my blankets and went to sleep while my mother tucked me in and shushed my father not to make a noise and wake me. When they went back into the hall I sat up and kneeled, looking at Big Nudd's half-lit shape lying out there on the cold hard dray.

It seemed like hours that I sat there, staring at him, watching the light ebb and flow across a square bulge in his hip pocket as he breathed his great beery snores. The noise inside the hall rose up in laughter and shouts and the thumping rhythm of accordion and piano. There was a lot of drinking, I could tell by the sound of the bursts of laughter that poured from the hall every now and then. Big Nudd could hear none of this.

Suddenly there was a figure standing in the dark beside Big Nudd's dray. In the shadows just beyond the light a shoulder, half-lit. I thought Big Nudd was going to be robbed, but the shadowy figure began to struggle with his shoulders, as though he was going to wake him up and invite him into the warm hall before he caught cold. The strange tussle went on for some time, and then there was a slight thump and a halting snort in Big Nudd's snoring, and suddenly his face appeared upside down, framed in the light between two of the big wheel-spokes.

I was first surprised and then frightened as the figure in the darkness bent forward momentarily into the light. It was my father.

I must admit that I was only frightened to see one of my own parents so close to someone like Big Nudd, whom everybody was so afraid of. My father withdrew into the darkness and even the glow of his white shirt was no longer visible. Only Big Nudd's huge face, illuminated between the spokes.

I remember wondering why my father had bothered to touch him in that strange way, and how he could be lying with his face upside down like that with his jaw hanging open upwards. In fact I lay back across the car seat to try it for myself.

When I looked back towards the dray where these strange things had taken place, I heard the shuffle and creak of Big Nudd's horses beyond the light in the darkness. Suddenly a horse snickered and shuddered in its harness, with several quick nervous stamps of hooves, and Big Nudd's face was suddenly snatched out of sight and carried away on a plunging rattle of sound that receded into the cold blackness of the night, along the rough mill-road that joined the main road at the hall and had fallen into disuse since the Depression had closed the mill.

Although my memory of all this is very clear, I did not then realise the implications of what I had witnessed. The sounds of Big Nudd's dray had scarcely rumbled away into silence when I saw a figure, my father, move mothlike through the light from a window down the side of the hall towards the rear door.

After what seemed like a long time, a man came out of the hall, looked around, and then began to move back inside.

'I thought I heard a noise out there,' he said to someone just inside the door.

'I'm sure I did,' said another man, pushing past him.

Suddenly there were people everywhere, milling in the light and demanding to know what was going on.

'It sounded like horses,' said a lady.

'Hey! Big Nudd's wagon has gone', called a man from over where it had been.

'His horses must have bolted with him. He was in no condition to drive them away.'

'Is that kid all right?' asked my father, pushing his way through the crowd towards the car.

I got quickly into my sleeping position and lay listening, and wondering.

'She's okay,' said a voice near the car. But my father and mother both came to make sure.

'Better make sure that Big Nudd's not hanging around somewhere,' warned a voice. 'He'll be in an ugly mood by now if he is.'

'He might have woken up and just gone off home,' suggested my mother, moving away from the car.

'What about all the noise we heard? It sounded as though his wagon was out of control.'

'We'd better have a look,' said one of the main men. 'He was pretty drunk, and those horses of his are skittery enough to have bolted with him.'

Nobody was very concerned about Big Nudd really, and nobody could blame them, but they brought lights and some of the men moved off to look for him, reluctant to bother but brave in a group. I sat up as my mother opened the door of the car and told me we were leaving. My father said goodbyes to some friends who had to wait for the bus at midnight, and we drove away, leaving people standing in little groups outside the hall, with glowing cigarettes and getting ready to leave.

We weren't even there when they brought Big Nudd's almost headless body in and laid it in a corner of the hall under a blanket. And nobody even asked me if I'd heard or seen anything. Never a whisper of suspicion about the way Big Nudd died. It was put down to a simple accident and forgotten about as quickly as possible in the relief everybody felt at his passing. As far as most of them were concerned it was a matter of him having received his just deserts.

(**from** 'His Just Deserts' **in** *Warm Beer and Other Stories*, **1969**)

§

3.
a strange kid

1945

The boys are worked hard, especially Bill and Barry. When other little boys are tucked, cosy, in their beds on frosty mornings, the Crump boys are out in their bare feet bringing the cows in for milking, standing in cowpats for the warmth. Then coming in for breakfast and a long walk to catch the bus to school. After school, they'll be home starving, to do the same work all over again. There is little energy left for school.

'Barely average,' Barry's teachers write on his school reports. He flits from school to school, 16 in all, while his father flits about as a sharemilker, from farm to farm, house to house.

Barry is almost totally disinterested in his studies, an attitude that causes him a lot of trouble with teachers who find him hard to handle. Barry finds himself hard to handle.

'I don't fail many of my exams, but I think that's only because the teachers are afraid to keep me in their class another year. Even though I'm young, I know I'm a strange kid, different from the others. I have my fair share of friends, but I don't keep them for long because we're not really allowed to take friends home and, anyway, we're always shifting to another school, another and yet another.'

Barry can be his own worst enemy at school anyway. A teacher will tell him to pull up his saggy socks and put his cap on and he'll bung his cap in his back pocket, push his socks even lower and wander around until he's hauled off for a strapping. One day he comes home after a thrashing feeling a bit sorry for himself. 'What the hell's wrong with you,' shouts the old man. And when Barry tells him the teacher gave him six straps and it's still hurting a bit, Wally drags him off and gives him six more. 'No teacher knows how to flog a man properly' is the explanation.

Barry wants to fit in and be a good pupil in the early days, but he's convinced himself he isn't capable of learning, a conviction most of his teachers share. Then one day, when he's at a school at Papakura, the class is given an essay to write at home. Barry goes home a worried boy and talks his mother into writing it for him.

'The teacher accepts it. It was okay and I can see he's pleased and real surprised that at last I've shown some ability at something.' Then the class is told to write another essay — this time about rabbits. 'Now rabbits is something I know something about. I've done a fair bit of rabbiting with Dad and I'm familiar with the subject, so I write this one myself.'

'The teacher feels my story's really got something, that it's one of the best in the class, but while the subject matter is all there, it's badly written.' The teacher tells Barry to take a second shot at his rabbit essay and the rewritten work pleases the teacher. 'It gives me confidence. I've gotten all the way to high school without ever getting anything right and now I've staggered the bastards. I know words.'

But the big word for Barry's childhood is lonely. He likes sport, but to his frustration finds he's not much good at games. It adds to his feeling that he's different, that he's stuck on the outside looking in. It makes him feel as if he's failed at something and not as good as everyone else. It's as if they know something he doesn't. 'When I'm older I'll find out that Mum and Dad had been celebrating my birthday a few days before it was actually due. How could they forget the date of my birthday? I feel like I can't trust anything and I wonder what's wrong with me. I seem to be apart from other people, even my brothers and sisters. I feel like some sort of freak.'

Barry's feelings of rejection intensify during school holidays when his father lends him to an uncle and aunt to help with the milking. The Crump kids are farmed out to relations regularly, never knowing if the old man will even let them ever go back home again. They worry for the ones left at home, about their mother. It's another extension of not being wanted.

As the boys grow older, the pressure comes on for them to get out. They're getting bigger and stronger, becoming a threat. They aren't going to sit back and let the younger ones suffer the sort of foul treatment from the old man that they did. They have no option but to go.

After leaving school at 14, Barry vows to make a new life for himself and, although his last school refuses to give him any sort of useful reference, he starts as an apprentice cabinet-maker at an Otahuhu factory for a shilling an hour. (Decades later, the same school will write to him asking if his name can be included on the roll of honoured old boys.) He doesn't like the job. 'I'm expecting to learn French polishing and cabinet-making, but instead I'm taught to put the dits in pencil cases, assemble rattles and make draughts by the millions.'

It gets to where he hates it, but doesn't have enough money to buy his way out of his apprenticeship bond. So he agitates for the sack and gets it when he sabotages some of the firm's equipment. 'I feel trapped. I'd burn the bloody place down just to get out. When they finally fired me, I thanked them very much and set out to conquer new fields.'

As the boys grow older, the old man's physical violence decreases, but the awful mental cruelty never does. The older boys go. First Bill gets out. And then Barry — out of the hell-hole of a home and into the world unprepared, with his sad little bag of possessions, without any true sense of loving family values and without ever any prospect of looking back, never mind returning if things don't work out. His family won't see him again for two years.

'I mount the trusty bicycle I paid off at ten bob a week working in the factory and delivering papers and with the rest of my worldly possessions in a sugar bag, I leave the family home and pedal off down Great South Road.' A few miles down the road he picks up a pretty girl and doubles her on the bar of his bike. She's going to visit her boyfriend south of Auckland at Papakura Military Camp.

Thirty miles down the road he sees a small dairy farm and impulsively turns his bike up the drive and asks the bloke standing outside the house if there's work going for a good farm hand and the bloke's not sure but he takes the boy inside for a cup of tea and bread and jam. Then Barry offers to bring the cows in for milking and he's got himself a job as a farm labourer, getting a weekly wage of two pounds 18 shillings 'and keep'. He spends most of his hard-earned money on ammunition for his .22 rifle, shooting 'rabbits and birds and anything that's going. Through sheer practice and enthusiasm, I get to be a good shot. I was always attracted to the bush. At home it was a place to run into, to escape. I'd look out at those bush-covered hills and see them as a way out, another world. Freedom. I don't really want to work on farms. Really, my dream is of becoming a deer culler.'

After working on a couple of farms, milking, fencing, tractor-driving, scrub-cutting and horse-handling, young Barry gets a job as a teamster working horses, a job he finds he likes because of his affinity with animals, but the job comes to a sudden end when he's arrested for the petty thievery of a few cans of food from a deserted house used by hunters. It's a minor offence and Barry gets off lightly.

It's another good reason to move on. Another early job involves working for a city council reserve ranger in the Hunua Ranges who gets them both into trouble with his habit of flogging off mutton he's shooting on the backs of farms in the area and raffling them off in local pubs on Friday nights.

Barry's early working life is hit and miss, but he's not bothered. He's already a nomad and his big nose leads him to Rotorua where he finds a job as a shepherd, but he's constantly surrendering to his growing habit of abandoning his charges to go bush in search of wild pigs. Finally leaving the sheep to care for themselves, he heads for the Kaimanawa Mountains, where he's accepted by the Forestry Department as a professional deer culler, after lying about his age and his experience. 'Tell them you can do something and by the time they find out you couldn't, you've already learned how to.'

... I'd trickled into the Internal Affairs Department in town to ask about a job shooting deer for the Government. I'd been sent to see a bloke called Jim Reed, who had a little office at the back of the building. He was about 45 and looked as fit as a buck rat. Parked in the yard was a light truck with Wildlife Branch painted on the door. Underneath it three dogs rested quietly in the shade.

Jim Reed was the kind of man who only talked when he had something to say.

'After a job, eh son?'

'Yes sir.'

'How old are you lad?'

'Eighteen,' I said, adding two years.

He wrote on a bit of paper.

'Done any hunting before?'

'Too right! Been after goats and pigs in the Hunuas for years!'

'You'll find deer a bit different from that sort of stuff,' he said. 'You got any dogs?'

'Yes, picked up a pup from a rabbitter at Taupo on my way through.'

'OK,' he said. 'You fill in this form and take it round to the main office; they'll fix you up with the rest. Then you'd better come back here while I work out what we're going to do with you. Oh, and by the way — you'd better tell them you're nineteen. Eighteen's a bit young for this caper.'

A clerk in the front office had given me a hand to fill in the application form, and asked who my next-of-kin was in case of accidents. 'Right, you've had it,' he'd said, and sent me round the back again. Jim Reed had given me instructions how to get to a base camp near the headwaters of the Whakatane River, and an envelope to hand to the Field Officer when I got there. He'd also handed me a list of gear I'd need, half of which I found later was superfluous. Then he'd unlocked a store-room that reeked of unvarnished wood, grease and gun-oil, and helped me select a rifle — an ex-army Lee-Enfield — from a rack which held about 20.

'We pay you seven-pounds-ten a week and ten bob a skin,' he'd said. 'Five bob if you just bring in the tails. You'll get five shillings a week dog-money if your pup turns out any good. We supply all the ammunition, but if you use more than three rounds a kill, you pay for them. Anything else you want to know before I boot you out of here?'

'No sir.'

I'd hitched a ride by timber truck, and arrived at the base camp not far from the end of the mill road the next afternoon. Nobody was about, so I'd dumped my gear in the hut and had a look round the place. Eight deer-skins and two tails hung on rails under a large canvas tent-fly just inside the bush. The hut consisted of four walls made of slabs from the mill, with a roof and chimney of rusty corrugated iron. Four bunks in two tiers stood against the back and end walls, a table and door took up most of the third wall, and a fireplace all of the fourth. A blackened billy over the dead ashes of the morning's fire held stewed dregs of tea. Outside the valley looked grey and wintry, and a stack of firewood stood waist-high beside the chopping block. There was little enough to see. Flynn had sniffed around, getting exciting whiffs of all the dogs which had recently lived there. I'd sat on the wood block, dredged out the letter Jim Reed had given me, and worked the flap open with my knife. The note read:

Stan,

This is Barry Crump. He looks to me like a good keen man. Give him a workout and let me know how he gets on.

Regards,

Jim.

PS: It might be worth putting in another camp at the head of the river. They were getting quite a few deer up there this time last year.

I couldn't get the flap of the envelope to stick back again, so I'd tucked it in and hoped Stan wouldn't notice.

Three blokes had come down a track by the river just on dark and introduced themselves as Stan, the Field Officer, and Trevor and Pat, who were shooters. They'd been surveying country or something and Pat had got a stag. We'd fed on boiled spuds, venison steaks, and tinned peas, with bread that Pat had baked in the camp-oven. Trevor had baked another loaf after tea to show me how it was done. He'd forgotten to wash his hands before kneading the dough, but none of the others appeared to notice. Pat and Trevor had complained of how few deer were about, but Stan said they were always a bit late moving into the area. Pat was leaving the job and had only been waiting till they'd got a new mate for Trevor before going. Stan hadn't seemed to notice anything wrong with the note when I gave it to him; he'd read it in silence, then gone to sort out some tentage which Trevor and I would take for the new camp at the head of the river. I'd wondered where Stan's truck was, why Pat was throwing the job in, and whether Trevor ever had a wash.

(from A Good Keen Man, **1960)**

§

4.

just groping around

1952

He works in the Kaimanawas and later moves across to the east to hunt in the mysterious Urewera forest. He sets a pattern to his life from the early 1950s to 1958 — shooting deer in the summer and hunting pigs, goats and possums during the winter. During this period Barry drifts around, travelling as far north as the Coromandel and as far south as South Westland, trying his hand at fencing, horse-breaking, bushwork, post splitting and scrub cutting. Learning. Soaking up the world as he finds it.

Barry doesn't stay in one place longer than a few months. 'The second I get to know the place and get good at the job, I split for new territory.' It's during these early days in the bush that the physical beauty of it makes a profound impact on his mind and imagination. He loves the peace and the solitude more than he ever thought he could love anything or anywhere. But he learns swiftly about the other side of it too — the loneliness and the fear of illness, injury or ailment, without anyone to offer comfort.

And, despite his fears and that nightmare of a childhood, he even goes home — perhaps to show the old man he has survived, that he's making something of himself, though he's not entirely sure what. Maybe just to see his mother and his sisters and brothers. They're living in the State house now. Lily and Shirley are at work upstairs in a building in the main street of Otahuhu when they hear a terrible commotion outside.

When they look out, they see a figure they don't readily recognise. There with three dogs, almost mad tied up outside the Post Office, is a chap who looks like a mountain man. Hair down to here and wearing the rotted remains of a Swanndri. It's Barry trying to find his mum. And as soon as Lily recognises him, she's running outside shouting for the world to hear, 'Look, my little boy.' Shirley's so embarrassed by the terrible sight that she hides. Barry is growing into a rugged, handsome man. And he's man-sized now, heading for a six-footer, with eyes that are always looking to the horizon and the start of a crackly, gravelly voice, helped along by the cigarettes he rolls and smokes almost non-stop.

They take him home, where the old man's just the same, only less so now that Barry is nearly full grown and obviously able to take care of himself. But Barry's wild dogs drive everyone crazy and then they run across and eat the neighbour's chooks. After a few days a darkness descends. He finds being in the city — even on the edges of the city — hard. The air tastes dirty and now he's so used to being lonely he can hardly bear people around him.

Anyway, they don't have anything he wants any more. If they ever did. But there's a strange old pull to them that he doesn't quite understand. And his little sisters and little brother Peter, the youngest, adore their torn and frayed big brother with his crazy dogs, big gun and his big grin, his long hair and his tall tales.

But he doesn't stay for any more of his mother quoting scripture at him and the kids nudging him for more stories. He gathers up his pack and his rifle and runs to catch the bus south, back to the Urewera. Carol wants to play one last game of tig and she runs after Barry because he's tigged her last. And she tigs him and he tigs her back, trips her over and runs to jump on the bus and he's off, waving to her out the back window till the bus disappears.

And when he gets back to trees for company, one of his deer-culler mates spots him in Ruatahuna, walking in half an hour after the bus. He jumped off a mile up the road so he could stuff into a culvert a sugarbag full of religious tracts his mother had given him to hand out to his new heathen friends. That's what he tells his new mate Jack Lasenby and Jack, knowing that his new mate Crump is at least half full of bullshit, wanders up the road and there, in the culvert under the road, he finds a sugar bag full of religious rubbish.

Jack had got wind of Crump even before he met him. Jack had been shooting at the north end of Lake Waikaremoana with a mate and when they reached their base hut there was a verse writ large in charcoal across the wall: 'If I ever come back to this one-eyed shack I'll be cussed by the world for cringin'. You can stick the lot up your big black bot, the boat, the lake and the engine.' It was an adjustment of an old Aussie shearing verse which went 'the sheep, the board and the engine' and was a reference to an old dinghy the cullers used and its notorious Seagull outboard engine. Someone had obviously had a hard time out on the lake. Jack said to his mate, 'Who wrote this?' and he said, 'Crump'. Jack asked who Crump was and he said, 'Oh, he's a bomb' in the vernacular of the time. And a bomb is just what Crump turns out to be.

Jack runs into Crump, who's on the road to Waikaremoana, poaching. He's young, about 18, maybe even younger, Jack thinks. Certainly younger than Jack and he has a little goat-like tuft of beard under his chin. It's all he can grow and it wobbles as he talks — and he sure can talk.

Within five minutes, he has Jack convinced he's one of the shooters who's come back from Korea and various other bullshit that Jack swallows and filters out over the next year or two.

In the bush when often the only conversation is a morepork saying the same thing over and over, almost everyone talks eventually, lets some personal secrets out — and some, like Crump, talk like entertainers and, in the grip of the urge to talk, sometimes some of the truth spills out.

He says his mother is mad on the Bible and his old man is in love with the racehorses and that Wally has trained a whole string of colossal failures and poured all his money into them. He also mentions that the old man knocks his mother about, but he doesn't make him out to be an ogre. Though, once, at a low moment on a lonely night he tells Jack about lying in a ditch face down and how he can smell the rubbery smell of a gumboot and it's booting him in the side of the head. Crump tells it so vividly that Jack will never forget it and always takes it to be a story about Crump's old man.

From the first time he meets Barry Crump he knows he's in the company of a natural con, a bullshitter supreme who'll never let any dull details stand in the way of a good yarn. Crump is a con, a magpie, a natural criminal who'll never really need to resort to breaking the law. He's living outside it already and to survive he needs to know everything, he reckons. Certainly all the stuff that seems interesting. He's busy learning anything that puts itself under his nose and furiously forming opinions about life, even if they're other people's. 'I have this feeling of injustice. I don't know what it's about yet, but I'm on its trail. I'm just groping around, but something is driving me to keep moving around and see as much as possible. I don't feel like I have a lot going for me, but the one thing I do have going for me then is that I can always laugh and I seem to be able to make others laugh with me.'

They're a strange bag of all-sorts, the men pulled to the deer-culling life, signing on with Internal Affairs to kill wild animals in difficult places for the Government and for the good of the forest. It had been set up in the 1930s by an ex-soldier called Major Yuricks, who went by the nickname 'Skipper'. As a result, it was organised along semi-militaristic lines, though it was marked by extreme informality in the field. At the outbreak of the Second World War, Yuricks called all of his Field Officers from throughout the country to a meeting in Wellington and marched them across to Parliament where they — all of them — volunteered for the Army. After the war the survivors came home and, unable to settle back into civilian life, many of them returned to deer-culling.

By the 1950s, it's not the life for everyone, though. One joker gets off the Railways bus in Ruatahuna, takes one look around at the bush surrounding the place, which is half-cleared anyway, and gets straight back on and goes on to Wairoa and relative civilisation. Others make it down the river to camp and then refuse to go out of sight of the camp or even leave the hut or tent. They're frightened by the bush. Not Crump. He loves it.

'Our rifles are ex-Army Lee-Enfield .303s. As soon as we get one, we strip two-thirds of the wood off it, the magazine cut-off, the clip-holder, the sight-guards, the sling-swivels, the safety-catch — everything that isn't absolutely essential. We sharpen one end of the magazine-spring in case we lose our knives, put two rounds and a piece of candle in the cleaning hole in the butt, shoot her in at 200 yards, stick 10 in the mag and one up the spout with the bolt half-closed and you're in business as a fair-dinkum government deer-culler.'

Some of the current crop of deer-cullers are blokes back from the Korean War, who've learnt to shoot and are happy to keep their finger on the trigger. Some are farmers' boys like Barry. Some are even university boys with thick books in their bags and big words on their lips. Keen-to-learn Crump is open to anything. Even education. And Jack happens to be one of the university boys, a young academic chap who is doing a spot of deer-culling. They pair up to go across Lake Waikaremoana to put in a track from the south-western corner of the lake. Jack has a little light reading in his pack — Ezra Pound, James Joyce's *Ulysses*, Edgar Allan Poe's *Tales of Mystery and Imagination*.

Crump reads them all from front to back and discusses them with Jack and wants to know about more books like these buggers. He's not impressed by the fact that Jack has been to university or even faintly regretful that he's barely had any education at all himself. He reckons education's all about telling you how to think and he's having none of that. He has the advantage of not having been warped by too much teaching, he tells Jack and any other over-educated blokes he runs into.

Crump has a very low boredom threshold and this brings out the best and the worst in him, with very little in between. He can be moody, but he's never had the freedom in his life to be such a thing as moody before. He finds the isolation that is part of the other-worldly shape of life in the forest hard. He's the sort of loner who prefers to have someone else around.

He has a lousy sense of concentration. If a job doesn't seize his attention and hold it tight, he just takes off from it. He doesn't see a job through unless it has some fascination for him. And he detects the beginnings in him of a feeling that will grow — a terrible thing really, a strange desire that, when things are going well, he wants to break them up.

Crump is a good shot, standing or kneeling, though not necessarily a good hunter. Good hunters are energetic and Crump isn't always terribly energetic. He's unreliable and even untrustworthy in some respects, he's starting to get heavily into the booze and even the bootleg stuff, the white lightning, but he's a good enough bushman and he puts up good kill tallies. He seems to need to be amused or to be amusing, doing something interesting or being the centre of attention. In the midst of an irresponsible bunch of footloose young men, Crump is more irresponsible than most, washing less, drinking more, spinning bigger yarns.

In reaction to the trim and tidy tent camps of the time, Crump prefers the crumpled look, making an already-small space even smaller and more cave-like by letting his tent fly swing low so he has to bend over to get inside. He admires the trouble some of the men go to with their personal camping touches and added sophistications — split timbers for chimneys and handmade doors turning on old condensed-milk tins driven into the ground and he studies them for future reference, but he can't be bothered himself.

He's pretty good in the bush. Early on especially, he gets lost, as everyone does, and he frightens himself and saves himself and doesn't talk much about it afterwards. He doesn't talk much either about the immense loneliness that sometimes fills his heart like ice water. But, on the other swing of the pendulum, his sense of fun can be so large it invades everyone.

He's in awe of, in love with the bush and respects it because he can't take it for granted. 'I spend a lot of my time on my own that first season, or maybe I notice it more. The first few weeks are the worst. I don't know what I'm doing and have to make it up as I go along. I rig up a disgraceful tent-camp on a beech bushline at a place called The Hoggett and make disgraceful loaves of camp-oven bread over disgraceful fires. Even the camp is in a disgraceful place.'

Crump loves his life, the dirt, the danger, the adventure. And his life loves him.

It lights him up, and he has a glow about him anyway, an ability to make things seem bigger and more intense, a sort of glamour that makes him hugely attractive company. He can be dangerous company too. His carelessness makes him so.

And he's a natural storyteller, ever on the search for more tales to inflate and adjust. The deer-cullers live the sailors' life — months away, lost on the deep ocean of forest, and then ashore for short periods and into town with their pay cheques in their newly scrubbed hands to drink it up in the pub and tell boastful yarns about their bush exploits, make the acquaintance of some of the local ladies. Then, once the money is gone and the novelty of drinking themselves silly every day wears off, it's back to the bush for another long, strange voyage.

There are one or two blokes who sensibly save their money, but most of them don't — least of all Barry John Crump. After a week in town he heads back into the bush with several months' worth of good yarns to spin out of what he's experienced.

Crump is a borrower too of other people's experiences, other stories, other attitudes, even the way others speak. He's looking for something and he assumes all the other rough boys in the bush are too. Years later, he'll ask Jack, 'What was it we were after, all us young jokers? What were we looking for?' Jack comes up with various answers — the adventurous life, the do-gooding principle, fighting the erosion the deer cause by chewing out everything in the back country, and so on. But one by one to his various replies, Crump says, 'No, think a bit harder. Think a bit harder.'

And finally he says, 'Come on, you needed one as much as I did. We were all after that one thing.' And Jack, lost on this one, asks what the hell it was they were after then and Crump says, 'We were all in search of a father and we picked on the Grey Ghost, the poor bastard.'

The Grey Ghost is their senior field officer, Ted Rye, an immensely capable older man who makes a profound impression on some of the — temporarily anyway — fatherless boys in his charge. He is a luminous storyteller with a touch of the Baron Münchhausen about him, who tells tall bush tales that sometimes go on all night and half the following day with the boys shouting encouragement.

Many of the impressionable young men model themselves on old Ted and Barry is one of them. Old Ted isn't really all that old at all, but he offers a powerful role model as a storyteller. Barry always talks a bit about his big brother Bill. But now it's 'me brother Bill', just like old Ted always refers to 'me brother Bert'. Barry takes it like it's his for the taking.

And then he's off on his own to his designated block killing deer again, or not bothering to kill them because he doesn't feel like it. Jack drops over one time and poaches deer on Crump's block. He crosses one of the lakes in the region and comes up the Waiau shooting Crump's deer left, right and centre. They shouldn't be out in the middle of the day, but they are. Crump hasn't been doing any shooting at all. There are bloody deer everywhere.

Jack gets to Crump's camp and here's Crump building a diving board over a big water hole in the river. Jack stays and plays with Crump for a few days, swimming and diving and lying around yarning before heading back to his own block where he should have been all along.

'This river's too good just to shoot, eh?' Crump tells Jack and that's the difference between them. Jack has his fun with the deer-culling life, but essentially he sees it as a job to be done. Crump, now that he knows how to do the job, sees it all as an endless opportunity to have a good time.

'There isn't always a town to head for to unravel those pay cheques. Sometimes it's a timber town and the timber towns are wild places full of hard men and women in the 1950s. They're cutting all the native timber, rimu, matai, totara, single people and families moving on from mill town to mill town. It's a way of life that's vanishing with the trees.

'The pubs are few and far away and they tend to close at six o'clock in line with the law. The main social life these timber town people have are parties, with the booze supplied by sly-groggers, often the local taxi driver. There's some wild homebrew around too and sometimes the parties last for days with everyone howling along to "Dear John" or "The Bubbles on the Beer Keep Haunting Me", accompanied by an old guitar with several strings missing.'

At the end of a deer season, Crump and three others who've been shooting out of Ruatahuna take jobs over at Murupara, felling pine trees for the logging company there. They're desperate for bushmen. The company has just started logging and they've built a whole village of houses and single men's accommodation, flasher than anything Crump and his mates have seen.

But they have no workers, so they send to Canada for 300 lumberjacks and have them sign up for three years in return for their fares to New Zealand. 'They get their 300 men all right, but none of them are lumberjacks. We never see one who's ever swung an axe in his life. There are a lot of alcoholics and perverts and criminals and other misfits among them. A year after they've arrived, there are only a handful of them left in Murapara.'

Things are changing in the bush, with the Forestry Department taking over the control of noxious animals. Tracks are being cut in all over the place and there are huts everywhere. The life is getting softer, with supplies now being airdropped in by plane. The deer-culling life isn't what it used to be. Forestry brings in a token system for possums, at two and sixpence a pop, and Crump and a mate toss in the bush work and head off to parts of the Urewera where they know there are big numbers of possums.

With cyanide and traps, they cut a swathe through the possum population and make themselves a tidy sum of money. Crump hops around the country, setting trap lines whenever he needs money. He buys a Norton Dominator motorbike and heads north to Auckland where his mate with the books, Jack Lasenby, introduces him to another breed of buggers altogether.

§

5.
a wonderful kisser
1957

'I'm a bastard,' Crump tells the woman he's about to marry, the first time they meet. 'Oh, OK then,' she says, knowing she's never met one like this one before — all tumbling blond curls, sticks stuck in his hair, rotten teeth. He's hilarious, intriguing, sexy as all hell. Even plays the guitar. Plays up too, probably.

It is Jack Lasenby who, at the end of one of the deer-culling seasons, hits Auckland with Crump and introduces him to a circle of artistic friends in the city. This is a different sort of a scene for Crump altogether. His wild energy, his sheer wildness make him stand out like a firebrand in a roomful of assorted small torches. He plays up the bushman bit to the hilt and regales them with wild stories and epic versions of the great porno-poem, 'Eskimo Nell'. They lap him up, and he's amused and uplifted by this interesting new company.

They are Auckland's arty underground and they drink and shag a bit like bushmen, as it happens. It's just that they use bigger words. 'They're what we call arty-crafty parties,' Jack tells Crump, who knows little of the big city, though he's learning fast and acting like he knew it all along.

Scratch the city's grey surface and things are seething. The whole art, architecture and writing scene is exploding and the young would-be movers and shakers socialise, in downtown coffee bars and especially at parties where they drink and fire each other up. Crump is surprised and grateful that such a band of big-city intellectuals seem to accept him for what he is. 'It's amazing. Some blokes I meet have jobs lecturing at university, but they treat me just like one of the boys.'

One of his new mates is a bloke called Kevin Ireland. He takes Kevin back to the Urewera to pick up a bit of money trapping possums. Crump's a loose unit in the bush by now and only there out of some sort of impulse. He'll spend weeks killing and collecting possum tokens, hundreds of them in a sack, but then he decides to go off somewhere else for some bloody good reason or other and he forgets about them. When he gets back, the flies have blown into his hard-won tokens and the maggots have walked off with them. But he doesn't care. He has learned not to look back. Not to regret. What's the point? He has little tolerance of his mates' sets of personal values. If Crump will drop everything and drift off to chase an adventure or a booze-up, then why shouldn't they? Why should the fact that they think they should be home with the wife and kids stand in the way?

He's dangerous fun in other ways too. With Ireland once, out possuming, Crump takes along enough cyanide to knock off the North Island and he's frighteningly casual handling a big pot of stuff that will kill you with only a grain or two. It was the talk of the bush at the time that some joker died simply from handling cyanide and rolling a cigarette and licking across the finger he'd dipped in the poison.

There are non-life-threatening moments too.

Kevin and Crump are out there in all that wildness and Kevin says to Crump he doesn't understand why deer-cullers and possum trappers don't take chess sets with them. 'They're the easiest thing to carry and, you know, it's a wonderful game for the evenings,' he says.

'Teach me,' says Crump and Kevin tells him that, contrary to his own advice, he hasn't packed a chess set. 'Well, I've got a pen,' says Crump, who's not about to give up easily. And he gets a slab of timber and, with Kevin's guidance, marks off the 64 squares and colours in the alternate ones. And for pieces, he grabs a couple of candles. 'Right, we'll warm these up in front of the fire, you shape the chessmen and we'll colour one lot of them with the ink from the pen.

And within an hour they have it done. The pawns are easy, the King and the Queen and the others are harder. They decorate some with bits of wood in the top. Kevin teaches him the moves, and Crump swiftly becomes addicted and insists on playing every night. One morning Crump wakes up groaning. 'Christ cobber, I'm euchred. I couldn't sleep properly for dreaming of chess moves.'

But the pull of the bush is fading for Crump. He's been possuming regularly with Jack Lasenby in the north-western side of the Urewera out the back of Galatea, but now Crump will be away for a month or two and he'll come back and work for a few weeks and then he'll take off again. Gradually, the absences grow longer and longer. Crump's got new ground to hunt.

In his new social circle, as he did in the bush, Crump swiftly sets about picking up the new skills — the paddle to take him across these deeper waters. And in the middle of all this, he meets the very spirited, dark and beautiful Tina Anso and they fall for each other just like that.

'My mother, Ruby, was a laundress at a boarding school and then we came to Auckland when I was 12. During the first four years we didn't have a home at all because my father, Willy, was completely hopeless at making a home, or anything else.

'I was born up north in Mangonui and Willy dug drains and people's cows would fall in them and disappear. He was very good at digging. It was a hobby of his. Frank Sargeson, who was a friend of the family, wrote a story called *The Hole that Jack Dug* about my father.' Tina is precocious and she's used to the company of unusual people.

She's grown up with them all around her. All sorts have been through her family home in Astley Avenue, New Lynn, all her life. She met Rewi Alley as a kid, knows writers like Sargeson and Janet Frame. Almost everyone she knows is a writer or something.

At 12, with her long black hair and fringe, she has a job selling programmes at His Majesty's Theatre. Then, later, she joins the Young People's Club, an arm of the Communist Party. They march up and down Queen Street protesting and unsettling the citizens. That's fun, because Tina is a bit of a show-off, likes making a splash. She's a keen dancer too, winning a silver medal for ballroom. She says she wants to be like ordinary people, but she can't quite manage it.

Crump remains unclear about what an ordinary person even is. Tina is intrigued by him and Crump knows this and contrives to lounge around acting as interesting as he can and looking like he's certainly interested in her too. He turns up to visit Tina at her family home in the suburbs of Auckland. Tina's doing the housework. 'I see you can do housework then?' Crump seems surprised. Impressed. And he's attracted to her, which of course makes him seem even more attractive. She hops on the back of his motorbike, and they hit the party circuit. They go to a lot of parties. It's a blur after a while. Barry sure can drink. He's a new sort of unusual person to Tina. He's got a boredom threshold that can be as short as the crack of a horse whip. She never knows what he's going to do next and that seems kind of exciting. And he's a wonderful kisser. 'You're very talented,' she tells him.

He's also very resourceful. Once, driving the car through Avondale with six aboard, they get a flat tyre. Crump goes behind a shop and comes back with a plank of wood, puts one end under the car and says, 'C'mon girls, you're the cantilever' and gets them to sit on the other end, all giggling while he changes the wheel.

No one ever has to worry about the car breaking down if Barry's around. He's a keen man in that sort of way. He likes impressing people too, of course, though many of his new mates are keen blokes too. It's the way in the 1950s for young intellectual and academic thrusters to study and attend lectures and finance the studious side of their lives by doing any available manual work for money — they're on building sites, off to the bush hunting, up in fire-watch towers, growing vegetables to sell.

They're a talented and unlikely bag of people, all moving around like a loose tribe from shindig to shindig, feeling like this party life will go on for ever. And Barry's not the only wild one. Within two weeks of meeting, they've decided to get married. Tina makes him wait till after his birthday, so that he'll be 22.

Tina's friends have been faintly amused about her attraction to Crump, but now they're a bit appalled. 'What on earth are you marrying him for?' is the general consensus. Barry doesn't really want to get married, but it's the only way they can be together. Tina has a son, Dean, who was born when she was 17.

They get married in a registry office. Crump's uneasy about it all and keeps asking Tina, 'What do you want me to do?' He has no idea what being married means and the truth is that marriage means little to him. 'I don't mind who marries me and I don't mind if they have kids already. It's all the same to me. I'll do my best to be a father and a husband, but I'm not sure I'm cut out for it.'

They move into Tina's family home in Astley Avenue and Tina swiftly discovers that among his other rapidly surfacing failings, Crump is as mean as piss. Her mother says he's the meanest man she's ever known. He wrecks the family car and sponges off his new family. It's all pretty bloody unimpressive. Except, of course, that some of the time he's so charming he lights up the lives around him.

He says he doesn't want children and Tina, who already has her young son, lies to him, saying that would be very unlikely. And life thunders on, Crump working in various easy jobs, labouring on building sites, felling trees, waving a spade at garden work, trapping possums out in the Waitakere Ranges, west of Auckland. There's not much fun in the work and he's not that taken with life in the city, but there's no end of fun in his new social circle.

Tina teaches him to dance rock'n'roll and he dances. Everyone dances. Barry's funny and he picks things up quickly. He'll pick up other women quickly too, if Tina's not careful, and Tina's not all that careful. Who the hell wants to be careful?

It's a strange scene. She and her friends are very close, very intimate, but without sex.

Sex hardly seems necessary. They feel like they've slept together, even though they haven't. There is a great deal of drunkenness. Everyone brings bottles, everyone dances, everyone talks his and her head off. Barry is very good at drinking non-stop and staying on his feet. And being funny. He's very funny.

He's a knockout with the ladies. Jack takes him to an exhibition at an art gallery in the city only to have Crump disappear with all the best-looking women in tow ... these well-dressed young matrons from the conventional, well-to-do suburbs of Auckland, spirited away by bushman Barry. And next thing there are these great shrieks of hilarity coming from round the back of the building. Crump has as many people as can cram in, crammed into the dunny and he's sitting on it, with his strides on, telling his stories and punctuating them by flushing the dunny.

He has a dangerous amount of charm. He walks into a room and the women's heads turn and it gets under some men's skin. The charismatically challenged among them are jealous and sometimes it's all a bloody nuisance because, with his hot temper, Crump sometimes finds himself lashing out, punching and kicking and realising that this sort of savagery isn't quite the way in these more refined circles. In these circles, savagery takes other forms.

Crump's dangerous to be around. It's the old lack of self-regard. One night in Avondale on his motorbike with Tina hanging on behind he's so drunk he tips it and the two of them skate along the road and come to a halt right in front of a cop car. Crump gets to his feet and sets about charming the cop. Another time, he's so drunk he can't see properly, so Tina steers for him. They get home alright.

At their parties, people get drunk and spew or just plain collapse in their tracks. Women lose the plot, get all emotional and hysterical and fall on the floor, but they all look out for each other, share the few cars they have between them, their cash, their booze, their dreams. It's very intense and some people can't handle it.

Crump enjoys saying rude things to people. He can be foul, cruel, confrontational in a way he almost seems to be working at perfecting. He'll be downright silly, stopping his motorbike beside a woman who happens to be walking down the road — a woman he's never seen before — and asking her, 'Do you know nine out of 10 film stars use Lux soap?' He seems to love making completely ridiculous remarks to people.

Tina meets his mother and father. It feels to her like he's very distant from them and she can see why. She hates Wally instantly. 'He's a fucking bastard.' She hears a story of how he broke one of his daughter's arms at the dinner table because she made a noise with her knife or fork that annoyed him. He terrifies her. Barry's mother doesn't fare much better. Strong-minded, quick-to-judge Tina despises Lily for hiding behind her religion and for her apologies, and her constant assurances that everything will be alright when it obviously isn't at all.

To Tina, Barry seems frightened of a lot of things. Going into the bush and being on his own so much was him trying to prove something to himself, but he remains afraid of many things, especially his father.

Meanwhile, Crump's becoming quite attracted to the idea of this writing thing that some of his new friends take so seriously. Some of these real writers and poets are telling him he should write down some of those stories he's always telling and cracking them up with. He really should, they say. Just don't write down 'Eskimo Nell', his big party turn.

He's not so sure and he reckons he needs to do some more reading before he sets about writing, so when his new mate Kevin Ireland tells Crump he can borrow any books he likes any time, Crump turns up with a truck and takes away the lot, which he promptly sets about absorbing, the way he once absorbed bush skills. 'I soak them up almost as he recommends them — Dickens, Lear, Mark Twain, Lewis Carroll, Banjo Paterson, Saki, James Thurber, Dylan Thomas, Kingsley Amis, James Joyce, Aldous Huxley, Nancy Mitford, Wodehouse and many others.

'I can't tell what influence all this reading is having on me or what I might write, but I like Roald Dahl's short stories. He has to be one of the best at it. I've been reading some stuff too by a bloke about the deer-culling life. He's an old deer-culler himself and he knows what he's talking about. He's probably a better hunter than me, but it's dull going. I reckon I could do better. A side of the story hasn't been presented and it makes me anxious that this book not be the complete history or record of our lives as cullers.'

Some of Crump's new friends are about to introduce a new literary magazine they've put together as an outlet for all this burgeoning writing talent around them. They give their magazine the homely name of *Mate* and when Crump — treading as close as he can to actually outright asking them — tells them he'd been keen on writing essays as a schoolboy, he's told, 'Fine, write a short story for our magazine.' Crump decides that's just what he'll do.

Kevin Ireland, particularly, is convinced that Crump has what it takes to be a writer and encourages Crump into being convinced too. Not that it takes much to convince Crump. Kevin even gives him writing lessons, sitting behind a big Imperial typewriter tapping out a version of one of Crump's yarns, with Crump dictating and Kevin translating. 'I proceeded ...' intones Crump. 'No no no,' shouts Kevin. The last bloke sitting behind a typewriter who Crump had made a statement to was a policeman. A light goes on upstairs in Crump.

'I had the idea that you couldn't put it down on paper like it came out of your mouth, then I realised that was the trick. Well, mine anyway. That's where I might have something, if I can just get it down on the page like I tell it to people.

I reckon that's all I need to do. It's just that it's taking a bit of getting used to doing all this concentrating.'

But he manages to concentrate enough to squeeze out a story that runs to four and a half pages in the November 1958 issue of *Mate*. He's alongside names that will have some shine in years to come — Frank Sargeson, Maurice Gee, Kevin Ireland.

Kevin takes Crump to meet Sargeson, a writer who is busy tapping out the template of New Zealand short story writing, when he's not growing vegetables or entertaining disciples and visitors. Sargeson is astonished by Crump, the shape of his character, the way he talks, everything about him. He tells Kevin later, 'You know, that man's a living anachronism. He's like an echo of our past.'

And Crump's story, in the second issue of *Mate*, is an anachronism. A tale from another place, another time. He calls it *A Good Keen Man*, after a key phrase in the yarn, and it starts out:

'After spending a placid week at the home of my very respectable parents, I abandoned the finer things of life in favour of the usual soul-blistering addictions of an off-season deer-culler.

'A fortnight of bright women, bad beer and bumble-footed horses saw me borrowing a bleary fiver off the publican for a new pair of boots and thumbing a ride towards my summer job, a bonus block at the Haumoana Lake. Jim, my Field Officer, had told me that he was putting a good keen man on the lake with me, which I thought was pretty rotten luck as I'd probably have to poach on every other block in the area to get a decent tally....'

And it spins on into a laconic yarn told by a loveable know-it-all deer-culler about the hopeless, unloveable 'good keen men' his boss keeps sending him to work with. The loveable laconic deer-culler is Crump, of course, or how he wants to seem. It's dialogue-free and told in a plain, humorous tone. Everyone tells Crump he should stick with the writing lark and, in the face of nothing much else interesting to do, he decides to string a few more deer-culling yarns together and see if they don't make some kind of book.

Ireland's happy to keep helping Crump out, staying over when the sessions stretch into the night. One morning, early on in the project, Crump rises. 'Christ, writing makes you hungry, doesn't it?' and jumps on the motorbike to go off and get them the makings for a decent feed of bacon and eggs. And if Crump had no idea what hard work writing was, then Ireland had no idea of what Crump regarded as a decent feed.

He comes back with a great big bag full of stuff, bangs a couple of family-sized frying pans on the cooker and sets about making bacon, eggs, french bread. 'How many eggs,' he asks Ireland, 'one or two.' 'Oh just one,' comes the reply and with that, crack, crack, crack, Crump breaks one dozen eggs into the pan for the city boy with the modest appetite. Crump cooks himself two dozen.

Apart from the occasional boyish flash of fun, he's dreadful to be married to, but Tina really tries to stick it out for as long as she can. It isn't easy. Within a year she gives birth to Ivan. She wants something of Barry's. She knows the marriage isn't going to last. She knows there's no way she can hang onto him, keep him. He's just not for keeping.

The day Ivan is born his father is off working with a mate — one of the few jobs he's had in months. Tina has booked into the hospital under the name Mrs Hamilton. She and Barry hate the name Crump and occasionally call themselves Mr and Mrs Hamilton. Barry drops by later in the day to see his wife and first-born son and though he's interested — especially in the breast-feeding — he's hardly an involved father.

The only time he hits Tina is when she socks him 'a good one in the face'. He throws things at her when he's pissed off … nothing major, a matchbox or, once, a doughnut. The stain it leaves on the wallpaper at Astley Avenue stays for years, coming through every new layer of paper like a greasy reminder, till it's eventually painted over. He's an awful arsehole, with his selfishness and his casual cruelty, and it's two long, hard, bouncy years before things fly completely apart.

Crump wants to get away from the Anso house and rents a house for his new and expanding family to live in out on the lonely, rugged coast west of Auckland, at Piha. Tina moves out with six-year-old Dean and one-month-old Ivan. Her mother's not very happy about it. She doesn't like Crump, thinks he's an awful, wild and hopeless man who's leading her silly, strong-willed daughter a merry dance. All Crump has going for him is an old Ford truck and that's often not going at all. They're only out at faraway Piha a month or so and, in that time, the truck hits a bank, Tina puts her neck out, Ivan suffers a slight concussion and, finally, Barry buggers off. Tina wakes up one morning and he's gone.

Crump's ever-wandering eye has been caught by a friend of Tina's, a psychology student called Jean Watson, who is staying at the Anso house in Astley Avenue. He sleeps with her and they keep right on at it, until Tina eventually finds out. Crump comes round with one of his mates for moral support. Tina's only weeks away from giving birth to her second son with Crump.

He tells her he wants a separation. She tells him she wants a divorce and his face falls. He's shocked by this. He never thought being married could get in the way of him doing what he wanted — even if it is sleeping with Tina's friend. Former friend, that is, because Tina, in a rage, goes round to thump Jean one, but Jean snivels and keeps sitting down so Tina can't get a proper punch in. 'We call her Barry's dog,' says Tina.

Tina is seven months pregnant in 1959 with their second son Martin when Crump leaves, feeling misunderstood. He leaves a suit with five quid in the pocket. Tells Tina to keep the money, sell the suit. It's the best he can do.

He's out of here.

'I was green, straight out of the bush when we hitched up. I was prepared to marry the first person who loved me. But I felt trapped in this married situation and was doing odd jobs in Auckland factories and driving trucks before I took off opossum hunting in the Waitakeres. The marriage lasted about two years before it disintegrated, but actually it didn't last five minutes on a genuine, lasting basis.

'We simply weren't in love and I was unhappy. And when I'm unhappy I do what I usually do — I run. And that's exactly what I'm doing. I wanted our marriage to work, but it had no chance. I'm starting to think women are a completely different, unpredictable species.'

Sam Cash looked at his old woman the way a man looks at a steep ridge he's got to climb on a hot day. It was a long time to spend in one place. Time wasted with a woman who had come to represent only a tremendous amount of noise.

Too much money in her family for a man to have a fair go in the first place, he reflected. If a man had any go in him he'd take her at her word and head off down country again. Back to the old life with plenty of hard work and no nagging woman on a man's back all the time. He sat by the fire thinking about places he'd been and things he'd done.

'I'm going to bed,' she barked through the remembered noise of a woolshed Sam was working in just then. 'I suppose you're going to sit there smoking those filthy cigarettes all night. Why can't you be like other men and keep decent hours? Up half the night and waking up bad-tempered in the morning. You can sleep in the spare room if you're going to carry on like this. It's disgraceful! Always telling lies and skiting about the silly things you've done. Frittering away your life, that's what you're doing...!'

In his mind Sam rode a muddy horse through a gate in a long row of pines and dismounted by a small hut on a river-flat.

'You could clout a man if he talked to you like that,' he muttered to the horse, as the bedroom door slammed behind his loved one. Queer, though, how a man can get so used to a thing that he misses it when it's gone, whether he likes it or not. He'd probably even miss the Old Girl if he shot through on her, but it was hard to imagine. He dug the fire in the ribs with a piece of wood and rolled himself another smoke.

How long is it since a man stood on a jigger-board or boiled his billy over a manuka fire, or swore at his dogs or drank beer in a pub that didn't close at six on the knocker and shove you out on the footpath with nothing to do but go home and listen to the bitching? Close on eight months!

And what was it she said this morning? Something about how if it wasn't for her old man they'd be out on the street. And then Sam had to 'go and repay all he's done for us by threatening to do that with his truck and telling him to do it with his job.

Filthy language and wicked ungratefulness. Why don't you go back and live like the pig you tried to turn me into? I don't know why I ever married you. Never shaving and going round like a filthy hobo. No wonder you can't get jobs! And me having to ask Daddy for money all the time.'

Daddy! — What's happened to a man? Wondered Sam.

He sat looking into the fire for a long time. He slept there.

(from *Hang on a Minute Mate*, **1961)**

Crump does go back to Tina and tries to put the wheels back on their marriage, but it's an unimpressive attempt. He finds them another house, back in town this time, and even sets about building a bookshelf out of bricks and boards and makes a nice job of it too. The reconciliation is another matter, though. 'I'll be back Tuesday,' he tells Tina and the boys, never saying which Tuesday, and that's him out of there forever. He does come back to visit sometimes. Once he turns up for one of their wedding anniversaries and Tina bakes a cake and ices it beautifully with 'I Loathe You' written in the icing on top and presents it to him. Enraged, he takes it outside and throws it down a bank.

A few months later, a mate tells him Tina's just given birth to another boy and Crump turns up at the hospital wearing a conciliatory smile. 'Piss off,' Tina tells him and he takes her advice. He never ever quite lets go of Tina, though. And she never quite lets go of him. Every few years they track each other down and live almost like they're happily married for a few days. Once, when Ivan is three and Martin two, Tina puts them in her mother's car and drives south to Rotorua. She just has to go and see Barry and he tells her he feels the same way. They meet up and talk about getting together again. But they don't.

He visits her after their divorce goes through, brings girlfriends to meet her. They become friends of a sort, but that doesn't stop her from putting lawyers on his evasive uncaring tail for the money he never sends her and his abandoned sons. Tina knows she has to protect her boys from their father, from the charm that he turns on you and warms you with and fills you with promises and makes you float on the possibilities. And then he dumps you and never delivers and hurts you like hell.

Tina will bring the boys to see him over the years, but he never seems to care whether he sees them or not. He doesn't want the responsibility. He almost seems happier with other people's kids. Barry seems to care more for Tina's oldest boy Dean than he does for his own blood, the two little boys. When Dean is 14 or so he changes his name by deed poll to Crump.

Tina keeps in touch with Barry's mother Lily too, taking the boys to visit, with old Wally, menacing and grumbling away. But Tina's not afraid of that awful old bastard and he seems to know it and keeps his distance.

Jean Watson is the new wife, though Crump will never marry her. She's crazy for Crump and, like Tina, will remain in love with him in her way the rest of her life. Unlike Tina, Jean never draws a line in the sand on Crump's behaviour. She absorbs cruelty and neglect just as readily as she absorbs his sweet, funny little boyness, his companionship and his sex. She has none of Tina's firepower. But, like Tina, she's a bohemian, part of the Auckland crowd they call the lunatic fringe and a bit of a writer herself. A strange, droopy, dreamy, faraway girl who, like Crump, craves adventure.

Well, she's off with Crump now and he sticks to the city, living here and there and trying to finish this book of his. His new cobbers are all telling him he's bloody brilliant and he's feted and lionised. There are those who say, 'Oh, this is just yarning, just a bush story', but there are others who seem to see literary merit in his writing.

His whole life is starting to feel like a story. He and Jean rent a room in Park Road, posing as Mr and Mrs Richards. In Ponsonby they live in a boarding house and style themselves Mr and Mrs Havisham (they've been reading Dickens). Jean is working at a print shop and Crump is banging away at his book. 'I'm writing this bit about one of the characters being in hospital and getting the end of a toilet-roll caught in his dressing-gown belt and coming out through the ward with it trailing behind him. I want to see if it'll actually work, so I go along the hall to the toilet and pull the toilet paper out the door and round the corner. I'm part-way up the passage when the landlady comes in the front door with a bag of groceries.

'"Mr Havisham," she calls out. "What on earth do you think you're doing with the toilet paper?" It's just something I'm writing, I stammer. "I don't allow writing on the toilet paper, Mr Havisham," she barks back. "This is a respectable house, I'll have you know. I'll just thank you to roll it up again and leave it as it was."'

Crump knows what he should do. Could do. Might bloody well do. Might just ask her, 'What if I was to give you a nice fuck?' And she gives him a funny look and wiggles her finger at him to follow her. So he does and ends up giving her a really good seeing to on her big satin sofa with the curtains drawn and her big cream telephone off the hook and making her shout out the name of some bloke she used to know. There's no trouble for a while. But then he goes and does something unrespectable again and they're off again. But he likes the moving around.

They live, for a while, aboard a lifeboat-turned-houseboat moored to the sewer line at Hobson's Bay. They get on well when they're holed up together just enjoying each other's company. They read the same books, the same comics. They laugh at the same silly things. Sometimes it's as if they can pretend to be children. At times it's as if Barry can be a kid for the first time.

They dramatise everything, make up stories about people they see, go through the dictionary and play games asking each other what words mean. A lot of the time, at first, it's wonderful, though Barry can turn mean, be so cruel. Treat her like she really is a dog.

And all the time he's thumping away at this book of his. Crump will claim later he put pen to paper and, 'within a month', his great New Zealand novel was complete. But the truth is it's quite a slog and all the time he's trying to make a quid here and a quid there to keep their skin off their ribs.

One night Crump's on his way out with Jean and her sister for a Chinese meal in town when the police come by and take him off. He's been working with some joker in the car business and people have complained they're not getting the money for their cars that have been sold. Jean takes him toheroa fritters for dinner in his cell. But he's soon out on bail and back into that book of his which, like his short story, is called *A Good Keen Man*.

§

6.

as cocky as hell

1959

By July 1959, Crump has stretched out his deer-culling yarns to an epic length and he reckons the book's about finished. In it, the loveable, know-it-all bushman goes by the name Bill Davies and the story, somewhat plainly, begins: 'It was ten years ago when I first trickled into the office to ask about a job shooting deer for the Government and was sent to see a bloke called Jim Reed, who had a little office at the back of the building....'

Then it ranges out across a string of linked encounters with Bill Davies emerging as a Kiwi Superman with advanced bush skills. Crump thinks it's a flat-out winner. 'I'm feeling as cocky as hell about it. I've taken it to Bob Lowry at Pilgrim Press and he's stapled it for me. Now all I've got to do is find a publisher. I marched up to the publishers. Two rejected it as unsuitable and said such a story would never sell.'

Whitcombe and Tombs, one of the country's largest publishers at the time, turn Crump down flat. 'We thank you for submitting your MS which we have read with interest. We regret, however, we are unable to undertake the publication as the cost would not make it a profitable proposition for either you or ourselves,' they tell him, in a decision the company will live to bitterly regret. There's no stopping the would-be author, though.

'I bowl along to a third, Reed. The bloke there, Ray Richards, asks me if I have 50 friends who'll buy it. Bloody cheek. But, yes, they are prepared to accept it, provided I'm willing to make major changes and go to Wellington, where an editing bloke called Alex Fry will act as my literary guru.'

Someone had put him on to A.H. and A.W. Reed, the Wellington-based publishing house — and finally Crump was on good hunting ground. Reed had cut out a large and fertile niche for itself in the book-selling business, concentrating on local authors, and most especially those with a feel for high country adventure, sheep-mustering, deer-culling. And humour. The company had a hit with the hicks-in-the-sticks humour of Frank Anthony's *Me and Gus* stories, which had been a national hit as a radio series on the National Broadcasting Service way back in the 1920s before Reed turned them into best sellers in the early 1950s.

Reed had turned itself into something of an unstoppable force in New Zealand publishing by the time Crump came along with his elongated yarn. Reed's roots stretched back to the early 1900s, when it was founded by a God-fearing bloke down in Dunedin called Alfred Hamish Reed, who expanded his Sunday School-supply business into publishing books of a religious nature.

The memoirs of retired ministers didn't exactly sell by the wagonful, but Reed got a taste for the book business. It wasn't till the 1930s, when he took on his young nephew, Alexander Wyclif Reed, that Reed started to become a force. Young A.W. talked the old man into expanding into more popular lines of publication, feeding a hungry public historical and biographical tales and blackblocks memoirs. New Zealand was ready to explore its own past — and Reed was increasingly ready to supply.

Much of it was low-tone literature, roughly written and sometimes seemingly not edited at all. But a New Zealand with only crackly radio to take it outside its own four walls of an evening, lapped up the books. By the end of the 1930s, the first serious sproutings of New Zealand fiction were growing too. Crump would read some of these, most especially John Mulgan's *Man Alone*, which was published in 1939 and which drew the blueprint for the literary school of New Zealand blokeism.

That novel — Mulgan's only one (he killed himself in a Cairo hotel room in 1945) — has a much darker brew of violence, survival and misogyny, but it provides a powerful manure for Crump's angle on the mythic New Zealand male to grow on. Sprinkle on a trace of the gentler rural male humour of *Me and Gus* and perhaps there's a best seller waiting to happen....

Reed's Dunedin founding office closed in 1940 and the company's HQ transferred north to Wellington, where things started to take off under the control of the young returned soldiers like Ray Richards, who brought a focus and energy to Reed that would push the company to the forefront of New Zealand publishing, before television would come along and poke a stick in the eye of the nation's reading habit.

The company's success was partly due to the fact that the bulk of books sold in New Zealand bookshops had been British. No stock was held in New Zealand and the shops had to order ahead, not knowing whether they were getting a hit or a miss. And if it was a hit, they'd have to re-order and tell their customers to wait.

Reed, on the other hand, kept their books in three warehouses and if demand grew, so could supply. And the sort of things that Reed was supplying as the 1950s passed were books about footie, fishing and tough tales about leathery deer-cullers. A population that was beginning to move into town away from its country roots wanted to read about them, it seemed. The right sort of book — *Me and Gus*, for instance — might sell 20,000 copies at a time when a collection of poetry might sell (as now) only 500.

The word was out, and words poured in from potential authors. By the end of the 1950s, two or three or four manuscripts are coming into Reed's office every day and they are read and judged as quickly as possible. So it is no unusual thing when a distinctly scruffy, single-spaced typewritten and rather short manuscript turns up from Auckland. Crump has landed on just the right desk.

Richards has personal experience with shaping and creating best sellers. He knows his market and he knows what will sell. Humour will sell, hunting will sell, back country books will sell and books illustrated by artists will sell. This *Good Keen Man* manuscript is rough as guts. Rougher. But it contains virtually all of the magic ingredients. And it has a magic of its own. But it's a magic that needs a serious polish.

This Crump character's stories are as much fact as fiction, as much fiction as fact. They're funny and idiosyncratic. 'We can publish this,' Richards decides and sends off an encouraging letter to the would-be author. Richards' attitude is that there's no risk attached to publishing this book, once it's had a good reworking. It's a bit short too, so he thinks they'll set it in a larger-than-usual type size and get it illustrated. That way they might get it up to a reasonable 160 pages or so.

On hearing the news that Reed is prepared to take him seriously, Crump buys an ancient Chev and he and Jean set off on a breakdown-plagued trip to Wellington to get a close look at this Ray Richards fellow, along with further details on what he's to do next. He gets the impression his book needs a bit more work.

as cocky as hell

They rent a one-room flat in Aro Street, in downtown Wellington, under Crump's name and he gets a job working on the construction site of the new Wellington Airport. And into Ray Richards' office wanders a tall, thin, strangely featured man with a long nose, a calm air and a laconic turn of phrase, though he doesn't seem very sure of himself.

Richards tells him, 'Well, you know the thing that sells books more than anything else is word of mouth' and Crump tells him straight back, 'I've got a heck of a lot of mates'. And that's true, of course. But they're mainly mates left behind. Mates who, when they read Crump's Crumpish yarns will know who and where he fleeced them from. Some will be bitter, some jealous. Some, like Jack Lasenby, will recognise the yarns for what they are — drawn from the experience, folklore, bullshitting and skiting that ran like a river through their lives as deer-cullers.

Richards is used to dealing with deer-cullers-turned-authors and Crump is impressed by the way the pint-sized publisher handles himself. 'He tells me my manuscript needs something called editorial attention and that he's going to put me in the hands of a journalist called Alex Fry who's done this sort of thing before. He'll sort out the grammar and the punctuation and the way the story runs. They're going to get an artist to do pictures to go with it too. The most impressive thing is that they give me a fifty-quid advance.'

Richards runs Crump home to his flat afterwards and as they drive up Aro Street Crump confides to him, 'Oh by the way, I have to tell you this. I'm living with a woman', as if to explain and to shock at the same time.

Richards sends Crump's scruffy masterpiece round to Alex Fry with a note attached describing it as a 'bit of a sow's ear as it stands at present'. Fry isn't particularly enthralled with the subject. He's surprised that a book concerned with something as trivial as the slaughter of deer could be expected to command any sort of audience. It seems strange too that the book-to-be comes from a man who is living a life hardly anyone in New Zealand lives any more in 1960.

But he can see that there's a bright man lurking inside the almost-caricatured bushwhacking exterior. Crump might talk like a pioneer, but he's perceptive and he learns fast. He's written *A Good Keen Man* the way he thinks people write books. From his brief research, Crump has figured that the author is never a character in a book, though it's patently obvious that Crump — not Bill Davies — is the man in the middle of the story.

The unlikely pair of them work hard at it and Crump learns fast, helped by the fact that he has a fresh and natural flair for storytelling. The combination of his offhand style and his huge personal charisma give him a marvellous unvarnished power. It's as if he's written a set of clothes that he's happy to wear — once Fry persuades Crump to make his book about the adventures of Barry Crump.

Fry isn't interested in the fee Reed offers him, but says he'll settle for a third of the author's royalties, thinking it might sell 5000 copies or so and that he'll be slightly better off with that. And Crump doesn't seem to mind that arrangement or mind taking instruction on how a book should be written, even if the bloke giving instructions doesn't know a bloody thing about deer-culling. Isn't probably even much interested in it. Crump doesn't protest at having his book extensively altered because he can see that the changes make it work. It's really got life now.

When *A Good Keen Man* is finally polished and presentable, Crump insists on a dedication that reads, 'for money', until Fry points out that it'll look a bit stupid if the book doesn't actually make any, so Crump settles for a slightly more subtle 'For L.S.D.', though, within a few years, that too will carry dodgy connotations. Then Richards commisions the gifted Dennis Turner to illustrate the book, builds strategically placed blank pages into its layout to fatten it up a bit and she's a goer.

Now the book begins with an evocative note ... 'Trevor trod heavily about the hut in unlaced boots building a fire and swinging the first tea billy of the day' and it ends with an almost mythical sense of mystery: 'I placed my mug upside-down on the table and turned in. The world of stone fireplaces, trees and rivers belonged again to the owl and the possum.'

Crump writes from his recent experiences and, cut to shape by the sharp pen of Alex Fry, his own tales come to glow with a reality and a shy love-of-the-life almost custom-made to entrance a city-bound New Zealand. There's a rough poetry in his writing when he talks of 'the mist lifting up out of the gullies and creek-beds in dirty bundles like Romney fleeces' and 'the graveyard effects of enforced idleness' when bad weather comes down in the high country. As he did in the bush, Crump learns this new craft fast so he won't need a teacher next time round.

As a result of being round the Reed office, the staff — and Richards especially — come to see a lot of this strange mock-rustic figure. He accepts invitations to Richards' home to parties and dinners. He usually comes alone, rubbing shoulders with other Reed authors and fitting in naturally enough — though casting a somewhat larger shadow than the other guests. One night he commands the floor in front of the fireplace, reciting dozens of verses of 'Eskimo Nell', which comes as a shock to the ladies because it goes on forever and doesn't get any nicer as it unravels.

Through Jean, Crump meets other, wilder literary sorts. He meets and gets quite matey with poet James K. Baxter and his wife Jackie when Baxter is working as a postman by day and drinking heavily by night.

Crump, a couple of times, goes round on a Sunday night to visit Richards, his wife Barbara and their three girls, sitting by the fire with them, sweetly fitting in with the family, almost a child himself, and never playing the show-off. Crump has a remarkable ability to let his imagination fly and astonish anyone who was a witness. He can spin a yarn woven from total fantasy with himself in the lead role and be so spell-binding as to enthrall and convince his audience, even though they know it's a pack of lies.

Crump is a performer in search of a stage. Maybe he'll find it in this book. Who knows?

Back in Auckland, Crump proudly takes his manuscript round for a visit to his old mate Lasenby, who's holed up in the little room with a gas stove he's been renting for years down in Grafton Road as his city pad. Jack reads it, mainly concerned to see himself and his mates reflected in it. He can't detect any literary merit at all, but he's hardly objective on the subject. He can see, though, that it's a bloody good yarn. Bloody good.

Crump's starting to think it's all bloody good too. Reed give him an escalating royalty on his book — 10 percent up to 3000 copies sold, 12-and-a-half percent up to 6000 copies and then a handsome 15 percent. Unusually, the publisher even coughs up for the costs of the illustrations. Crump's off and happy.

'I've got a big cash advance for the book and I'm feeling well-paid and more than happy with the transaction. I'm using the money as a down-payment on a V8 truck and taking off for other adventures with more freedom and confidence now that I've been accepted as an author.'

One of the other things Reed ask of Crump, the about-to-be author, before he buggers off back to the bush, is an outline of his life up to that point. Crump manages to fit that into a page and a half, listing his hobbies as 'women, beer, women, cars and women, keeping an antiquated vehicle on the road, staying out of town and getting advances off publishers'. He lists his favourite poet as Dylan Thomas and writes off New Zealand writing as 'too serious' with 'too many psychologists about'.

'I want to write about people — not what goes on in their minds, but in people's bloody lives. I'm going to write a new book based on this principle and I'm going to apply for a state literary grant I've been told about. And I'm getting out of town.'

Crump heads off rabbiting in the Wairarapa and on to the Taupo and Reporoa districts. Then strange news trickles through. To his astonishment it seems that *A Good Keen Man* is selling remarkably well. His royalty payments are trickling in. He has an income.

The success of *A Good Keen Man* amazes everyone. Ray Richards and Reed are confident that the book has the right ingredients and that it won't fail in terms of making them a profit. Richards knows too that Crump's string of yarns has something else. It's in the humour, the language and in the attitude. And Crump stands as tall as his tales. This is an author with almost lethal charisma.

There's no one quite like this man.

The man has to hide in the bush to keep his big head out of sight. He knows it makes a good target and he's got to figure out how he's going to handle all this success. Some of his old deer-culling mates aren't impressed by his show-off book, reckoning he's just a skite, pinching other people's yarns and exaggerating his abilities. It's hard for them to swallow *A Good Keen Man* as fiction when it's full of twisted fact and the main character is a factual character called Barry Crump.

'Jean and I are just getting into a routine and now all hell breaks loose with *A Good Keen Man* having to be reprinted over and over. I've got wads of newspaper clippings saying extravagant things about my writing. I got a cheque for hundreds of pounds. One journalist reckons I didn't even write it and I wanted to find him and rip his head off. I'm already getting affected by it.'

Crump is getting affected by it. He swiftly adjusts to his rising tide of income, spending it so fast and so mysteriously that he's almost always broke and looking for some new opportunity not to be. As the sales keep racking up, the thought of that third of the royalties from *A Good Keen Man* that he so casually signed over to Alex Fry is beginning to rub a raw patch on Crump, despite Fry's crucial contribution.

Over the years, Fry will allow his cut to reduce to a quarter, a fifth and down to a notional one percent until it eventually disappears altogether. He starts to feel guilty about how much he's earning from that one-off casual editing project.

Fry gets a blunt and violent message from Crump as to how the suddenly famous author feels about the deal. They run into each other occasionally in Wellington and Fry isn't sure what he's dealing with now that Crump's a famous author. The pupil is perhaps turning into a monster.

There's a party at a friend of Fry's. Crump has deliberately not been invited. He has earned a reputation for getting drunk and being foul-mouthed, insulting and generally unpleasant. Crump crashes the party, blissfully uncaring of what some — many — of the crowd think of his well-worn and increasingly unpredictable act of asking women if they want a fuck and loudly reciting 'Eskimo Nell'. He's at his foulest, it has been observed, when he's been too long in town and at the time of this particular party he's in sore need of solitude.

Fry, playing the decent innocent, asks Crump to leave the party. Crump invites him outside and Fry stupidly accepts. No sooner does he turn around than Crump cracks his nose, puts him down and gets in with the boot. Nobody tells Crump what to do, least of all leave. Least of all some bastard who's getting rich from his book. Fry comes round with a broken nose and three broken ribs for his attempted gallantry. After that, there was a natural rupture in relations.

Anyway, Crump isn't sure that he wants to be anybody's mate. Mates wear out quicker than cheap pants. They get to be a burden to haul around. You want to travel light and that goes for friendships too. They can be the heaviest of all. 'I'm an outsider. I'm detached. I walk the lonely path. It scares me sometimes how alone I am. But I feel like I see things with a clear eye being apart.' Crump's already mythologising his role in life. But there's something about the pain of it he likes. 'Sometimes when I'm lonely I feel best.'

§

7.

the fastest gun

1961

The Literary Fund Advisory Committee makes a grant of £150 to Barry Crump, of Taupo, to assist him in writing a follow-up to his successful first novel, *A Good Keen Man*, it is announced in the daily popular press, though Crump's not sure he wants this sort of personal information getting out. People might start thinking he cares about money, though of course he does. And now he's going to have to write another book to make some more of the damned stuff. It seems to run through his hands like water.

The publisher is dead keen. *A Good Keen Man* is so successful it's all Reed can do to keep up with the demand. However many they print, they need to print more. It will go on to be reprinted 14 times. There has never quite been anything like it. There never will be again. Well, not for Crump.

The publication of *A Good Keen Man* changes everything and opens Crump up to a level of attention he's totally unprepared for. He likes an audience, of course, but hell's teeth, this is ridiculous. Suddenly he seems to be immensely attractive to everyone — men and women. Now he's got well-off, well-dressed, well-educated women falling all over him, not hesitating to show how sexually attractive they find him. At first it's wonderful, but after a while it's something else altogether.

One night in Devonport, over on Auckland's North Shore, Crump and Lasenby head down to one of the pubs on the waterfront for a quiet drink or 10 and a bit of a yarn. A young joker comes over and wants to drink with them. Crump politely explains that he just wants to catch up with his cobber and 'no thanks very much', but the young man takes it badly, turns nasty and starts accusing Crump of thinking he's too good for ordinary people now — the people who bought his book and probably made him rich and famous. Crump and Lasenby end up having to walk out.

'I can't barely even go into a pub now without some young joker who thinks he's going to be the fastest gun in the west and pick a fight and beat up the older joker. I can see it stretching out ahead of me. I can cope with it now, but in 10 years I'm going to have younger, fitter, quicker blokes coming up to me and wanting to pick a fight in every boozer I go into. Life could become intolerable.'

Meanwhile, Crump's publisher is reacting the way any publisher would faced with the totally unexpected and runaway success of a first-time writer's novel. They want another book. Fair enough, says Crump, promptly moving to South Westland. 'I'm shooting deer for a bob a pound and trying my hand at other things such as whitebaiting and gold panning that I've picked up locally. I like the Coast. It's like 100 years ago down here. They're straight-shooting people, the Coasters.'

Crump comes to the writing life profoundly unqualified. He's bluffed and crammed his way past the usual apprenticeship. But he has an instinct for stories, not all of them his own. He carries a notebook and he scribbles down his improbable thoughts before they fly out of his head forever. He scribbles down stories and ideas he hears and tries to catch in words some of the characters he meets, pinching their best stories and painting swift word pictures of their personalities. He's now forever on the lookout for stories to string together for some future book.

He likes to make out writing a book's as easy as everything else he's done, but it's not and Crump's nervous about his next book. *A Good Keen Man* was easy in lots of ways — his own adventures as an apprentice deer-culler magnified, made up and thrown onto the page. This next one, though, is going to be more like proper fiction. Crump doesn't think of *A Good Keen Man* as fiction at all. But he's going to have to make this one up, make the main character someone other than himself. Someone real, but not real at all. He's got a name for him. Sam Cash. And Sam Cash is going to be a man a bit like Crump, a man who's finding it increasingly hard to find the space to be a man anymore in a world that's conspiring to fence him in and tell him how to live his life when all he wants is a little freedom and a few adventures, out of town where the world's still a bit like it used to be.

This will be Crump's ultimate shoot-through handbook and he's calling it *Hang on a Minute Mate*, the title a slice cut as fresh from Kiwi vernacular as its now-famous predecessor, *A Good Keen Man*, was. And, like its predecessor, this book is a thinly veiled string of yarns bound together by the strides of a larger-than-life character.

The book is a tale of two Crumps. There's Sam Cash, a man who looks 'at his wife the way a man looks at a steep ridge he's got to climb on a hot day' and promptly buggers off to chase a string of adventures. The spark that fires the cynical Cash to set off in search of life the way it should be is the arrival of Jack Lilburn, who represents the other, younger, Crump, a semi-empty vessel Sam Cash can pour his wit, wisdom and endless fund of yarns into.

The story starts with a real dazzle, capping Cash's misogynistic opening monologue with the arrival of young Jack on his doorstep in the hands of the local constabulary who've caught the young man red-handed trying to drain petrol from the car outside the Cash house. Cash responds by telling the cops that the young man is a family friend who's welcome to help himself to petrol. It's a lie, of course, and having sent the confused cops packing, the roguish Cash packs in his troubles, packs some gear and a gun and hits the road with Jack in search of adventure and a life away from the wife and outside the law. The car parked outside, it turns out, isn't even his.

There's plenty of work to be found out there on the road, Sam tells Jack. 'There's mustering and shearing gangs this time of year. Fencing and scrub-cutting, packing, logging — any amount of jobs going. Never tell them you can't do a thing. Get stuck in and have a go. By the time they find out you've never done it before, you're doing it.'

Hang on a Minute Mate is a kind of western, with Sam Cash as a dodgy sort of John Wayne and Jack Lilburn as the Kid, grabbing all the laconic advice the older man dispenses. It's Sam the teacher and Jack the pupil and Crump jams the book with hands-on detail as they drift from one rustic short-term job to the next. Sam's cynicism and his criminal mentality give this story much darker tones than Crump's first book. Mostly they surface in the exchanges between Sam and Jack.

'Where are you thinking of settling down, Sam?'

'Anywhere suits me, Jack. As long as it's not more than a few weeks I'll tackle anything there's a quid in.'

'Sounds like a good idea, Sam, but do you think there'd be enough jobs for us to do?'

'More than enough,' said Sam. 'If we run out of a job we'll make one by wrecking something that'll have to be fixed.'

'We couldn't get away with that too many times.'

'Anything's better than being tied down to one place,' said Sam decidedly. 'That'll kill a man quicker than a cut throat.'

Then Sam is off into a vaguely illustrative yarn from his bottomless bag. 'Y'know this reminds me of ....' is a favourite Cashism as he slips sideways into someone else's story. Crump even borrows one from the domestic life of big brother Bill for the story of Sam's mate whose wife locks him out of the house one night, obliging him to cut a new front door with a chainsaw. But there's a quieter voice too where Crump's love of the bush life and fear of the city life surfaces.

In the cold mountain days, Jack learned how to sneak up on deer and shoot them with Sam's old shotgun and the candle-grease cartridges. He learned how to bake a loaf of bread in the iron camp-oven, tickle trout in the creek, and how to guess whether it was going to rain or not by the way the cloud lay along the range in the mornings. In the cold mountain evenings Sam told him how in the big cities they work by hours and minutes and save their money to buy things they don't want because they've already got everything they need. And how they wear small shoes because they don't want anyone to know they've got big feet, and ladies are more important because of their sex and men have to let them go first through doors and things. How shop windows are for seeing what you look like in, and a job writing letters is more important than a job fixing fences, and you pay more for a leg of meat than a good knife. How flash cars are for paying off and insurance companies. And when you buy a house you still have to go on paying for it after it's paid for, because of rates and things. And if you don't watch it they'll get you for income tax and sock you a hundred quid right off.

Hundreds of things Jack learned off Sam in the days they loafed and waited until the big mob poured down the main valley in a rolling, surging cloud, soaked up Sam and Jack's mob and carried it along. The other musterers climbed the ridge to the hut for a boil-up, then the eight of them rode down to the river and set the big mob moving again. Sam and Jack were sent out to one side to watch for strays and keep the mob from spreading. Jack felt more important then than he'd ever felt before. He galloped back and forth shouting: Speak up Moss, and whistling Nigger to go and head off a straying sheep, then riding round it himself because Nigger took no notice of him and refused to leave the horse's heels. It was a waste of time trying to work Nigger but Jack worked him just the same because it sounded good.

(from *Hang on a Minute Mate,* **1961)**

They live life by the Sam Cash prescription and never stay anywhere long, Crump justifying this footloose stance with mythic phrases. 'We've seen where this road comes from, Jack me boy,' said Sam as they climbed back into the cab. 'Let's see where she goes to....' Or, on the fraught matter of women and marriage and the dread prospect of settling down, 'No, Jack me boy, the woman caper is a crook one....

'Once a woman gets you she hangs on like a rata. There's kids and telephones and boots off before you come into the house and you've had it! You've got as close as you can get but it's not close enough. And you can't go back and have another go at it because you're too busy telling lies to keep yourself out of trouble to even remember what being a man is like.

'No, Jack me boy, she's a grim business. I only wish you could learn from what happened to me, but you'll have to see it for yourself or it won't be real,

'But you don't have to marry them,' said Jack uncertainly.

'If they want y', they'll get y'. Don't worry about that lot! They've got all the gear to do it with,' answered Sam, 'definitely.'

And the story darkens as it lengthens, Sam, drunk as a skunk, landing up in jail for pinching a Ministry of Works grader and towing a car down the main street of Tokoroa. He also owes hundreds in maintenance to his abandoned wife. When young Jack tracks him down to Mt Crawford Prison, Sam refuses to see him, as good as his word, a loner to the end. *Hang on a Minute Mate* is printed with the dedication, 'For L.S.D. again.'

After the runaway — and continuing — sales of *A Good Keen Man*, the booksellers of New Zealand are enthusiastic about Crump's follow-up, which they hear is even better. One bookseller in Masterton buys an ancient second-hand car that more or less looks like Sam Cash's vehicle in the book and parks it at the parking meter in front of his shop. He leaves it there day after day and fills the shop windows with Crump's books. He orders 1000 copies and Crump turns up to sign some. After the 1000 sells, the shop orders more.

Month after month, Reed are ordering another 5000 copies. Things get so confused with all this reprinting at Reed's printers over in Sydney that when an order comes through for 5000 each of *A Good Keen Man* and *Hang on a Minute Mate* they print them in the wrong covers and ring Ray Richards to report the technical misadventure and allow, 'Well, we've lost a bundle over this little mistake'.

But ingenuity jumps in and the printers are instructed to pop all 10,000 wrongly jacketed books in the guillotine, chop off the spines, glue them in pairs and call it *Two In One*, a best of Barry Crump. And that swiftly sells 5000 copies too. And so it goes.

Reed want a steady supply of new Barry Crump books for the hungry personal market he — and they — have created.

By 1962, *A Good Keen Man* and *Hang on a Minute Mate* will have sold nearly 100,000 copies between them. Crump is big in the backblocks, in the towns in the days of the personality booksellers who relate to a personality like Crump. Reed want a new book a year, thank you very much Barry. They like to put them out in October so they can sell out and the shops can restock and then sell out again. And then it's Christmas and everyone buys one for the husband and the father and the teenage boy.

It becomes part of Ray Richards' job to get these books out of Crump. Often the first problem is finding him, though Crump's always sure to leave them an address to send the royalty cheques to. And he's forever shouting out for more cheques. Richards finds him roaming the country rabbiting and deer shooting and doing odd jobs and having a good time. Often he's not quite in the mood to write a new book.

But the pattern will be established in the 1960s for Crump, the writer of no fixed abode. This will give him an income of about $70,000 a year during those years, though the amount of money Reed pays him appears to be of no consequence to Crump, who gets through it rapidly and never bothers about paying his taxes. He doesn't believe in taxes. This attitude eventually brings him serious grief and what with Tina chasing him for support money and now the Inland Revenue Department, Ray Richards takes the radical course of putting Crump's chaotic financial affairs into the hands of a public accountant.

The publisher pays Crump's considerable royalties to the accountant, the accountant pays the tax and then pays Crump. And Crump howls like hell about this, but he promises never to breach the arrangement. Reed figure that eventually New Zealand's seemingly endless appetite for his first two efforts will be sated and they'd like the next book. But Crump is feeling perverse and has other ideas.

A 'good keen man' has retired at the rather premature age of 28, according to a story in the *New Zealand Herald* in February, 1962. 'Mr Crump admitted that he had "pots of dough". He made a "few thousand" last year and it would be more this year.' Four English and four American publishers are seeking rights to his two books, he reckons.

'I have retired on what I have made,' says Crump, who then goes on to confuse the whole retirement issue by announcing that he's working on his third book, 'to be titled perhaps *Situation Vacant*.' It is to be, he tells the newspaper, a 'quality' writing job.

Crump's finding it easier and easier to get bored these days and suddenly feels tired of the bushman's life. Travelling up the West Coast, he and Jean have a flaming row. They make it to Wellington where he dumps her and one night goes to a party where there are some of the literary set. There he meets the sort of

Lily and Wally — a saint and a monster.

Three cherubs — Bill, Barry and Colin.

Crump (third from left) roughing it with the rough boys and learning everything he could — deer-culling in the 1950s.

Mike Bennett

Crump with deer-culling mates and trophies. From left, Alan Duncan, Crump, Jack Lasenby (booze in hand), Roy King, Bob Young and Rex Newton.

Crump and first wife Tina all dressed up in the 1950s — he was no lapdog.

Crump and baby Ivan — not a doting dad for long.

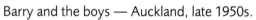
Barry and the boys — Auckland, late 1950s.

Chapter one.

------I Become A Deer Culler.

~~It was~~ Ten years ago ~~when~~ I ~~first~~ trickled into the office to
ask about a job shooting deer for the Government.₫ was sent to see a
bloke called Jim Reed,who had a little office at the back of the
building.He was about forty-five years old and looked as fit as a
buck rat,which he was.Parked beside the door was a little grey truck
with a canvas canopy,a full load of dogs and 'Wildlife Branch' painted on the doors. Jim was the sort of bloke who only talked when he
had something to say.

After a job eh son? he asked,waving towards a chair.

Yes Sir!

How old are you Boy?

Eighteen,I said,exaggerating by two years.

He wrote on a bit of paper.

Done any hunting before?

Too right,Been after goats and pigs in the Karakatai for years!

Well you'll find the deer a bit different from that sort of stuff.
You got any of your dogs with you?

No,a mate of mine at Riverside is looking after them for me.

O.K.,well fill in this form and take it round to the main office,
they'll fix you up with the rest.Then you'd better come back here and
I'll work out what we're going to do with you---Oh and by the way,
you'd better tell them you're nineteen,eighteen's a bit young for
this caper.

A bloke round the front gave me a hand to fill in the application
form and asked me who my next-of-kin-was,in case of accident.Then he
said 'right,you've had it', and sent me back to Jim,who gave me an
envelope to hand to the Field Officer at a base camp at the end of a
road ~~that a milling company~~ had put up the ~~Waitenui~~ River.He gave me
instructions as to how to get there and a list of all the gear I need
ed (I found later that half of it was superfluous). Then he unlocked
a big store room and helped me to select a rifle from a rack that
held about a hundred of them.

We pay you seven pounds ten a week and ten bob a skin and five bob
if you just bring the tails in. We supply all the ammunition,but if

The manuscript for *A Good Keen Man*... 'bit of a sow's ear'.

Whitcombe & Tombs Ltd

PRIVATE BAG C.P.O.

TELEGRAPHIC ADDRESS

"WHITCOMBES"

TELEPHONE
ALL DEPTS. 32-650

PUBLISHERS, PRINTERS AND
MANUFACTURING STATIONERS

AUCKLAND. C.1
NEW ZEALAND

WAREHOUSES:
AUCKLAND
HAMILTON
WELLINGTON
LOWER HUTT
CHRISTCHURCH
TIMARU
DUNEDIN
INVERCARGILL
LONDON
MELBOURNE
SYDNEY
PERTH

13th July, 1959

Mr. B.J. Crump,
"Pilgrim Press"
75 Wakefield Street,
AUCKLAND C.1.

Dear Sir,

We thank you for submitting your MS which we have read
with interest. We regret, however, we are unable to undertake the
publication as the cost would not make it a profitable proposition
for either you or ourselves.

Yours faithfully,
WHITCOMBE & TOMBS LTD

NP/DM

per:

A Good Keen Man rejected.

Young, hungry and topless — the best-selling author in the 1960s.

Ray Richards

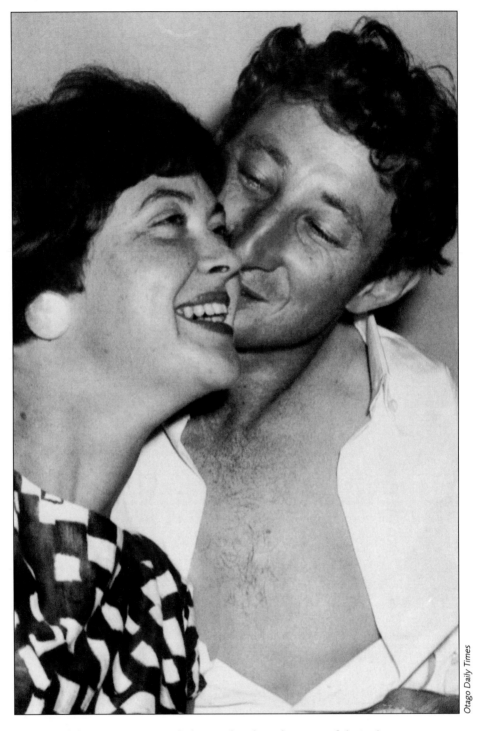

Dizzy with lust — Crump and Fleur Adcock at the start of their short, ridiculous marriage.

woman he hasn't run into before — and whom, for lack of anything better to want, he decides he wants. She is a talented young poet called Fleur Adcock and she is probably as close to a total opposite of himself that Crump has come across. It's a match made in hell, but they strike it for the sheer madness and physicality of it.

It turns out to be physical alright. Right from the stupid beginning, it's physical. It's immediately apparent Crump doesn't much like the idea of sharing his considerable proximity with a woman who is not only bloody hopeless in the kitchen, strong-minded and argumentative and disinclined to do what he tells her, but also maybe smarter than him. She knows Greek, for Christ's sake.

§

8.

a vague
contempt

1962

Fleur has a vague contempt for people who write the sort of thing Crump writes. It's all just boys' talk to her. And Crump thinks Fleur's a bit too bright and flash for her own good. But she's a gorgeous looking woman, the sex symbol of the literary set, once married to the poet Alistair Campbell and she's with their five-year-old son, Andrew. Everyone's as drunk as always at the party and there are a lot of complications and unpredictable emotions. Crump and Fleur are in the process of escaping other relationships, put things behind them a bit. Crump tells Fleur that Jean was practically sending out wedding invitations and that she'd even told her parents they were getting married. He's not having any of that, he says.

She's never met anyone like him before, being more used to studious academic types. Barry is so colourful. And he has a certain charm, she thinks. And he's sexy. He gives her so much attention it makes her glow, cracks little jokes, says the most outrageous things. He seems so … exaggerated. She never knew there were people like this.

One Sunday afternoon, Crump and Fleur and little Andrew turn up at Ray Richards' house and sit with the family on their terrace with tea and cakes. It's all nice and almost nervously normal until one of the little Richards girls asks, 'Well, Mr and Mrs Crump, how many children do you have?' and Barry and Fleur don't seem to know how many children they have. The girls are amazed that Mr Crump appears not to know how many members of the family there are.

Crump continues to court Fleur, comes to her home, and when she goes into the kitchen to make a cup of tea he says to her mother, 'I miss her when she's out of the room'. He's very good at charming old ladies. They think he's delightful. Then Crump follows Fleur to Dunedin where she has worked as a librarian for four years — and where he marries her.

'I don't like her poetry and she doesn't like my books', but nonetheless New Zealand's best-selling author Barry Crump and 'the poetess Mrs Fleur Campbell' announce their engagement in Dunedin in February, according to the Press Association. 'Take your glasses off,' Mrs Campbell tells the author when a photographer asks them to pose. 'But they make me look intellectual,' says Crump.

When asked who has the upper hand in the relationship, they reply together, 'It's a partnership'. Mrs Campbell will continue her work in the Otago University library and Mr Crump will be 'engaged on his third book', his first two having sold more than 100,000 copies between them.

In June, 'Wellington author' Barry John Crump is granted an unconditional discharge from bankruptcy in the Supreme Court at Auckland. Crump's counsel tells the court that creditors have been paid in full. Crump is present in Court with his wife.

But the marriage is ridiculous from the start. From even before the start, really. They only did it to horrify their friends. 'Don't get married,' Fleur's friends whisper. 'Have an affair instead.' But she's had affairs already and they didn't prove anything and anyway, she's tired of her quiet life. They get married the day before Fleur's twenty-eighth birthday and this is definitely the end of her quiet life. For a while, anyway. Crump can't even wait till after they're married before he cheats on her. The night before the wedding, he disappears with another woman, a nurse, and doesn't return, leaving her sitting in a coffee bar.

Next morning she has to go and drag him out of some pub to even go to the Registry Office — Fleur with a bruised lip where her husband-to-be belted her, and little Andrew all dressed up in a clean shirt with a little bag of confetti his grandmother has bought him. It never really gets any better. She's never been part of a scene where the women stay in the kitchen and get a feed ready while the men go down to the pub and get tanked up, but now she's in it, deep. Someone rings Crump a few days after the wedding and asks, 'How's Fleur?'

'I'm turning her into a doormat,' says Crump, but Fleur isn't doormat material for very long. And of course he doesn't have a job because he's a writer now. But really he is totally disorganised and at a loose end. His accountant is only feeding him his royalty money in dribs and drabs. He's often in the pub by nine in the morning, while Fleur is off to her respectable job as a librarian, Crump mocking her librarian clothes, the little white blouses with collars.

Fleur never quite knows where her new husband is. He often disappears for days and nights at a time and it doesn't pay to quiz him too closely on where he's been and with whom. If he gets annoyed with you, Fleur quickly learns, he hits you. He doesn't like people answering back, least of all women. Least of all his brainy bloody wife, who seems to know a lot of things he doesn't, though mainly the sort of things education teaches you. He insists that she teach him Greek, but he loses interest after learning how to spell his name in it.

He makes an effort with Andrew, in that way that he seems to with other people's kids. He larks about, sillier than a kid himself. Sometimes too silly, too big and physical and intense, too frightening. This sudden stepfather is exciting, takes Andrew trout fishing and on trips to the backblocks in a Land Rover. But sometimes when he's yelling at his mother and she's yelling back, Andrew looks up at the shotgun Crump keeps on the wall and fantasises about ripping it down and defending his mother.

One night Fleur decides to get Barry once and for all, get him back for the violence, the lies, the awful arrogance. She waits till he's asleep and creeps up with a huge Latin dictionary she intends to bash his head in with. Her arm's in plaster, broken in a recent domestic incident, so it's not easy to lift the dictionary. But as she does, about to bring it down on his damned head, his arm shoots out in his sleep and grabs her. There's something a bit spooky about him sometimes. He can do all sorts of things in his sleep. One night, in his sleep, he tells Fleur the dream he's dreaming, as he's dreaming it. He's completely forgotten it the next morning.

Fleur just can't cope with this creature she's married. He is just not constructed like other people. She — no one — has any idea what he's going to do next. He's completely unpredictable. He can be unexpectedly charming, unexpectedly generous, unexpectedly cold, frozen. The only thing that can be predicted about him, she's deciding, is that he'll always shoot through. Head for the horizon.

Crump quickly tires of the gentle charms of Dunedin. Fleur lines up a job at the Alexander Turnbull Library in Wellington, but has to work out a month's notice in Dunedin. But Crump's not waiting round for her and shoots through for Wellington, leaving her to pack up their flat and organise the move.

As soon as he's back in Wellington, Crump looks up Jean. He sets her up with a job in Sydney, with Reed's print people there. Fleur, suffering her way bewildered through each painful month of this awful marriage, finds out about Crump's philandering by accident. The Post Office rings asking for a Mr Crump who's sent a telegram that morning and paid a shilling too much. Fleur pops into town to pick up the shilling and discovers the telegram has gone to Jean Watson in Australia to say he'll be on his way over shortly, ready for his next adventure.

So's Fleur. She wants to ship out to England, where there's no such thing as a bushman. She wants to put this unfortunate experiment behind her. The marriage has lasted five months.

Crump had seen Jean off to Australia at Wellington Airport, her only luggage a flax kit with some books in it and a copper teapot she'd found in a second-hand shop to keep her papers and money inside. He'd have gone with her, only there was a mix-up with his passport and he couldn't just disappear the way he wanted to.

Meanwhile Crump is about to knock out another book.... Well, that's what he's told his publisher, who are dead keen on a third best seller from the hand of their rough-hewn new literary star. But then Crump decides what he needs is a new adventure, something he's never done before. Something no deer-culler he knows has done. He's off to Australia to hunt something a lot more unpredictable than deer, possums or rabbits. He's taking himself off to the Gulf of Carpentaria in northern Australia to be a crocodile hunter. There should be a bloody good book in that. And a bit of humour to be had.

Meantime his third book, *One of Us*, is due out and he doesn't care if he's round for that. In fact, he's so offhand about this book that he fails to supply an ending and goes bush leaving Ray Richards a chapter short of a book. The printers are screaming and Crump's off the map, so Richards sits down at the typewriter and bangs out an ending. No one notices, least of all Crump.

One of Us is the further adventures of that hobo philosopher Sam Cash, who's off again running away from everything in general with a useless cobber or two in tow, filling every silence with a yarn and never sticking to anything for any longer than he needs to. It treads familiar ground in its footloose male, woman-fearing world, though it does it with the now-established Crump cheek and charm.

> The early morning sunlight shone through Ponto's big ears and lit them up like a pair of late-model tail-lights. Behind him Sam was transferring some tobacco into his pocket from the pocket of Ponto's coat hanging on the door of the shed they'd slept in. Ponto hadn't got much sleep. He'd sat huddled in a corner, shaking like a dog on a river bank all night. Sam had squatted by the door smoking and thinking and dozing on and off.
>
> They were somewhere north of Murchison. How far neither of them was certain, though they'd agreed it was somewhere between twenty and a hundred and fifty miles.

It was a half-fine morning, with bush all round and the raining-on-leaves sound of a creek somewhere nearby or a big river in the distance. Ponto was sitting on a clump of fern on the bank above the road brooding.

'That's definitely the last time I'm sleeping on the ground,' he complained in a voice as stiff as his knees. 'It's no bloody good to a man my age. I'll end up getting rheumatism or something and have to retire. And I'm hungry,' he added.

Sam leaned against the wall of the hut watching the way Ponto's ears wiggled as he talked. Not getting an answer to what wasn't really a question anyway, Ponto turned to Sam and said, 'Do you know where this road leads to?'

'Well there's several ways of looking at it,' answered Sam, pinching the ends off a thin cigarette and lighting it. 'It could lead us to a dead-end, for one thing. It could take us to a flash job and a business of our own. Or it could lead us into a whole swag of trouble. It could lead us into the sea or into those mountains up there. It could lead us into the grave — anywhere. Y'see, Ponto old boy, it's not the road itself but the way you travel it. Some blokes bowl straight past some of the best things that are ever likely to happen to them because they don't see them. They're too busy looking towards the end of the journey to get a kick out of the travelling.'

(from *One of Us*, 1962)

Before he shoots through in pursuit of Australian adventures, Crump goes to visit Fleur and invites her out for a drink and, while they're sitting in the pub being polite, she asks him for a separation agreement. 'Sure,' he says and they stroll round to his solicitor, wait while he fills out the forms, sign them and go back to the pub to toast their own end. All Fleur wants from him is the fare to London she's booked for herself and Andrew. With a great sigh of relief that she's not going to go him for alimony, he hands over £140 or so.

He stays around for a few days and they have a pleasant enough time, now that they've buried the whole dreadful marriage business. Later, he'll sign across some of his royalties to her. She's just grateful to be shot of him. She's an Anglophile anyway and now — and perhaps forever — Barry Crump will epitomise a certain aspect of New Zealand she'd be only too happy to be half a world away from.

Crump doesn't have to travel half a world to get away from what's holding him down. All he has to do is get to Sydney where Jean is waiting with a flat to stay in and a Land Rover to shoot through in.

... whenever we loaded the Land Rover there was a great performance. Mainly because of all the junk she accumulated and wouldn't part with. One of these days I'm going to have a real clean-up but I haven't got around to it yet.

Anyway she hadn't even been officially invited on this trip. This croc-shooting was supposed to be a pretty dangerous game. A man wouldn't want to be tearing round all the time seeing that she didn't get into trouble. I was thinking of leaving her in Sydney till I'd had a look if it was suitable for a woman up there. I'd even wondered about jacking up a mate to go with me. But the only blokes I knew in Sydney who'd be any good were tied up with women or down with jobs, and they probably couldn't get away or weren't trying to....

(from *Gulf*, 1964)

Crump and Jean set off north from Sydney. They leave at seven in the morning and the rain is pouring down. There's nothing of interest until they reach the Blue Mountains and they're only interesting because they're so small. Heading north past a place called Warren, in New South Wales, they call in at a sheep station to inquire if they can camp and Crump can take a crack at shooting some kangaroos.

'Wangrawally is the name of the station and Yeaman is the name of the people. And no, we cannot under any circumstances go shooting kangaroos on their 30,000 acres. But I set to work on the boss for a while with my astonishing charm and when that doesn't work I tell him about being a writer.

'He literally gives me the station — takes us shooting in his Land Rover, gives us flash quarters to stay in and more food than we can possibly eat. He even suspends work on the station for the duration. The kangaroos are so thick there that you get tired of shooting at them. It's quite common to see well over a mile of 'roos spread out in a long hopping mob. Thousands of them. I've shot enough skins to make a rug. I've blown some emu eggs which I might try and hang onto to impress New Zealanders with. I like emus. They're good-looking birds. They're everywhere and they make good dog tucker.

'After a while it looks as though nothing short of armed resistance is going to get us away from the Yeamans, but a bit of the tactful Crump diplomacy prevents bloodshed and we leave for Lightning Ridge vowing eternal friendship and promising to keep in touch, as people always say and never do.'

At Lightning Ridge they dig for opal. Beautiful stones. 'I've got two real high-class opals and dozens of beautiful opalised potch. From there, we shoot over the border into Queensland and camp at a place called Hebel. In the early hours of the morning I was awakened by a truck roaring like a furnace.'

They find the truck stuck in the mud at the side of the road. There's a drover, his cook and shepherd. They're drunk as Aussie skunks, on their way back from the pub with 2800 sheep camped down the road. Crump and Jean come to their rescue, towing them out, though the drunk drover repays the favour by backing right into the Land Rover and smashing one of the parking lights. Full of thanks and apologies, the drunk Australians go back to the pub, buy a great stack of canned beer and come back, light a campfire and pour good Aussie beer down the throats of their rescuers. Crump begins to recite 'Eskimo Nell', but everyone's fallen asleep and he's left tailing off into thin air.

'At daylight the cook and the shepherd are out the monk and the drover himself, Darby Neale by name, not far behind them. I break up his camp and drive his truck to the next camping place. When I catch up to the mob, Darby has fallen off his horse and he's lying in the grass like a dead man. I wake up the cook and he and I take the mob onto the camp where everybody flakes out.'

Next day they go to the nearest pub where Crump gets paralytic, while Jean stays cold sober and takes notes in her travel diary. They get back to their camp by sheer luck. Crump flakes out and little Jean has to drag him, an inch at a time, into the Land Rover.

They travel north, occasionally delayed by encounters and adventures. They've been aiming for Normanton, in the far north of Queensland, but take the wrong road and land up well to the west in Burketown. A big notice says, 'Drive Slowly, Town Ahead' and they approach a shabby collection of worn-out buildings scattered over a flat area of bare dirt. One of them is a pub.

It's in this pub, at 8.30 in the morning, that the pair stumble upon a croc-hunter called Harry Blumenthals, or 'Harry Blue', a Latvian bloke who's been 10 years shooting crocodiles in the vicinity. He's a solitary sort of joker, but he's friendly enough. This is a man who might demonstrate the art of killing and skinning great big dangerous reptiles and he says he doesn't mind showing Crump how it's done. So they load up their vehicle with supplies and follow Harry Blue's old truck off towards the coast.

Harry Blue is an interesting character — so interesting, he leaves Crump feeling slightly shy and understated when faced with his new mate's exploits. He claims to have fought in the war, sold diamonds in Germany, lived with the Aborigines in the far outback, cohabited with the unpredictable natives of Torres Strait, been gold mining, opal mining, copper mining. You name the mining, he's done it. He's fascinated by wildlife. In fact he's almost a form of wildlife himself, wearing only ancient shorts or a loincloth made out of what looks like an old curtain.

They hunt crocodiles by night, drifting in a dinghy along a deep, slow river draped with spooky trees, made spookier by the spotlight Harry Blue wears, coal-miner style, atop his head. When they spot a croc, eyes red in the light, they drift towards it until Harry takes a shot with one of his rifles between its eyes. Crump, suddenly the eager apprentice again, tries sitting on the river bank with his rifle, waiting for crocs to surface. He manages to nail a couple.

'Harry likes having Jean and me around. We're real bushmen, he reckons.… He's a hard-case piece of work, the crocodile. He hasn't altered in 300 million years, they reckon. You'd never tame one, there's something prehistoric about them. You have to make sure you do everything right when you go after him. One flick from that tail and you're history. He doesn't run away from you because he doesn't know anything about being attacked.'

They go hunting the big salt-water crocs, hunting in a manner as primal as their prey — with 12-foot harpoons spiked with nine-inch barbed spikes and 80 feet of rope attached. He and Harry stab the crocs in the neck, the crocs go straight to the bottom and they wait with their .303s for them to surface. Then they shoot the croc in the side of the head until a bullet finally penetrates its dense skull and finds its tiny brain.

Then they rope its jaws, chop through the spine at the back of the neck with the axe they keep handy and float it back to shore for skinning. Harry tells Crump most people who ask him to take them croc hunting get taken to the worst, wettest, most-mossie-infested place he can find. Mostly, they go home quickly. He tells Crump he didn't put him and Jean to the same initiation because they didn't come from town. They were country people. 'Your wife is even a bushman.'

Crump even manages a letter back to his publisher, telling them he's started 'already' on another book. It's about 'ingeniousness', he says. 'How was the last book? I hope to hell it isn't a flop. Let me know what she turned out like and then I'll be able to sleep at night. Will now write to the accountant about needing more money. God save us — Barry Crump.'

Mike Bennett, an old Crump pal from the deer-culling days, joins up with Crump and Jean, who have made their way across to the eastern coast, to Cooktown. It's a struggle for Bennett to even get through in his Land Rover on the shattered road to this half-forgotten outpost on the edge of the wilderness. Cooktown is a tough little joint 200 km north of Cairns at the end of a road that disappears in the rainy season. The easiest way to get anywhere is by boat. But Bennett gets through and even finds the right pub in this three-pub town. It's called the Half Sovereign. It used to be called the Sovereign, but then a cyclone blew half the pub away.

Crump's in there leaning up against the bar as if no time has passed and there's nothing unusual about finding each other in this godforsaken place. 'Don't give that bloke a beer,' Crump instructs the barman. 'He won't pay.'

Crump has bought a 30-foot auxiliary diesel sloop, *Waterwitch*. He's never been much of a sailor, but not knowing much about something has never stopped Crump from giving it a crack and somehow he and Jean have managed to get the boat to Cooktown without sinking or running aground. They have it moored on a lugger wharf at the mouth of a stream, right opposite the Cooktown police station. Bennett moves in.

Nothing about the chaos of Crump's life surprises him, apart from the only thing about Crump that isn't chaotic — something new since he was last around Crump in the bush. There is now a discipline in Crump's life, just a tiny corner of it, but it's a discipline nonetheless. Wherever they are, whatever else is going on, Crump sits down most mornings and types a chapter of a book. Most extraordinarily, the book he's writing is another Sam Cash epic, set a world away from the heat and the strangeness of this temporary life in Australia's far north.

Crump decides that to earn themselves some diesel and drinking money, they should become tour operators, catering to the few hardy travellers who make it as far out of the way as Cooktown. They don't get many customers, but they do pick up a bloke called Miles, an Englishman who turns out to be a gentleman's gentleman — a butler — whom they bring on board for a look at the other side of life. They even show him how to skin a croc.

It's big dangerous country where they are, the sort of place someone as uncontrolled and downright foolhardy as Crump is bound to get himself into trouble in sooner or later. Once, when they find themselves cruising through half an acre of migrating coral snakes, Crump insists on jumping in the dinghy and trying to land a deadly nine-footer with a fish spear. One night, pissed as a newt, he falls off the Cooktown Wharf and lands in the mud. Bennett is tempted to leave him where he's lying. They've been fighting, as they have been quite a bit. Crump's a bastard when he's drunk. Especially to sweet, long-suffering little Jean, who persuades Bennett to climb down into the mud with her and drag Crump, safe from drowning, above the water mark. Crump repays this kindness, when he comes round, by accusing Jean of pushing him in.

Cooktown is a wild place. Get up early enough and you might meet a pig, a dingo or even a passing snake in the main street. One time or another the Crump gang are banned from every pub in town. They retaliate once by throwing a live python through the front doors of one of them. The police sergeant asks them to move the *Waterwitch* downstream so it's not moored opposite the police station. He says he'd rather get some sleep than listen to them drunkenly trying to make their way through the mud and onto the boat when the tide is out.

Crump's not very motivated about making money. They try collecting oysters off the rocks to sell and collect seashells to flog off to passing tourists, but his royalty cheques stop him from being poor enough to really give a damn about earning. They even catch the occasional crocodile, though their carelessness almost costs them dearly. Once, a 12-footer comes back to life as they're sliding it up the mud to the river bank. With a great flick of the tail it sends Bennett flying and almost gets its great jaws free of the rope Crump's holding around them.

Crump tends not to take this sort of thing very seriously. Or anything very seriously. There's a problem with the *Waterwitch*'s propeller and Bennett hops overboard with a mask on to take it off. It's a tricky job involving the removal of a pin with a pair of pliers, so Bennett is set up with a bit of half-inch garden hose to breath through. On board, Crump amuses himself by putting his thumb over the end of the hose to cut off air to his friend.

His friend becomes less and less amused by Crump's attitude and antics. He's running out of money and Crump doesn't care, and Bennett's not impressed by Crump's casual violence to Jean, the way he'll just give her a clip round the ear for something as trivial as burning the toast. Occasionally Bennett takes his protests across into trying to give Crump a clip round the ear himself, ending up with at least one black eye for his trouble. And never an apology. In the end, he takes himself off, tin mining.

Crump returns to New Zealand briefly and catches up with big brother Bill, who now has a steady job in Putaruru and who's married with eight kids. Barry regales him with his amazing Australian outback adventures. 'Why don't you come back with me?' he asks Bill. 'Hang on,' says Bill, 'I'd better go and get my boots. No, bugger it, I'll go as I am.' Bill won't get back to New Zealand for years.

One of the bosses from Barry's publisher drives Bill out to the airport separately from Barry. He begs Bill to make sure Barry gets his next book done because they want to get it out in time for Father's Day. 'Just make sure he finishes the thing will you Bill? And if you ever want to put pen to paper yourself, I guarantee to print it for you.'

Cooktown is full of raw material for Crump, just as the whole Aussie adventure has been. There's characters in this town so wild and eccentric, they almost make Barry Crump seem ordinary. There's Rum Jungle Jim, who accidentally blew the brains out of one of his divers trying to scare sharks away with his rifle when he was skippering a pearl-lugger in the Timor Sea. Now Jim works hard drinking schnapps and beer in one of the Cooktown pubs trying to blot out the memory.

'He recounts experiences round the coasts and islands of north Australia that make me feel I was born too late for real adventure, dropping it on me for a loan of a quid until pension day before staggering off into the dark, still chuckling at his own last joke, to be beaten up by a wallaby he surprises on the porch of his shack down by the river.

'Then there's Quiet Eddie from Bundaberg, fishing out of Cooktown with Big Andy the bully, who arrives down on the wharf mad on rum and threatening to get Hungry Hogan (his triggerless .45 six-gun) and shoot Quiet Eddie for forgetting the bread. Eddie gets into a bit of a panic and grabs a .303 out of the dinghy and blows one through the leg of Big Andy, who goes down on a bollard and puts a rib through one of his lungs. No one notices the hole through his thigh, all they can see is the blood round his mouth and think he's at least lung-shot. They take him up to the hospital on the back of Jack Stewart's old green International truck. Eddie thinks he's killed a bloke and goes along and gives himself up to the sergeant, who tells him that if Big Andy lives he's going to arrest Eddie and charge him with failing to stamp out a public nuisance when he had a chance.'

Despite the considerable charisma of the locals, the Crumps and their cronies conspire to take over Cooktown. Crump is amazed by the place. 'Things here are unbelievable! For example, Jack is the local undertaker but the rattly old '38 International truck he usually roars out to the cemetery with the coffin shaking around in the back among a few drums and ropes, gets stuck in the mud. So he uses our Land Rover. He holds the record of 20 minutes from the pub out to the graveyard and back to the pub.

'The informality of everything is incredible. The bank manager wanders into the pub in a pair of dirty shorts and a singlet. Never wears a tie, even at work. And the shops! Jack's got a hardware shop. I was having a cup of tea with his wife in there when an old bloke came in. "What the hell do you want?" she demanded. "Nothing," he said. "Have you come to pay me some money?" "No." "Well bugger off you miserable old bastard!"

'Then the sergeant's wife came in to weigh herself. She's trying to take off a bit of weight. "What do you want you old bitch?" asks Jack's wife. "I want to use the scales," says the sergeant's wife. "Well take your bloody shoes off, you cheating old bitch."

'The other day I drove the one passenger out to the airport on the T.A.A. bus. Halfway out there half a dozen little heads pop up from behind the seats. Half the kids in town are in the habit of stowing away on the bus for a ride out to the airport. We had two of the Stewart kids, one of the bank manager's and one unidentified black kid.

'If I can just get a regular 100 quid a month from New Zealand, we might settle in for several years. It's a real carefree outfit here. Only about one in 50 people work round here and there aren't that many people round here in the first place. There's more swaggies and lotus-eaters than I'd ever have thought existed.'

Barry and Bill and Jean are doing a bit of crocodile hunting, shell collecting. They stuff the little crocs and sell them. They shoot crocs from a 16-foot clinker at night with spotlights. One night Barry, Bill and Jean are out hunting. They've already got one big croc on board. They've chopped through the back of its neck so it's got every right to be stone dead, but it suddenly whips its massive jaws open and whacks them shut again. Jean thinks it's come round and throws herself backwards into the dark, crocodile-infested waters. She can't swim. In water she just floats around.

The Crump brothers know she can float, so they leave her there, floating, while they let the boat drift on into the darkness to take a look round the corner just in case there's a good one lurking there. Barry tells Jean not to make any bloody noise. They find her later, on the way back, still floating there.

The three of them become very close, little Jean looking after the needs of two hulking great men. It's a strange life. Not like a life at all. Like living in a book. A stinkier sort of fairy tale. The only time they ever have to connect with the real world is when it comes to money. And it's while he's in Cooktown that Crump breaches his sacred agreement with his accountant back in New Zealand and puts a cheque through his local bank. Outraged, the accountant withdraws his services forthwith. Bloody hell and buggeration, thinks Crump. We'd better get that next book out pronto.

§

9.
loveable,
of course
1963

Crump's fourth book is out, his third in a straight line of Sam Cash adventures. It's called *There and Back* and it's a slim volume, even with Dennis Turner's characterful line drawings. But it's a ripping string of tall tales and loose living, with Cash now lurching round the country like a twisted sort of Robin Hood — taking from the rich and giving to the publicans. And Crump's writing now has a poetry to it. He knows for sure that the truth lies in the detail and, in telling the detail, he convinces his readers that he has lived what they're reading. And that maybe he's as big a ratbag as Sam Cash. And, like Sam Cash, a liar and a skite and a helpless exaggerator. And loveable, of course. So loveable that he gets away with it.

One last cloud lay across the sky like a rotten hunk of wood falling slowly to pieces. The yard below the house looked like an old battlefield with its scattered hulks of old truck-cabs and chassis standing untidily about. Sheep on the hills beyond were already grazing their way towards shade and water. It was going to be a stinking hot day.

Someone moved in another room. Sam smoothed over a couple of folds in the roughly-made bed and climbed quietly out the window, lifting his suitcase out after him. He circled the house at a respectable distance in case of dogs, then went back up the path and knocked loudly on the back door. Sure enough, a mangy old cattle-dog ran belatedly out from under the tool shed, growled once, woofed twice, sniffed Sam's trouser-leg and waved his tail in reserved approval.

The door opened and an untidy kid looked shyly out.

'Your father up yet?' asked Sam.

'He's still in bed,' announced the four-year-old boy.

'Well nick in and tell the lazy hound that Sam Cash wants to see him, will you.'

The young fellow ducked out of sight and ran through the house calling, 'Daddy, the lazy hound wants to see you.'

Sam grinned and put his case on the porch. There were voices and sounds and a big man in pyjamas and overcoat came to the door.

'Sam Cash, you old sod! Come on in! When did you hit town? I heard you were up north with Goldson's Transport.'

'Just arrived,' said Sam blandly. 'I got your telegram okay but one or two things held me up.'

'Telegram?' said Joe puzzled. 'Oh, I remember. But that was over eighteen months ago! We finished that contract just before last Christmas.'

'Yeah,' agreed Sam. 'As I said, I got a bit side-tracked. How's tricks anyway, Joe? Still on the logs?'

'Yeah. I've got four logging units on the road at present. And if I get another contract I've put in for I'll be buying a new outfit for it — I'll need a good driver, if you're interested.'

'Hell,' said Sam disgustedly, 'I wish I'd known, Joe. They've just got me talked into taking over a mill up Pohukawa way. Twelve bob an hour. I've practically accepted it — er — what are you paying just now, Joe?'

'Well most of my chaps get eight bob or eight and six and they work their own hours. A good man can knock out his twenty-five notes a week.'

'Hmm.' Sam looked thoughtful. Then: 'Tell you what I'll do with you, Joe. Make it nine bob an hour and I'll try and put this mill crowd off. It won't be easy but I think I can swing it. You gave me a fair swing on that bulk-lime contract and I wouldn't like to see you put a crook driver on a new truck.'

'I don't know whether I can afford nine bob,' said Joe. 'It's pretty big dough.'

'You can't afford not to pay good money, the way things are in the logging business,' corrected Sam. 'You need a man who knows timber from felling to classing, in this caper. Half the blokes on the trucks these days don't know one end of a spanner from the other. I've seen contractors go broke through drivers who put their trucks in the garage every time they get a loose battery-terminal or a spark plug lead comes off.'

'You've got something there,' admitted Joe. 'Anyway you'd better stay and have a bit of breakfast with us and we'll talk it over. I should hear about this other contract today or tomorrow. Where are you staying, by the way? There's a spare room out back you're welcome to use till we get you settled into a hut out at the job.'

'That's decent of you, Joe,' said Sam, 'but are you sure I won't be in the way?'

'No, there's tons of room here. The spare room hasn't been used in weeks.'

(from There and Back, **1963)**

But Sam Cash can't get away with it for ever and Crump closes the door on Cash's hoboing days. He's doing this because he's about worn Sam Cash out for the time being. And anyway he's already got his story together for the next book and it doesn't involve Sam Cash. It involves a big brave crocodile hunter and it's going to be written in the first person. So, at the close of *There and Back*, Crump returns Cash to where he started at the beginning of *Hang on a Minute Mate*, the first Sam Cash book. Back to living death in suburbia.

Sam dug spuds for a week on the Canterbury Plains and then flew across Cook Strait in a Viscount because he didn't go for the type of people who travelled on the ferry these days.

In Wellington he drove a fork-lift on the wharf till he had his plane fare to Auckland and a few quid to spare. Then he boozed it up, borrowed a fiver off a taxi-driver he'd met and caught the bus to Napier.

He operated a drag-line for a Napier firm until he had enough money to pay his plane fare from Napier to San Francisco, and that got him as far as Gisborne. He cut lawns for the Gisborne Council for a few days, sold the mower to a publican who'd done a mate of Sam's for his cheque in the old days, stole it back, drew his pay and caught the bus to Opotiki. Sam distributed a good slice of his hard-earned cash among the publicans of Opotiki and decided to make a straight dash for it, to get home before he went broke again. So he set off to hitch-hike north and very soon got a lift to Whakatane. That night he was in Tauranga, the guest of a shopkeeper who'd picked him up in Matata and taken an immediate fancy to him. For the price of listening to an endless round of bad and badly-told jokes, Sam got a feed, a bed on the sofa and a lift to Paeroa the next day.

'It's only about forty miles from here out to the main highway,' said the shopkeeper, shaking hands with Sam at the turn-off. 'You'll have no trouble getting up to your place by tonight,' he added. But he was wrong — it took Sam two months to

a life in loose strides

80

get from there to his 'home', a house his wife lived in that belonged to his father-in-law, who didn't think Sam was everything a son-in-law should be by a long shot.

Sam strolled along the suburban road from the bus stop, past the neat rows of houses with trimmed gardens and lawns and hedges, until he came to the right number. After looking round the garden for a few minutes he went inside. His wife was at the kitchen sink.

'Oh,' she exclaimed when she saw him, 'you did give me a start! Where on earth have you been?'

'Have I got a clean shirt?' asked Sam, lifting the lid of a steaming pot on the stove and sniffing the contents.

'Look at you,' she cried. 'Filthy! I just hope none of the neighbours saw you like that. You just get straight into the bathroom and give yourself a thorough going-over. Then you've got some explaining to do. You can't come in here after five years asking for clean shirts. The cheek of you!'

Sam went into the bathroom, rinsed his hands under the tap, shook the water off them and patted them half-dry on a clean towel. Then he went out into the sitting-room and began to build a fire out of the heap of smouldering sticks in the grate.

'You've burnt me bit of wood I use for a poker,' he said. 'When will tea be ready?'

'Tea will be ready when it's cooked,' she said sharply, coming to the sitting-room door. 'You needn't think you can march in here and order tea whenever you like — I knew you'd be back as soon as a bit of extra money began arriving. I know you, Sam Cash!'

Sam had pulled up a chair and sat in it with his feet on the mantelpiece.

'How about swingin' the billy?' he asked, getting out his tobacco.

'I'll put the kettle on when I'm good and ready,' she said, going into the kitchen and putting it on. 'You can't come lording it round here just because I haven't seen you for five years. You're lucky I'm still here. Daddy offered to pay for a holiday in Australia for me. I nearly went, let me tell you.'

'You've planted flowers in me lettuce-patch,' said Sam.

'Of course I have!' she said indignantly. 'Do you think I'm going to keep your lettuces going for five years while you loaf around the countryside, hardly ever working, not sending any regular money — where have you been, anyway?' she demanded.

'There and back,' said Sam. 'And I might have to go out again later, so see if you can hurry that tucker up a bit will you, I'm starving.'

(from *There and Back*, 1963)

And Crump's fans back in New Zealand lap that one up too, though they have ceased to lap up the quantities of Crump's books they used to. *A Good Keen Man* especially and *Hang on a Minute Mate* continue to sell. But *There and Back* —

loveable, of course

like *One of Us* before it — will go on to sell less than a quarter of the extraordinary *Keen Man*. Not that Crump knows, or even particularly cares.

On the steamy edge of Northern Queensland, Crump's great Australian adventure is starting to run a bit ragged. You can only do something for so long, even something as wild and amazing as the life Crump's been leading in crocodile country. Crump loves the boat, though, and he'd be reluctant to leave her behind.

By the second half of 1963, Barry and Bill and Jean are getting some occasional business running the *Waterwitch* out to the Great Barrier Reef and its islands as a charter boat. But a wary tourist might be wise to look closely at the unlikely crew offering their boat, their services and their hastily acquired skills for a cruise on the unpredictable seas off Queensland.

In August, under large headlines in the daily press, comes the story that six castaways, 'including the New Zealand author Barry Crump', have been rescued from a coral island in the Great Barrier Reef by the New Zealand yacht *Tuarangi*. The party has spent 36 hours on the desolate island without food or water after a charter trip on Crump's 30-foot launch went disastrously wrong.

They stranded when the boat dragged its anchor and drifted out to sea with one member of the party on board and unable to start the motor. The Invercargill-based yacht *Tuarangi*, which had left New Zealand for a world cruise, spots distress signals on the island and picks up the castaways. The launch is later found wrecked on the Australian mainland and, after a search of the rugged coast, the missing member of Crump's party is found unharmed, but thoroughly sunburnt.

The crew of the *Tuarangi* spotted the distress signals on the largest of a group of islands known as the Three Isles, about 50 miles north of Cooktown. A fire had been lit, a large 'SOS' scratched on the beach and a red flag was 'being waved violently', said one of the crew.

'Those on the shore,' reports the *New Zealand Herald*, 'were Barry Crump, his brother Bill, Mr and Mrs Dudley, from Melbourne, with a friend and one other woman.'

The 'other woman' is Jean Watson and though they were stranded on the island for only a day and a half, the castaways were beginning to show signs of thirst. The only liquid on the island had come from one palm which had only nine small, bitter coconuts. When rescued, they considered their situation would have been desperate if they had not been picked up within 24 hours. The average temperature in the area is 80 degrees at this time of year and the island had no shelter, save the skinny coconut palm.

Crump tells his rescuers he's been based in Cooktown for the previous year crocodile shooting and running charter trips to the Barrier Reef, and that he had taken the party, which included a retired police commissioner, on a shell-collecting expedition to the island. Starting to fry under the merciless sun, the retired police commissioner had taken the dinghy out to the *Waterwitch* to get a shirt. While he was on board, the anchor dragged and he was unable to start the engine. A south-east wind blew the boat away from the island, towards the mainland.

The old policeman had a nightmare trip, drifting in heavy seas across nine miles of open water to Cape Flattery on the mainland. There the *Waterwitch* grounded in the breakers about midnight. The hapless passenger then made about 15 trips through the surf, salvaging all he could from the yacht, which was valued at £1000. By morning, she was a total wreck with pieces of her hull scattered along two miles of beach. Only the engine and dinghy could be salvaged and the boat wasn't insured.

After picking up the castaways and being unable to get ashore at the beach where the launch was wrecked, a rescue party, including Crump and brother Bill, sets out by foot from Cape Flattery to reach the missing policeman, in the dark and through country that is some of the worst Crump has ever tramped. It takes them four and a half hours to reach their lost customer whom they find wearing white-striped pyjamas, the only personal belongings he has managed to save from the wreck.

Despite his ordeal and his age, he's fit and cheerful. Next morning, the party returns to the *Tuarangi* by a different route, which seems easier than the first, but takes six and a half hours to cover. Two snakes are killed on the way and thousands of inch-long green tree ants, which bite like red-hot needles, fall upon the party as they walk.

This is an outrageously embarrassing thing to happen to Crump, who has taken to putting himself about as being pretty much idiot-proof and indestructible. Among themselves, the Crump gang blame the stupid old cop for blundering about and pulling the wrong rope. But Crump is an uncertain sort of sailor, known to sling his anchor on the first attractive bottom that presents itself, never thinking that a rising tide might lift it.

Crump is profoundly upset about losing the *Waterwitch*. She was a beauty and he'll never get another one like her, damn it. Confused about whom to blame and perhaps even wondering if he isn't himself partly to blame for her loss, he retreats inside himself, turning morose and dejected. He's not nice to be around on an ongoing basis. And he doesn't particularly want company anyway.

He's even fallen out with his publisher back in New Zealand. On a trip down the coast to Cairns, he spots a couple of his books in a bookshop window. People from all over the country he's run into have mentioned they've seen his books too. He's recently had a letter from Reed saying they haven't been able to arrange for any of his work to be published in Australia, to his annoyance. They have had *Hang on a Minute Mate* published in Britain. Crump had signed over British royalties on that one to Fleur and she has recently been forwarded a cheque for

£100. It's not a best seller, but she appreciates the money and writes a warm letter thanking him and filling him up with news about London he doesn't really care about and telling him how she loves it there.

And that's all very well, but now Crump has all this information that strongly suggests he has books on sale in Australia when his publisher says otherwise. So there's been an angry exchange of letters going on. There's never enough money and he's in the shit with the tax department and over bills for maintenance payments to Tina. He's had a savage letter from his accountant telling him he's had it too easy in the past and that the slap-happy days are over. And now his publisher's at the end of their bloody tether about his work habits. They send him one last advance — they say — and virtually order him to finish a new book and say they'll pay on the results and not on the promises. And it had better be a book about his Australian adventures too, they say.

Reed are also getting angry about Crump's ill-natured, money-hungry attitude. When his earnings go up, he displays an uncanny ability to upwardly adjust his spending so that the latter is increasingly threatening to run right past the former. He's forever firing off letters wanting to know where more money is, crying poor, crying tough, crying threats to change publishers. Between April 1962, and December 1962, he managed to chew through £14,000 in royalties in far-off Cooktown to the extent that he has less than £200 left. And out of that he owes 40 quid, plus 50 in overdue maintenance to Tina and a little over £2000 to the tax department.

Crump is stuck in a mire of self-pity — a pity so selfish that he sends the ever-decent Ray Richards a telegram that reads, 'You have let me down'. He signs one angry letter to Reed, 'Faithfully, but no longer yours'. There are people at Reed who are starting to think along the lines that unless Crump comes up with something bloody exciting about his crocodile shooting adventures, then the great shooter has shot his bolt. *There and Back* is a slow mover and there's a growing feeling that Crump's glory days as a man who moves mountains of books are over. Now all he'll be left to move is that giant ego of his.

Reed resolve that trying to be friendly and supportive is the last way to handle the demanding, difficult Crump and that things should forthwith be approached on a proper businesslike basis. 'But I'm stuck here,' thinks Crump, 'with no means of making a quid and facing a return to the drinking, getting-in-debt existence that I tried to get out of before and couldn't. I can't even get a job here because there are none. I'm starting to feel sorry for myself. It's the frustration of not being able to do anything. And now I'm up for maintenance and likely to get six months in jail. Next it'll be the tax people.'

He slings off a letter to Ray at Reed telling him he's got a new book coming which he's been rewriting about half of, though he hasn't touched it for a week or two. It's not a Sam Cash job and it's quite a different type of thing to what he's done in the past. He's not going to know if it's anything special until he sees how the rewrite goes and then he might leave it for a month or two to mature and see how it looks after that.

Reed write back promising him that several thousand pounds in royalty payments will shortly be on their way to him, via his accountant and the tax department. And expressing gratitude too for all the publicity surrounding his recent shipwreck, two days after the launch of *There and Back*. And mightn't that make a bit of a story, perhaps?

Crump doesn't think so. He's still hurting from the loss of the lovely *Waterwitch*. But despite all that and even without a boat to float it on, there's a grand plan hatched one night in Cooktown, involving a local fisherman, his wife and kids and a couple of others and a scheme for them all to start a bit of a tourist resort on one of the easy-to-reach islands out there. There's a beauty called Lizard Island, with a lagoon. So they sail out to take a closer look, but the 10 of them have trouble co-existing and they sure get through a lot of tucker. Then Crump has a row with the fisherman and then that spreads to a row with everyone. He tells them all to bugger off and leave him there, so they take him at his word and sail off, thinking they'll go back in two or three days. There's plenty for him to eat. There are wild yams. He could catch fish. He's got a couple of rifles to shoot passing pigeons. He knows how to look after himself.

But two days after Crump launches into his Robinson Crusoe phase, two cyclones in a row hit Lizard Island. 'Suddenly there's no food around. The pigeons stop coming out to the island and the turtles and fish all disappear into deeper water. The last food I ate was some honey in water, and then there was just water, heaps of it, pouring out of the sky.... I'd been sleeping in a canvas hammock slung between two trees, but in this rain it'd fill up in minutes so I crouch among the roots of a huge tree as the rain roars over me.' He suffers several days and nights, naked because his clothes feel so cold and clammy.

Maybe the others forget to go back for him, or they're just still fed up with him, but Crump is found by passing strangers alone, naked and 'almost starving'. Crump offers various people a variety of explanations. He had gone to the island a month earlier with a companion or companions to investigate the possibility of deep-sea fishing in the area. His companion (or companions) left him on the island and either just didn't return or were prevented from returning, as planned, by engine trouble or bad weather.

He had a book he wanted to get finished and he thought being marooned might help him get on with it. He'd been living on those bloody yams and whatever fish and turtles he could spear. Then he accidentally got himself rescued. He decides he wants to call it a mishap. But the newspapers, especially the ones back in New Zealand, like the look of the word 'Marooned' in the headline.

Crump's island rescue this time comes at the hands of the captain and crew of a small trading ship, the *Darega*, who report that Crump is weak from hunger when found. Brother Bill hears about the rescue on the radio and the local police tell him that Barry has been taken to Port Moresby, in New Guinea, and is under arrest as an internationally distressed person. Bill figures Barry can sort himself out and stays on in Cooktown and won't see his younger brother again for five years. Jean shoots through and gets a job on a sheep station and then moves round a bit, having adventures.

Crump is in the news again, but the confusion of explanations he offers in the face of all the excited attention results in some of the stories being slanted in such a way as to suggest that he was deliberately marooned on an island by one of his friends.

Then the Australian papers run another story when the fisherman from Cooktown who Crump had fallen in and then out with points out that he didn't desert Crump at all and, angry that Crump should apparently make such an allegation, shouts grouchy things back at Crump through the newspaper columns. This experience, Crump reckons, is likely to make him deeply suspicious of journalists and he stores it away for future reference.

§

10.

leaving her pregnant

1964

After recuperating for a bit in Port Moresby, Crump returns to New Zealand and announces himself 'as fit as a buck rat' and says he plans to settle in New Zealand and will be discussing with his publishers the writing of a new book.

Crump has come home to hunt new territory, but this time it's the rugged and treacherous terrain of his own success and notoriety that he's exploring. There's a great view from the top, but the footing is always uncertain. In the two years Crump has been away, he's become a celebrity. Everyone's heard of him and everyone wants a bit of him. Luckily Crump has grown a personality big enough to fit the clothes his fame has fashioned for him.

He's more than a writer of best-selling books. He is the books. One look at him, all six strapping feet of him, and one listen to that rumbling Kiwi voice of his that fuels his endless yarns, tells almost everyone who meets him that Crump is a natural star, one too bright to cope long with merely being filtered through the pages of books.

He hasn't been back in New Zealand long before Crump takes up an offer to travel to the West Coast of the South Island to play the role of what is described as a 'backblock character' in a Pacific Film Company feature film called *Runaway*. Director John O'Shea is convinced about Crump's star potential and wants him to play Clarrie, an eccentric individualist who lives in the outback. And so he does, giving a somewhat unsettling performance as an unfriendly hillbilly type whose few lines are rendered in an unsettling bird-like squawk.

Crump goes back up to Wellington where he settles for a bit. Jean is back and has a flat. Crump moves in and lives and sleeps with her for a couple of weeks. But he moves on, this time leaving her pregnant with what will be Crump's third son left behind. Jean will call her baby boy Harry, after Harry Blue, the man who showed them how to hunt crocodiles.

Crump slides back into the city life, running into and jousting with larger-than-lifers like the wild-haired medical guru Erich Geiringer. In the back bar of the old St George Hotel, downtown, they drink beer and tell jokes at each other non-stop for two days, competing in shifts as they move from the pub to Geiringer's place and back again.

Crump buys a Jaguar and moves into Geiringer's flat for a while. Then he shares a house for a bit with artist Selwyn Muru. Young brother Peter comes to stay for a while. There are a lots of parties and a lot of shagging with all sorts of women. Crump meets loads of people, almost everyone who reckons they count. He puts out another book.

This one's different. It's called *Gulf* and he claims he wrote it in only five days and nights in his own handwriting. The way a bushman would write a book. It's a lie, of course. *Gulf* is a notebook novel. It's a bent sort of journalism. Gonzo before it was invented. Crump leads the story in the first person and everyone else from his recent Australian outback adventures is thinly disguised. Jean is 'Fiff' and she represents the first time Crump has written even semi-sweetly about a woman. Harry Blue is Darcy and Darcy gets to tell some vivid yarns and spin some tough philosophy.

... Darcy told us how some of the Myall aborigines in Arnhem Land cross the rivers. When families of abos on walkabout have to cross a river, they stop half a mile before they get to it and have a breather and sort themselves out. Then they run to the river, dive straight in and swim across. The oldest and weakest get left behind and are the only ones left in the water by the time any crocs around get into action.

'A croc will nearly always take the last horse or cow or person in a bunch.'

It's a handy way to weed out the weak, but I wouldn't like to be an old abo — or, come to think of it, it wouldn't be so bad at that. At least they don't kick you out of the family as a reward for growing old, and leave you to die among strangers, like we do. An abo knows what to expect and why to expect it. There's nothing personal about it.

Darcy told us, too, about an eighteen-foot croc parading up and down in the river in front of a blacks' camp with a screaming girl held in its jaws, ducking her under every now and again and then holding her up kicking and screaming again. When the croc got tired of this it closed its jaws and sank. The last they saw of the girl she was sinking slowly into the spreading stain of her own blood.

That story kept me quiet for a bit then I asked Darcy, 'Why didn't you shoot the croc?'

'I could not have hit the croc without the danger of hitting the girl,' he replied. 'And my eyes were almost blinded by what they were seeing.'

(from *Gulf*, 1964)

Gulf makes it five books in under five years and it's well received, some reviewers liking its slightly autobiographical style, its new location and the broadening of the old Crump approach. 'Like Mr Crump's earlier books,' says the reviewer in the *Auckland Star*, '*Gulf* has a solid backbone of good humour and wit. But *Gulf* also contains marked differences from the first four Crump novels and, in some respects, breaks new ground for him.... Unlike its predecessors, *Gulf* does not belong to the oral tradition of the "tall story". On the contrary, its characters are ordinary people and thoroughly unpretentious.

'Secondly, *Gulf* contains none of the sometimes-bitter mysogyny which animated Sam Cash. Indeed a woman (statistics 32½-24-33) is present right through the book. Her feminine cunning and equally feminine naivete towards her "big fierce lizard-skinner" providing some of the book's most engaging moments.'

And third, says the reviewer, *Gulf* isn't 'a collection of unrelated tales which have been tacked into the rickety and all-accommodating picaresque of the earlier books'. The 'larger-than-life' approach of *A Good Keen Man* had been followed by three books in which Crump's Sam Cash character managed to 'pile one absurdity on top of another, until Mr Crump became one of the most engaging point-blank liars who ever gate-crashed into the New Zealand literary scene.... It is almost disconcerting to find the humour of understatement in a book by Barry Crump!

'*Gulf* may not be the best novel Mr Crump has written ... but it is a lot better entertainment than television or a night at the pictures.'

Crump goes all out in *Gulf* to write a commercial book, even offering a gentle ending. It's as near to happy families as he's written himself so far.

We'd done what we set out to do and now we'd reached the stage where each croc we shot was reminiscent of another. As the Wet drew closer we began to wonder

leaving her pregnant

where we'd go next and what we'd be doing. I first noticed it when Fiff said one day, 'I wonder if we're going to be pioneers, in a wild place where I'll have to do the cooking in a big open fireplace till you get the house finished? We might even have a baby?' No comment.

(from *Gulf*, 1964)

But while Crump comes back to New Zealand, Jean Watson remains in Australia, going off into the Australian desert in search of Lassiter's Lost Reef. 'It's still lost,' Crump tells an interviewer. 'She didn't find it.' Back in Wellington now, what Jean has found is a life stuck in one place, bringing up one of Crump's sons and later giving birth to another, though he isn't kept.

But Crump will come and go from Jean's life, sometimes parking his truck or whatever he's driving across the road from her house and come across for a meal and to drink and play the guitar and talk about old times, talk about all sorts of things. Even God sometimes.

He's a funny old never-quite-grown-up sort of boy, is Barry to Jean and Jean sets about writing a book inspired by her own younger life and by her encounters and her love for someone she calls in her story Abungus, but who in real life is Crump. She calls the story *Stand in the Rain* (1965) and when Crump gets wind of what she's up to, he's not at all happy. He likes private things kept private. There's enough people too nosey about him already without someone like Jean writing a book and feeding them more things to gossip about. She's not really going to do this to him, is she? He wants to know. Jean would be the last person to betray him. Hang out any dirty laundry in public....

Crump has been living, off and on, in Auckland with girlfriend Lenna Rainger and her three kids, two girls and a boy. He's happy playing father to someone else's children. It's a strange thing, but it feels better this way. He's strong on discipline and initiates weekly family meetings to air grievances and straighten out differences. Crump hits it off especially well with the younger girl, Simone, who loves his love of fun and that he'll build them a tree-hut and take them to the pictures. He teaches her chess when she's five and loves playing that game of tig he once played with his little sister. He calls it 'Touched you last'.

She's young enough to love his impulsiveness, too. An impulsiveness that can have him getting Lenna to wake the kids in the middle of the night with the news that Barry wants to go bush and they're all going with him. Now. They do quite a bit of camping out in the bush around the central North Island. He's lovely to live with about a third of the time and when he turns really dark and distant and nasty, he generally takes himself off for a week or two. And after a year or two, he takes himself off and doesn't come back at all.

Anyway, Crump is having a bit of trouble with being Crump. The myth he's built of himself is, not unnaturally, getting in his way. He can't believe how many strangers walk up and tell him who he is. 'You're Barry Crump.' The drinking is part of the game too. Solid, hardcore boozing and all the madness that goes with it. He could write a book about the lines on the faces of the barmen he's seen.

Instead he's written a story about a pair of big-city rubbish collectors with the unlikely names of Dinny and Watcher. He calls it *Give a Bloke a Yard* and Reed aren't very impressed. In their opinion, he's fast running out of creative steam. He'd started out with such a hiss on *A Good Keen Man*, but that was largely autobiographical. Then he went on to the Sam Cash books, basically a cunning way of stringing together yarns he'd picked up and embroidered and he was still good, but his material was thinning out the further he stretched the Cash concept.

In their opinion, *There and Back* was so thin it was barely a book at all, but things picked up with *Gulf*, mainly because it took him back to the autobiographical approach. Then, early in 1965, he sends them a collection of short stories he's pulled together and they are openly unimpressed. And offended by some of the content. Crump seems to be letting his coarse side out of the sack, setting Reed huffing and puffing about their reputation. And Crump's of course. It's an undistinguished collection that they wouldn't consider for a moment if it hadn't been written by Barry Crump, they feel.

The 'callous and appalling' content of several of the tales disturbs some at Reed to the point that they want them either held out or censored and modified out of recognition. One story, *A Stroke of Luck*, even has a sort-of sex scene involving a barmaid. Crump has never previously tackled sex on the page and Reed would rather he stays that way. The opening piece in the collection, *Fingers*, is the tale of an ancient eccentric who feeds the remains of her dead husband down the dunny. The story with the bedded barmaid also features a spectacularly revolting opening scene that was too strong for some of the sensitive stomachs at Reed.

Windy Long had had a stroke of luck and wound up at a party at Ngongotaha.

There was a bloke, mill-worker by the look of him, who'd latched on to them. Everyone thought he was with one of the others. Windy didn't go much on the look of him in the first place, but it wasn't him who'd invited him to the party. Nor had anyone else, as far as they could work out later. He just tagged along and when things were starting to get warmed up, around one o'clock in the morning, this bloke whose name nobody knew decided to get crook. He was sitting in a big old armchair that everybody reckoned later should have been given to one of the women, only no one thought to say anything about it at the time.

He started getting a bit wild in the eye at first. Then he looked around worried and swallowing and shifting his bottle of beer around from one side of his chair to the

leaving her pregnant
91

other. Then he got to gurgling and waving and trying to get out of his chair.

Puketu and the boys would have just shunted him outside for a look around and a bit of fresh air and left him to it, but not Mrs Puketu. She fussed around him like an old mother hen, telling him what was wrong with him and what to do about it.

'A nice big feed. That's what you need,' she said, helping him onto his feet. 'I'll just bet you haven't had a decent meal all day. Now you take this plate and go out to the stove and help yourself to some lovely hot stew. There's a whole big pot of it. Nice mutton stew, with carrots and parsnips and kumara and puha.'

The bloke took the plate and spoon as though he was hypnotised and wandered into the kitchen. He lifted the lid of the pot on the woodstove and as soon as the steam from the stew hit him in the face he cut loose. All over the hot stove. Then he sat down against the wall by the stove and passed out, dribbling all over his shirt as though it happened every day. Everybody crowded into the kitchen doorway, looking at this character and the terrible mess he'd made. Then it started to pong.

It pongs a bit when you burn rubber or hair. It pongs when you're stripping the wool off a dead sheep, or the knife slips when you're gutting a poisoned cow. Cattle trucks pong and so do rotten cabbages. Everybody's got their pet pong that they can't stand, but this was the pongingest pong Windy had ever tried not to smell. It was so bad that he was scared to take his next breath, and then it didn't matter because he couldn't. It went through the house like rotten steam under pressure. Everybody reeled back into the sitting-room. Puketu threw a couple of buckets of water at the stove but it was as much use as trying to put out a fire with diesel oil.

The party was a goner. It occurred to Windy at the time that it'd be a hell of a good way to bust up a party that wasn't going too well, but a bit on the drastic side. It would have stopped a riot.

They took the beer outside and stood around Windy's van, drinking and arguing who ought to go in and drag out the bloke who'd done it before he got asphyxiated and pegged out all over Mrs Puketu's kitchen floor. That was when they found out he'd never been invited in the first place.

In the finish, Windy ducked in and dragged him out to the porch and threw a coat over him and left him there to sleep it off. Then he shifted the van a little further away from the house and they carried on with the party, which was beginning to pick up a little. Puketu lit a bit of a fire and business was almost back to normal.

(from 'A Stroke of Luck' **in** *Warm Beer and Other Stories*, **1969)**

Reed send the 18-story collection back to him for in-depth revision and he's back to them with a big bounce accusing them of subjecting him to 'literary claustrophobia' and telling them that they're old-fashioned and out of touch. He refuses to remove the bedded barmaid and when Reed offer him the option of offering the book to another publisher, he rings in, sounding sober, and says he's taking the book back. He tells them he'll give them first refusal on his next novel, which he claims is nearly complete.

Reed are shitting bricks now, thinking if Crump finds a publisher for his dirty, drunk and violent short stories, they'll bribe him into staying with them for his next 'proper' book. But Crump doesn't find another publisher or, more likely, doesn't try.

And now he's offering them a shadow of a decent book called *Give a Man a Yard* and they feel it has few flashes of the old Crump spirit and while it might sell on the strength of his name, it would be a nail in the coffin of whatever he does next. There is pressure to reject the manuscript, but that would be two no's in a row and in the end Reed go ahead, rework the story, hire a new illustrator called Roger Hart, retitle it *Scrapwaggon* and out it goes.

It's his sixth book and it takes another swerve in direction. Now Crump's really trying to write a novel and it's a flinty, rough-hewn slice of the drunken vagabond life, full of the well-established Crump/Cash attitude. The women don't come out of it very well and the men are, of course, misunderstood. The dialogue is as vivid as ever, though the story is short and lacks the lift and the poetry of old as it tells the tale of a pair of roguish but loveable rubbish collectors, one of whom is unexpectedly visited by a grown-up daughter he'd left behind. In her, it's as if Crump has combined his fear of old wives and abandoned children.

His most lyrical writing, as often, is in relation to unlikely topics.

Dinny woke up very carefully with the feeling that his eyelids were stitched together. He had a hangover. But he knew how to handle hangovers. He had a method of sneaking past when they weren't watching. He lay very still for a few moments getting the hang of it. This one was a beaut, about a force-six on his private hangover-scale.

With the very top-front edge of his brain he thought about some plastic bags he'd brought home yesterday, and reached slowly out with one hand to feel along the side of the bed. His fingers closed round the neck of the bottle and he drew it slowly out of the boot it was jammed into. Then he sat up, swung his legs over the side of the bed, heaved one blurred eye half open and raised the bottle in a single smooth movement. Then somebody started knocking on the back door and ruined everything.

For a ghastly moment he was caught unawares. Before he could get his mind shut the hangover surged up from behind him, speared through his brain, arc-welded his eyeballs and short-circuited his whole nervous system. An alarm sang in his ears and his stomach fell up and down inside him as though it was in a washing machine. He put the bottle on the floor with a thump that ran up his arm and caused the walls of his head to cave in, and rammed a handful of blanket into his face to stop it from exploding. His heart tripped and fell and his own fists began shaking themselves in his face. He thought very hard about the plastic bags and waited for it to pass. Dinny was

leaving her pregnant

93

in a bad way, and somebody was still knocking on the back door. If he hadn't wanted to see who it was he'd have probably hidden in his blanket and waited till they went away. But he hardly ever got visitors.

The hangover eventually sank away and perched restlessly in the back of his neck, as though daring him to make a false move. He got to his feet and glided carefully to the bedroom doorway, with his eyebrow held hard high on his forehead to hold back the headache. Down the hall and out through the kitchen. He throttled the door handle for a few moments to get control of the shakes and then drew the door open. There was a girl standing there....

She didn't speak at once and Dinny wasn't in any hurry, so he left it to her. He rarely had a visitor like this, even if she had come to the wrong place, which nobody had ever done before. Maybe one of the Jehovah's Witnesses? — No, they always hunt in packs. Saleswoman? — Not a very good one if she was. He remembered the Welfare Officer who'd called in once to see if he had any kids living there. Could be, but a bit innocent-looking for that caper really. Quite a tidy carcase on her, by the look of things.

No, he couldn't place this one at all. He was just about ready to give in and ask when she spoke.

'Hello Father,' she said.

'Uh — What??'

'Don't you remember me? I'm Leila.'

'Er — Oh yeah. Sure. How are you?'

'Aren't you pleased to see me?'

'Yeah, 'course I am. You just took me by surprise for a moment.' He looked around and up the junk-lined path towards the gate. 'Where's your mother?' he asked suspiciously.

'Mother died two months ago.'

'Hell,' said Dinny. '— I mean, that's real tough. 'Struth. You'd better come in and sit down for a while.'

He had to let her carry her own bags. If he'd bent over to pick them up just then his head would have rolled off his shoulders, slopped onto the ground and seeped away. He led her into the kitchen and managed to pull a couple of chairs out from the table. They sat down.

'I didn't know about it,' he said. 'Haven't heard from any of you for — let's see — eleven, nearly twelve years. You were only a bit of a ...' Dinny's voice trailed off as the hangover thundered back again. She reached over to put her hand on his arm and he pulled away so sharply the jolt set his eyeballs on fire.

'I understand how you feel, Father,' she said gently.

(from *Scrapwaggon*, 1965)

But this is old-fashioned stuff in a land being conquered by the Beatles and where most boys dream now of an electric guitar rather than a rifle. Crump's market is shrinking, along with his grasp on the modern world. His grasp on the day-to-day world is shaky enough.

He's living in Auckland, with a girlfriend, Mercury Theatre actress Helen Smith on a 33-foot launch called the *Sunray*. 'She's not as good as the *Waterwitch*, and there's a petrol engine instead of diesel, but she's better to live on. There's a toilet, a galley, four bunks, two radios, a depth-sounder. We've had her out on the gulf a few times and she goes like a bomb. Luxury.

'I've had a very strange letter from John O'Shea. A European producer is interested in filming *Gulf*, even has an actress jacked up for the Fiff role — Peter Seller's wife. But John wants me to let him have back his lapsed film rights for which he still owes me 500 quid so he can bargain with this producer. It doesn't appear that he'll be having much to do with the production anyway.

'So I've reasoned that if this European producer is interested in filming *Gulf*, I'll be hearing all about it in due course. So with typical Crump efficiency, I've decided not to reply to John's letter. That way I haven't ballsed anything up.'

If there's any hint of ready money, though, Crump's prepared to balls up whatever he needs to balls up. He's seriously money-hungry. So money-hungry he's trying to find a job. *Scrapwaggon* is selling at half the speed of *There and Back* and that sold at half the speed of *Hang on a Minute Mate*. He's starting to lose heart a bit in the writing game. 'Christmas is coming up and I don't see how I'm going to eat let alone drink unless I start bludging. They're going to repossess the boat in three months at the outside. I've tried getting a job under a different name, but they recognise me like a shot and want to know what the hell I want with a job. I just haven't got any interest left in writing or anything to do with it.'

Even if he felt like finishing off the book he's supposed to be finishing off, he can't because he's broken his finger. Inland Revenue has cut off a good chunk of the cash he was due from the *Weekly News* for some bits of books he sold to them, much to the annoyance of his publisher. Any change he had left has been spent repairing the bloody boat, which is due to be repossessed anyway.

He sends Reed a poor-me letter, telling them not to expect any new book soon — though he reckons he's got two on the go and some advance money would be nice — and signing it with his customary kiss-off, 'God Save Us — Barry'. The tax department, now on the aggressive with the always-evasive, ever-moving Crump, are onto Reed for half of Crump's earnings before they get into Crump's leaky hands.

Someone — one of the 'Auckland phonies' Crump bitches about — tells Crump that Jean's book is out and being plugged 'with Crump all over it'. Crump is approached by someone at a party inquiring, 'I understand you're having a

leaving her pregnant

biography published', meaning Jean's book. He's very tense about it.

But the rumours about Jean's debut novel, *Stand in the Rain*, are slight exaggerations of the truth. Crump is in it alright, in the character of the eccentric Abungus for those in the know, but there's no mention of the famous bushman writer anywhere, though the book's publisher, Pegasus, push as close to the Crump legend as they can without crashing. On the book's liner notes they announce, 'Here is the woman's side to a New Zealand legend. Here is the girl behind the good keen, deer-killing, possum-trapping, pig-hunting, rabbit-shooting, scrub-cutting, hard-case, dinkum-type Kiwi....' Which is about as close as they can get to saying 'Barry Crump's ex-girlfriend tells all' without actually saying it.

Pegasus tell Reed that it's all nonsense about their using the honourable name of Crump to sell Watson's book, though people who know them both might think the story is based on fact. But that happens with any novel. Barry need have no fears, they assure Reed.

In a sudden mood swing, Crump tells Reed he's finished his version of the great New Zealand novel and that it's 'a shocker' and that they'll be pleased to hear it's 60,000 words. Well, it's certainly more than 50,000. The working title is *No Reference Intended* and he wants to rewrite the second half of it. He sends the publisher a detailed synopsis, the tale of a dull ambitious newspaperman who rises to the top through mishaps and lies. It's remarkably cynical. But Crump's remarkably excited about it. He's done his research with no end of journalists. He knows their game.

§

11.

woman to woman

1966

The Compton Group, of London, has acquired British rights to the next Pacific Films feature, *Gulf*, freely based on the novel by Barry Crump. Shooting of the film is to begin in the Gulf of Carpentaria later in the year. The Australian actress Tanya Binning, notable for her recent appearances in such B-graders as *Mondo Cane, Carry on Cleo, Runaway* and *Repulsion*, has already been signed for a part in *Gulf*.

Crump might despise the city and its buggered-up values, but he's learning to hunt it. He's gotten onto this new medical stuff that helps you stay up and gives you the strength of 10 men. It's called amphetamine, or speed, and some medical friends put him onto it. Anyway, it helps. It all helps. At a book launch Crump meets Brian Easte, a television producer responsible for the popular bright and breezy local magazine series *Town and Around*. Crump tells Easte he'd be a bloody fool if he didn't hire him — Crump — to go on the show.

And Easte knows who Crump is and knows his power. He's seen him walk in a public bar, lean in towards the people he's with and say, 'I met a bloke once…' in a voice that cuts through the room so that the bar goes quiet while Crump entrances a roomful of strangers with one of his yarns. So Easte thinks if Crump can do yarns, like skits, on television, it might just work.

Crump reckons he can manage that and starts with a guest appearance on *Town and Around* just a few days later, joining the personality-driven show, alongside its resident stars Keith Bracey and Barbara Magner. Shortly after, Easte announces that Crump has a 'roving commission' to 'find other individuals and bring them back alive'.

In announcing Crump's arrival in the relatively unexplored world of New Zealand television, one newspaper critic observes that *Town and Around* has been finding it increasingly difficult to find the offbeat items and interesting people that are its lifeblood and there are 'dangerous signs' that it might be running out of steam. 'With Crump around, the chances of the show falling flat are considerably reduced.'

Crump modestly allows that he is 'very pleased to be involved in some of the brightest and most entertaining interviews ever staged in New Zealand television'.

Crump's job is to cover the 'Around' rather than the 'Town' end of the show, tapping into his country contacts and his endless fund of yarns for material, connecting city-bound Kiwis with their rural roots — and especially with a rustic, blokey sense of humour that they haven't previously seen on their television screens. Until Crump's rowdy arrival, the voice of New Zealand broadcasting has been a plummy Pommie one with little sense of local vernacular, humour or attitude. He arrives with a big bagful of all three, especially the attitude. And on screen, he throws out to New Zealand a characterful, caricature reflection of itself. Crump's self-mythologising is penetrating the electronic age. Now he isn't just on all the bookshelves. He's grinning his laconic grin into everyone's living room.

His producer knows that if he sends Crump off into the backblocks with a camera crew, he'll head for the local pub, corner some of the local identities and squeeze a few good yarns out of them, which he'll then bring back home to his masters. Eventually. Basically, he feeds them a load of bull, buggers off, gets on the piss and comes up with a story. He gets heavily into the booze these days. And he's a competitive drinker who'll drink anyone under the table with pleasure. He meets his occasional match. But not often.

But this is the life. He's being paid to have fun. It's a hell of a lot easier than writing books. And in a way it's like writing anyway. He just doesn't have to bother putting it down on paper. Putting himself out there in the public eye like this helps sell the books he has written anyway.

Crump's *Town and Around* pieces go out regularly on Wednesday nights.

They're mostly one-note symphonies, based around the Crump character or world view. There's Crump, the laconic hero who comes to the aid of a damsel, played by Lenna Rainger, in distress on the highway. Her car has broken down, but under her rescuer's tender ministrations it starts falling to bits, pulling completely in half when Crump goes to give her a tow. Crump and his mates had an old car cut clean in half for the skit. Crump holds out a playing card sideways for sharpshooter Tex Morton to cut in half with a bullet from 120 yards away. 'Spare me days,' growls Crump when Morton hits the target. It's all he needs to say, in the voice of his with that crooked grin on his handsome, big-nosed face, for all those living rooms to love him.

In another one of his pieces for *Town and Around*, Crump does a droll interview with his mate Bill Moller, who lives the rustic life in the Waitakeres, west of Auckland. Moller has suffered a dramatic accident. 'So Bill, I hear you had a bit of an accident,' says Crump, and Moller tells him — and an astonished television audience — that he was out in 'grunt grotto' sitting on his longdrop, which he'd recently tamed by dropping half a can of petrol down it.

'I was sitting there having a cigarette, Barry, and you know how it is, you finish the smoke and drop it down between your legs and next thing I know, woosh, I'm blown 50 yards away.'

Then there's one where Crump kits himself up really nice in a dinner suit and black tie and turns up to take a woman to a ball. She comes out in a lovely gown and everything looks relatively classy until Crump's truck won't start and he gets under the bonnet and starts fiddling around and rips off a bit of her dress to clean oil off something.

Crump is loose talent, though. He has to be told to desist when, one day, he lights up a joint on the job. He's discovered marijuana now. And LSD. He's a drinker first and foremost, and he likes throwing a good piss-up when a royalty cheque comes in, but he'll give anything a go. That LSD's quite a go, alright. Things are getting pretty loose with the ladies now too. Crump always liked shocking people and now one of his tricks involves asking a total stranger, preferably in front of some of his straighter mates, whether she might like a fuck. It's amazing how often they'll not only not be shocked, but either invite him home or even, once, when he asked this good-looker in a lift, she said sure thing and they just went upstairs in a building and found an empty office and had a shag on the floor.

Crump's getting a surprising amount of everything done. The large jar of amphetamines he keeps on hand helps. The rejection of the short story collection still rankles with him, so he takes a character called Windy Long who features in a couple of those yarns and inflates him into a lead role in a full-size story and sends it down to Reed. It's that next book he promised them, he says.

It's called *The Odd Spot of Bother* and it's full of slivers of Crump's life and old fears. It's the tale of serial loser Windy Long, a man so down at heel in the good luck department that even when he wins a fortune in a lottery, things turn bad for him. And, of course, women aren't to be trusted at all, least of all when they're friendly.

A funny thing happened to Windy one day. He discovered a drink he liked the taste of, and it didn't seem to be very strong, either. It was orangy stuff, called Merry Widow, and he got quite merry on it. He was feeling so cocky after four or five of them that he armed himself with fifty dollars from his nearest bank and swaggered off to explore one or two of the other pubs around town for a change.

Next morning he woke up in a strange bed, in some pub or other, by the look of it, and with a shrieking hangover.

What happened yesterday? Was that the day he tried out the Merry Widow stuff? No, that was the day before — or was it?

He remembered lots of people going out of their way to be friendly with him. It must have gone to his head, or was that the drinks?

He pulled the sheet away from his face and leaned over the side of the bed to see if he could recognise the floor. No, he'd never seen it in his life before. He still had his shoes on, by the feel of it, but he couldn't be sure just yet. His pockets were twisted round his hips and his coat was bunched up around his shoulders. Hullo, what's this? No shirt on.

What the hell's a man been up to now?

Then he looked around and saw the woman in the bed with him. He stared at her, not believing a word of it. Blonde hair all over the pillow — one hand lying slightly curled beside her face — mouth a bit open and a glimpse of white teeth. A bit of a looker, as far as he could make out. Now where had he seen her before?

She began to stir and wake up with his moving in the bed and he had a moment of panic. Had he crept in here drunk the night before? She might wake up and start screaming at any moment! He began to edge himself out of the bed.

Then the woman suddenly woke up. Windy froze. She sat up, yawned happily in his face and then dived for a quick kiss on his horrified cheek.

Then he recognised her. The barmaid.

'What the hell?' he croaked.

'What the hell what?' she enquired contentedly.

'What the hell are you doing here?' he said '... are we doing here?'

Then he noticed that she was wearing his shirt, done up by only one button stretched across her bare front.

'Darling!' she laughed, grabbing him in a smothering headlock. 'Don't tell me you don't remember your own engagement party? I must say you don't give a girl much time to....'

'Engaged!' gasped Windy, tearing himself free.

'Yes, darling. Engaged. See, here's the ring, remember?'

And she poked him in the stomach with a sharp finger with a glittering diamond ring on it.

(from *The Odd Spot of Bother*, **1967)**

The previously banned bedded barmaid scene has been slipped back in. Crump has his dastardly way, his personal sense of power and honour are intact and Reed have their next Barry Crump best seller, except that it isn't a best seller at all. *The Odd Spot of Bother* is moving half the speed of *Scrapwaggon*. The new book comes dedicated, 'For Lenna and the Kids', though that's all over now.

As well as being a star of *Town and Around*, Crump also jumps aboard another Auckland-based television series, *Yo Heave Ho*, a children's show that has fallen on thin creative times and has its masters, the New Zealand Broadcasting Corporation, worried about its future. In a wild and imaginative rescue bid, Crump has been hired as scriptwriter and to play 'one of the characters on the beach'.

One critic isn't too excited: 'I am not sure that Barry, for all his gift as a storyteller, is exactly the discovery of the year as a television performer. He no longer mumbles, but his dinkum Kiwi lingo sounds a bit odd amid a host of largely theatrical accents. Nevertheless, Crump's engagement for *Yo Heave Ho* is an important development. Here for the first time we have a New Zealander, writing in the New Zealand idiom, for a New Zealand show.' Crump, all modesty as always, describes his emergence as a television scriptwriter as 'one of the fringe benefits of being a successful writer'.

In July, Crump takes up an invitation to make a contribution to Braille Week by recording readings from *A Good Keen Man* and *Hang on a Minute Mate* for blind talking books.

Shortly afterwards, Crump is reported hiding out ill on Great Barrier Island 'since he was heaved overboard, along with others, from the ill-starred *Yo Heave Ho*'. He goes missing from *Town and Around* as well. But Crump comes back and in August, it's announced he's been 'dispatched forthwith to the Urewera' where he will be shooting pigs — and film.

Crump's sick of the city. 'I'm getting bored with being successful. It sure has its points, but it's ceased to take me anywhere new or answer any questions. There has to be more to life than this. We surely haven't been put on this planet just to hassle each other for money and die.'

Also, Crump's careless bounce from woman to woman has come to a sudden stop, at least for a bit. Her name is Vanda, she's 22 and he meets her one night in an Auckland pub where he's being particularly charismatic. He does a real number on her, walks into the bar with some of his television mates, fixes his gaze on her and rumbles, 'You, stay there', goes to the bar and buys them drinks and then devotes his total attention to her to such an extent that she's almost hypnotised by him.

Crump is getting good at this sort of thing, getting under people's skins, inside their heads. It is a powerful thing, he's found when you're as notorious as he now is, if instead of letting people be interested in him, he's intensely interested in them. He has learned to keep a crowd at arm's length and under his spell by entertaining them with yarns and to put individuals under his considerable spell by beaming right in on them, disarming them, dismantling them and then putting them back together again, but sometimes with a bit of him in there. People around Crump increasingly speak his language, the colourful Crumpese he spouts. It's a kind of conquest and it's interesting to him.

He does it to Vanda in the pub this night. He tells her things about herself that he seems to have read in her face. He tells her she's had a traumatic experience in her life and she has — witnessing, as a child, her mother being swept to her death from rocks by the sea. He doesn't talk about himself. He concentrates on her and her life and her troubles.

Vanda is deeply impressed by his apparent knowledge of psychology and his concern for her. They meet up again and start a relationship. It's a little like the patient falling in love with the psychiatrist. Crump's very masterful with her and she's grateful and overwhelmed. She's in awe of his fame anyway. This is, after all, the legendary Barry Crump and he seems just the sort of stuff that legends are made of. If she ever paused to think about legends and their substance, that is.

'Don't ever dismiss anyone,' he tells her. 'Everyone's got a story within them and often if you sit down and talk with them you'll learn interesting, neat things.' He seems so good with people, so charming, drawing them out, getting them to tell him things they might never have told anyone before. Though he seems much more interested in what men have to say rather than women. And he seems so sensitive to the needs and troubles of friends, going all out of his way to help.

It's very flattering at first and that's why she goes out with him. He's a star and he's not at all like any other boyfriend Vanda's ever had, though he's not the most romantic of men. The relationship is a bit off and on at first, given the fact that Crump's trying to wriggle out of a thing with another woman. But then he does wriggle out and moves into her place and it's all on with Vanda, and soon it's even more all on because she's pregnant, though not by Crump. Though, of course, this doesn't seem to make much difference to him.

He tells her, 'Come on babe, we're moving to the country' and she thinks, Why not? She'd come from the country in the first place and maybe a change from the city will be good. They move down to Lake Rotoma, where Crump sets them up in a little bach on the shores of that big, beautiful piece of water and then he promptly buggers off to do a story or go on a bender with some of his mates or chase skirt, for all Vanda knows, and leaves her alone and pregnant. 'Just be there when I get back,' he tells her.

He returns in time for the birth of Alan, a good excuse to go on a bender with some welfare money Vanda's had to organise to support herself while he's been away. And while she's still in the maternity hospital, he drifts across to Te Teko where he turns up at the door of a bloke called George Johnston. 'They tell me you do a bit of hunting and fishing,' says Crump and Johnston tells him, 'Yeah that's right', knowing just who Crump is, but not saying anything at first. They don't get that many famous folk passing through Te Teko.

Crump tells Johnston he's in the area to do some stories for *Town and Around* and he's looking for somewhere to live. So they head down the pub, hit the piss and hit it off famously. Johnston's a bushman and a bit of a bad boy with a taste for adventure just like Crump and he reckons it's going to be fun having him around. He sets Crump and Vanda up in a house 300 yards down the road from his place and Crump immediately announces that before he can start having any adventures, he's got to get a book written and promptly locks himself in a room with a typewriter, not letting anyone inside, not even the increasingly mystified and unsettled Vanda. He tells Johnston, 'I'm out of piss money. I need to write a book.'

Then, Crump having come out of his writing cave, he and Vanda decide to marry and celebrate their honeymoon by going up the Rangitaiki River in a jetboat with Johnston and Vanda's dad and getting on the whisky and beer. Crump's not the most romantic of men. Johnston and Crump team up like the Lone Ranger and Tonto, doing a bit of safari work, catering to deer-shooting, trout-catching tourists and chasing the odd story for *Town and Around*. Crump teaches Johnston to light a fire in the rain and to light a fire under his life. Crump loves lighting fires. He also likes leading his new mate astray and all over the place and into more fun than he ever thought possible.

There are major bonuses to being around someone as famous and outrageous as Crump. The women just hurl themselves at him and Crump can only cope with so much. Though he can cope with quite a lot. They go to a party one night where all the men leave and Crumpy stays and plays with the women. And having the *Town and Around* camera and crew in tow is a real power tool. Then they can get away with bloody murder, and often do. Crump's asked across to Te Puke to address the local Lions Club and he turns up, gets up and starts up 'Eskimo Nell'. The Lions roar.

Once, on the road just south of Auckland, two chicks in a car recognise Crump and wave for them to follow their car. They do and end up at their flat in the eastern suburbs somewhere, all four them naked, drunk and just going for it. And another night, the two of them queued up in their bush shirts with their pants down and their dicks out, taking turns with this friend of Crump's, her on her knees wearing nothing but a sheepskin, her husband, an old guy, sitting in a chair with a brandy, watching, not saying anything.

Crump tells Johnston about the writing game and laughs about the things he's going to put into books. He makes it sound so easy. 'The way you look at writing a story,' he says, 'is that there's the way something happened, there's the way it could have happened and then there's the way it should have happened. And that's the way I do it and that's the way the readers like it.' He professes great knowledge of and instinct for what the public want and like and he tells Johnston he'll probably be using him in some of his stories. Adjusted, exaggerated and renamed, of course.

Crump often takes Johnston along on his *Town and Around* assignments, which he does only when put under extreme pressure by Auckland. The money's rubbish and he's getting bored by the hasslement from the people at head office. Crump's never sure where the fun stops and the work starts and it's always as hard as all hell getting out of the pubs once you're in them. But that's where he finds his stories. That's sometimes where he sets them.

Crump and Johnston and a television camera turn up at a pub outside Gisborne and announce that they want to set up a party scene that night for an item for the television. Everyone rushes round to oblige. 'We'll need lots of people,' says Crump, 'particularly girls.' Someone rings into town and organises lots of ladies to come out and they have a hell of a wing-ding, with a band and dancing and the publican laying on endless supplies of whisky and beer and thinking all the time that it'll be marvellous getting the hotel on television. But there's no film in the camera that everyone's dancing past and smiling at. There was never meant to be.

When he runs out of money, Crump lives out of Johnston's bank account in the spaces between his cheques arriving. Sometimes the spaces are long and sometimes Crump just gets pissed off with the whole deal and one of those black moods rises to the surface and drags him down. The boozing only makes it worse then.

Then one night, when little Alan is about four months old, Crump comes home to the family in their little farmhouse at Te Teko and takes his big fists to Vanda with such ferocity she's sure he's going to kill her. She's terrified and afterwards, when she can bear to face a mirror, she looks even worse than she feels. And she doesn't know what to do, whether to tell the neighbours, call the police or what. But, in the end, she feels defeated by her husband's fame, by the knowledge that everyone loves having him in the district and that they won't want to hear anything bad about their hero, least of all that he's a wife-beater. So she says nothing and stays indoors and out of sight till her bruises fade.

But when she is fit to go out in public, they go into the bush one day, Crump out in front leading the way as always and Vanda behind with her baby in a backpack. Crump gives her a loaded rifle to carry and she walks staring at his big back for an hour fighting with herself about whether to do what she strongly feels she should and shoot him in the back or not. She's that afraid of him and that close to pointing the gun, pulling the trigger and putting a big hole through him.

But where will that leave her? Alone with a young baby to support and no money and nowhere to go. So she doesn't. She carries that rifle, cursing herself every step, but silently cursing him more for doing this to her, putting such a dreadful impulse in her head. For Vanda, only 24 and from a loving, supportive family, the volatile mixture of having a publicly famous, privately violent husband and living in an out-of-the-way, hunting-shooting-fishing sort of place like Te Teko is a heavy burden. The local women are warm and helpful, but Vanda doesn't feel able to talk to them about the dark side of a man they have only seen the charming side of. Violence seems to be a hidden subject. It's something she's had no previous experience of and, after all, she's 'Barry Crump's wife' and she isn't expected to have this kind of problem.

So she shuts up and gets on with the life she's been dealt, living in fear, never knowing when Crump will be kind, loving and funny or when he'll lash out. He's as likely to turn nasty sober or drunk. There's something wrong inside him, she realises, two sides of the man fighting.

Things turn so bad again that she moves out and goes back to her dad, but he has remarried and has a young family now and it's not so easy and then Barry rings her and asks her to return. So she does, knowing it's never going to work and always fearing for herself and her little boy.

Meanwhile, Crump is putting the finishing touches to his follow-up to *The Odd Spot of Bother*, which he's claiming he wrote in a couple of spare days that he had 'in order to pay off several thousand dollars, $3800 actually, that the Inland Revenue Department and I discovered I owed them'. Crump's chaotic financial affairs have him teetering on the brink of bankruptcy. He's into everyone for cash, making promises he can't, or can't be bothered to keep. His publisher is becoming well and truly sick of Crump and his constant demands, his evasions, accusations.

And sometimes Crump crawls to the back of his cave and wonders what the hell this is all about. Why is it that those people out there who seem to like him so much and buy his books and pester the pants off him every time he stops to buy petrol or fill up with beer get the best part of him? He hears that part of him talking to them. He hears that part of him enchanting strangers he'll call cobber or mate rather than try to remember their names. He hears these people laughing and offering him another drink.

But he hears it as a stranger. Because the part of him that's left for him to deal with is the black awful bastard. The one who wants to be alone, but can't bear to be.

Out of the blue, Wally Crump sends a manuscript of a novel called *McDunnit Wunnit* to Reed, asking them if they'd be interested in publishing it. The story is the old man's second novel. He published his first effort, *McDunnit Dunnit*, himself a few years earlier and tried to flog it off around the place without any success. But Reed are unfailingly polite and mindful that he's Barry Crump's dad and write back, rejecting it in an encouraging sort of way. It's a bit old-fashioned, they tell him, and he writes back saying, 'I'm getting a bit long in the tooth myself, perhaps that's the trouble'. Reed even mention it to Barry by letter, telling him that it's easy to see where his own flair comes from.

This is the last sort of news Barry wants to hear, though he's having a pretty good time of it most of the time down in Te Teko, setting new highs in Kiwi blokedom with his mate George. They're often away shooting or fishing or filming. Their wives are never invited, though sometimes other women are. They get themselves involved with an outfit called South Pacific Safaris, taking American tourists on hunting trips through the Rotoma and Te Teko districts. Then someone gets the idea of running bush camps for city boys and using Crump's profile to promote it. Everyone agrees it's a tremendous idea and likely to do very well indeed.

Crump shoots up to the dreaded Auckland and holes up at the flash Intercontinental Hotel on one of his sporadic visits to the big smoke for a *Town and Around* piece. He rings Tina and she mentions to him that young Martin, their son as he might recall, is nine now and keen on carpentry. 'Put him on the phone,' says Crump. It's the first time in Martin's memory that he's spoken to his dad — and now he's got this big rumbly voice coming into his ear. 'Gidday Martin, it's Barry here,' he says. Not 'Dad'. It will never be 'Dad'.

Both their birthdays are coming up and Barry blows little Martin away by saying, 'How's about a night on the town, just the two of us, tonight?' Yes please, says Martin and Barry tells his excited son he'll pick him up at tea time. But he doesn't. He eventually turns up at 11 o'clock with two cheeseburgers and a hammer and buggers off again.

§

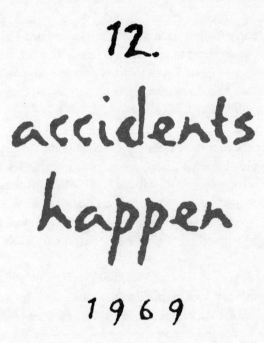

12.

accidents happen

1969

An edition of 100,000 copies of *Gulf* have been printed in Russia, but as Russia doesn't subscribe to the international copyright convention, they won't be paying Crump or his publisher a cracker. They are prepared to pay a royalty of sorts direct to the author, so long as he travels there and spends it there. Crump thinks this over.

Meantime, his eighth book is published. It's the short story collection that Reed's had previously as-near-as-hell rejected. It's been titled *Warm Beer and Other Stories* and Tony Stones has been hired to illustrate the 19 stories, some of which have been previously published. It's a powerful collection of tales, darker and more dangerous than Crump has been before. Some of the savagery that had disturbed Reed originally remains. It's dedicated 'For Alan, My Son'.

He's painting a grim picture of country life in this collection of out-of-town yarns and he paints it particularly in *Just Deserts*, the murderous tale of a terrifying West Coast mine owner, a character he told friends he based on his father Wally, down to his big hands. Violence is even more explicit in *That Way*, the nasty, vivid story of a rabbiter who doesn't just kill rabbits. It's not the Crump his diminishing public wants and after a quick sell it slows down rapidly. Like its predecessor, it will go on to sell around 10,000 copies, well short of his previous heroic peak. He blames the publisher for misunderstanding him. He's not going to put up with this much longer.

In September, 'Barry Crump, aged 34, of Te Teko' is fined $30 in the Hamilton Magistrates' Court on a charge of exceeding 30 miles an hour, reduced from one of driving at a dangerous speed. Crump admits the reduced charge and explains that he was overtaking two slow-moving trucks. 'It was just normal driving. I was sure I did the right thing,' he pleads eloquently.

The bush camps for boys turn out to be terrifically successful. Working with South Pacific Safaris, Crump and George Johnston are the front men for the camp, in the bush near Lake Matahina, up the road from Te Teko. Crump's work habits aren't always conducive to the task at hand, which involves teaching boys bush skills, from fire-lighting — a Crump specialty, he's obsessive about fires — all the way through to the fun end of things, guns. Though more and more of doing the same thing with other people's kids starts to put the old strain on Crump, the boredom.

It costs $40 for a week at the camp and boys who know all about Barry Crump the great bushman save up or nag their mums and dads to pay for them to get there. Bookings for the camps pour in and as each set of school holidays roll round, there are even more boys wanting to come — many of them wanting to come back for a second or a third visit. Hundreds of boys go bush with Crump and Johnston.

The adventure starts just driving to the camp, sitting in the back of a Land Rover as it bounces round the dark, forbidding Lake Matahina on a road full of holes, with the lake just down the cliff there. They live rough in little huts and one of the rules is that if you don't catch meat, then you don't eat it. Johnston and Crump split them into groups and take them pig hunting. They get filthy quickly. The toilet is a pit dug in the ground with a couple of bits of manuka across them to crawl out on and drop your business from. Crump's sons, Ivan and Martin, are at one of the camps. Some cheeky young lout is giving young Martin a hard time and Martin bleats to his dad. Crump stalks straight out to the kid, picks him up and throws him in the stinking dunny pit.

Alan Seay is 15 and he's a big Barry Crump fan. He's read *A Good Keen Man* and *Hang on a Minute Mate* and some of Crump's other books and he tries to catch him every time he's on *Town and Around* on the television. He sees an advertisement in the newspaper about the bush camp and that Barry Crump's running it and he's dead keen to go. It's not easy raising the $40, but he gets a job on a strawberry farm at Albany, north of Auckland, and he saves it up. In the end his cousins, Stephen and Mark, both younger than him, go too.

When they arrive, no one in particular seems to be in charge. There are kids milling around. They stand talking to them, when a Land Rover pulls up and Barry Crump sticks his head out the window and asks, 'Where are you guys from?' and someone says, 'Papatoetoe' and Crump says, 'Blow me down, I was born there.' And all the kids are blown away. This is the real Barry Crump. What a man. Then he drives away and they don't see him for several days.

The person who seems to be most in charge is a young guy the same age as Alan, called Gary Lett. He conducts what activities there are and drives them around in one of the Land Rovers. One day they pile into the Land Rover with a heap of rifles and ammo and drive to a clay pit area in the bush and just blast away.

Crump and Johnston put in an occasional appearance. Another man comes and shows the boys how to sharpen knives. Crump takes 10 or 12 boys off on a pig-hunting trip, setting such a ferocious pace with his dogs that one of the younger boys collapses gasping. Crump rounds on him, demanding to know what's wrong with him, has he got a crook ticker or what? Then, pissed off by the gasping kid, he grumpily leads them back out of the bush, the hunt cancelled.

On the second-to-last night, they're going out spotlighting for possums. The boys fill two Land Rovers, Crump driving one, Gary Lett driving the other, with nine aboard, including Alan Seay. First they drive over to Te Teko where Crump has to drop in to see a friend. He warns the boys not to start swearing and goes inside. He stays for ages and the boys get restless and boisterous and start swearing a bit. Next thing, Crump comes storming out, raging at them and swearing fouler than some of them have ever heard. He says he has a good mind not to let them go spot-lighting. But he changes his mind, jumps into his Land Rover and they're off.

Around 11 o'clock, the Land Rover with Alan Seay and his cousins in it, the one with the broken back door handle, turns back to the camp, swinging round past the dam at the mouth of the lake and round on the rough road high above the lake when there's an almighty bang and the next thing the nine sets of startled eyes inside the Land Rover know, it's going down the cliff towards the lake so slowly it seems that Alan Seay can see the headlights reflecting in the water. And then, woomph, they hit the lake, the windscreen shatters and a huge wall of icy water invades the Land Rover, battering the four boys in the front and then surging upward through the gun-racks and onto the five boys tumbling, trapped, in the back.

It's pitch black as they drift towards the bottom of the lake, but somehow Alan Seay manages to find the steering wheel, orient himself and get his head out the side window. His shoulders catch and he's running out of breath, but somehow he gets through. Just as he kicks free, a hand reaches out from the back of the Land Rover and briefly grabs his ankle. Then he shoots to the surface, where he find the three other boys from the front seat. Alan is badly cut across the chin, bleeding heavily and his mouth is full of loose teeth. Gary Lett keeps frantically diving, trying to get down to the five boys trapped down there. But it's no use, he's exhausted and has to stop before he drowns himself.

So the panic-stricken, terrified boys run down the road for help, heading for the village below the dam. Then a couple in a car pick them up and next thing police and ambulances are arriving and everything's turning to hell and damnation. Crump has arrived back at the camp earlier and turned in. Johnston is in bed at his home in Te Teko.

At the lake, the police send for a diver. He takes an age to arrive. And they send for Crump and Johnston. The two men come running, their world turned upside-down by the news of the accident. Crump races down from the camp and Johnston drives up from Te Teko. The diver arrives, but then it's found he has no gas in his tanks, so another diver is summoned from Whakatane. Crump and Johnston are filling their stunned heads with the detail of the crash, staring at the black lake, thinking of the five boys down there. After the police mention a boat would be useful, Johnston finds a jetboat and launches it on the lake. Then a fully equipped diver finally arrives, goes down into the lake and swiftly finds the Land Rover and the bodies of the five boys trapped in the back behind the gun-racks.

The dead boys are brought to the surface and passed to the grim onlookers at the lakeside. Crump feels like a stranger in his own skin. This can't be happening to him. 'We carry the bodies out on the back of a truck. One boy had managed to smash his way through the glass, but his Parka caught and he was trapped — and the other four boys trapped behind him, drowning pressed against the glass. We carry them into a concrete-floored shed as a temporary mortuary and that's when this thing happens. As I lower the boy I'm carrying, I let him slip so his head hits the concrete with a bump. That's the sound I can't get out of my head now. The bump. That and the fact that I did it deliberately.'

It's all over the newspapers and the radio and flying off everyone's lips the next morning — the awful news that five teenage boys attending an adventure camp drowned when their Land Rover plunged off a 25-foot bluff into Lake Matahina above the hydro-electric dam in the Urewera. The camp is being run, the stories and the loose talk stress, by Crump and his partner George Johnston. Four other boys in the vehicle who had struggled clear are in Whakatane Hospital suffering from shock, cuts and bruises.

The 15-year-old driver of the Land Rover, Gary Lett, of Te Teko, apparently dived repeatedly into the lake in efforts to save the five boys until he collapsed from exhaustion. Lett had been 'helping out with training' at the camp.

Mrs T. Coker, the wife of a Matahina Power Station worker, talks of turning her lounge into a first aid station after the four soaked and bleeding survivors — Gary Lett, Lawrence Hamilton and Mark and Alan Seay — came to her door after being picked up by a couple who found them running along the road near the dam. Mrs Coker used sheets to stem the blood from the boys' wounds and wrapped them in blankets while Mr Coker rang the Edgecumbe police.

'It was dreadful,' says Mrs Coker. 'I always thought I would be very good at doing that sort of thing and I suppose it was alright at the time, but it was awful after they had gone.' Together with neighbours, Mrs Coker gave the boys hot drinks. 'We had to help the boys drink. They couldn't do it themselves. One of the boys had a terribly cut chin. All we could do was wrap them up and stop the bleeding.'

Police inquiries into the Matahina Dam tragedy continue. Inspector J. Rossiter, of the Tauranga police, says the inquiry is centred on Whakatane and that dozens of witnesses have been interviewed there and at Te Teko, Edgecumbe and Matahina.

Crump goes home numb and overwhelmed, not understanding how such a thing could happen to him. Christ, this is the worst thing yet. This one blots out the sun.

On 12 December, Barry John Crump and George Vansel Johnston are each charged with manslaughter when they appear before Mr W.M. Willis, SM, in the Whakatane Magistrates' Court. No pleas are taken. The charges are that, on 4 September 1969, at Te Mahoe, near Te Teko, having undertaken responsibility for the care of David Stratton Izard, aged 13, Emrys Tangiora, aged 12, Timothy John Dyas James, aged 13, Stephen Murray Seay, aged 13, and Murray Richard Rogers, aged 13, the omission to do which was dangerous to life, did omit without lawful excuse to discharge that duty and caused the deaths of the said persons, thereby committing manslaughter. The accused are represented by Mr L.H. Moore, of Whakatane.

Crump and Johnston go into a protective huddle. Anger and attitude jolt Te Teko like a lightning strike. No matter how the two bushmen explain it to themselves and agree how it happened, they know they're already being judged and found guilty. The road was tight and rough where the Land Rover went off. Heavy trucks travelled it regularly, there was a quarry nearby, often rocks dropped on the road. The Land Rover must have hit one of those. The impact would have jarred the steering wheel right out of young Gary's hands. It was an accident, pure and simple, and it wouldn't have mattered who was driving.

Crump's not very good at confronting his emotions at the best of times and these are hardly the best of times. He clams up, goes into retreat. The two mates don't go out together much any more. There's a terrible chill in the air. A rumour goes round that Crump doesn't care, that he hasn't even bothered making contact with the bereaved families. That he's cut himself off. But he does make attempts, though they're up against fierce hurt and anger. He and Johnston are asked not to attend the tangi of one of the boys.

The adventure camp is cancelled.

In early 1970, the taking of depositions on charges of manslaughter begin in the Whakatane Magistrates' Court. On application by Crown prosecutor, Mr T.M. Thorp, the charge against each defendant is amended to apply only to the death of Timothy John Dyas James. Mr Thorp says each death would create a separate offence and the purpose of the prosecution is to establish the responsibility or otherwise for the event. In accordance with the practice of the Crown in multiple fatality cases, it is considered that one charge is adequate for that purpose.

Constable R.B. Gaskill, of Edgecumbe, who attended the incident, tells the Court that shortly after being called to the scene, he drove for two miles along the road above the lake and did not see any pothole or boulder. The weather was fine and driving conditions were good. Mark Seay showed him where the accident occurred. Gary Lett tells the Court he had been helping Crump and Johnston at the camp since they started in August 1968. The defendants placed him in a position of authority over the boys and he drove them regularly in a Land Rover. On the night of the accident, he was driving on the metal road alongside the dam between 25 and 30 mph when he felt a bump. 'Shortly after, it was a whole series of bumps and we crashed through tutu and gorse and plunged into the dam,' he says.

Another boy says that most of the time at the camp he went out with a group supervised by Lett. On 4 September, they went hunting in the morning and then had a swim. In the evening, his group went opossum hunting in a Land Rover driven by Lett, who he knew was an unlicensed driver. The hunting trip in the evening was arranged by Lett, Crump and Johnston. There were nine in his vehicle and another, driven by Crump, left first, but they met at Matahina.

'We went along the road a bit and then separated to shoot opossums,' the 13 year old tells the Court. 'We carried on with that until about 11 p.m. There had not been any arrangement to meet again after we separated at Matahina.' The return trip began with three boys in the front, including Lett, and six in the back, says the boy. After they had tried to shoot a rabbit on the road during the return trip, he sat in the front with Lett and Mark and Alan Seay.

Mike Bennett

The great crocodile hunter at work.

Crump's rocky profile overshadows Lake Coleridge.

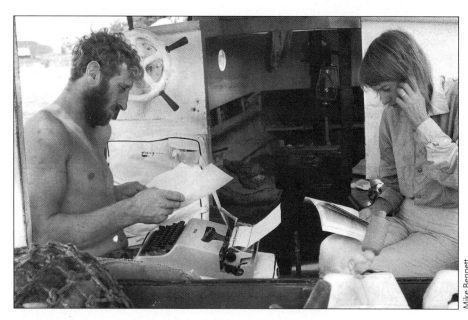

Crump writing about New Zealand at sea off North Queensland
with Jean Watson.

The New Zealand Herald

Recording his work for books for the blind in the 1960s.

Crump the cover boy — in *Mate* magazine in 1968.

Crump, in the midst of the sex-symbol years, turned his hand to many things
— including advertising carpet.

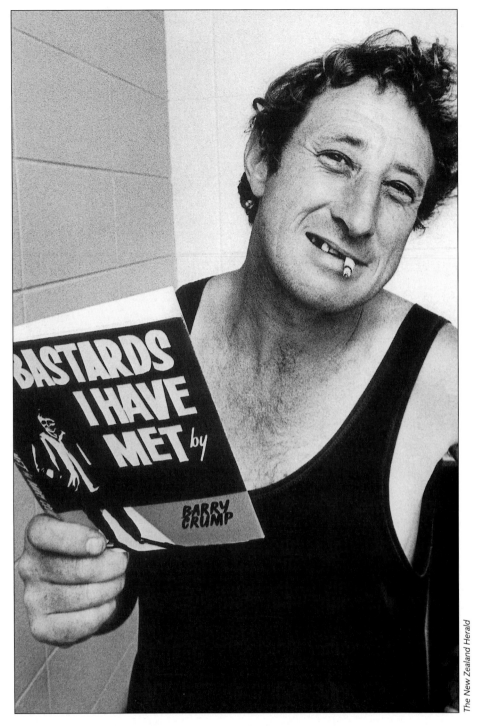

The New Zealand Herald

Rough as guts with a book to match — Crump goes it alone
with *Bastards I Have Met*.

Crump and his gun — Te Teko, 1970.

Playing croquet — here fully dressed.

Nelson Evening Mail

A bushman and his wife — with fourth wife Robin.

'Before we set out that evening I knew the rear door handle was broken on the inside. You could not open it from the inside. It had been like that for about two or three days. Someone in the front usually got out and opened the door. We drove back over the Matahina Dam…. We hit a bump or something on the road. It was a severe bump and there was a loud crack. The vehicle bounced and went over the side.

'When we went into the water there was a great splash and suddenly it was full of water. Between hitting the bump and going off the road was very fast. I was trying to breathe, but it was all water. We were all moving round trying to get out. I stopped after a while and then got out through a broken window. The other three in the front seat got out.

'Gary and I dived to try to help. We were able to reach the vehicle once with one dive. We could see the headlights under the water. We could not reach it on later dives. I saw the headlights moving further down.' Mark Seay tells the Court Crump was told about the broken door handle before that evening by one of the boys.

John Donald St Clair Brown, of Auckland, managing director and secretary for South Pacific Safaris Ltd, says his company handled the bookings, promotion and business side of the camp. The boys paid $40 for seven days' stay. He says an item about the camp had appeared on *Town and Around*. A form sent to inquirers included the sentences: 'New Zealand has more to offer in the way of back country sport and activity than any other country in the world and we show our boys how to enjoy these things safely and skilfully' and 'We meet the boys at the bus depot and from then on they are our responsibility'.

Sgt John Munro, of Rotorua, says that on 5 September he saw Crump at his home in Te Teko. 'I asked Crump if he was aware that the interior door handle on the Land Rover was broken and he said he was not aware of it.' In a statement, Crump said he returned to the camp at about 10.15pm. 'When I arrived back at the camp, I found George Johnston there with some who had stayed behind. I was not expecting Gary to return until some time after myself, but by 11 p.m. I was a little uneasy about them returning to camp safely, but I wasn't alarmed. I went to sleep.'

Crump and Johnston plead not guilty and are remanded, on bail of $500 each, to appear in the Gisborne Supreme Court on charges of manslaughter. Outside the Court, Crump runs into Alan Seay who has a vivid scar across his chin from the crash. 'Oh well,' Crump tells him, 'you'll be able to grow a beard over that.'

Then, six weeks later, a judge throws out the manslaughter charge against Crump and Johnston after legal argument in chambers in Wellington. There is insufficient evidence for the accused to stand trial, the judge rules.

At an inquest into the deaths of the five boys, concern is expressed by a lawyer representing the boys' parents that Crump, Johnston and South Pacific Safaris Ltd have not had to subject themselves to public questioning about the accident. The lawyer, Mr S. C. Ennor, says the proprietors of the camp had allowed a number of young boys to go with an unlicensed driver in a defective vehicle.

The defect was known to Johnston, he says. The vehicle was overloaded. Nine boys from the camp were allowed to go out with firearms when none of them was of an age when they would be entitled to do so. 'No doubt this has been a traumatic experience for Gary Lett, but he should not have been put in this position,' says Mr Ennor. 'Neither should these five boys have lost their lives.'

The parents of the drowned boys want to ensure that this sort of thing does not happen again, but the coroner, Mr S. Osborne, of Whakatane, says he doesn't feel he can make 'any useful recommendation'. He returns a verdict that the boys had been accidentally drowned at Lake Matahina. Crump and Johnston don't attend the inquest.

A week later, bereaved fathers Hayward Izard and Neil Tangiora tell the national scandal rag *Truth*, 'We don't want a witch hunt — just to see that it doesn't happen again'. All the parents of the dead boys receive cheques for $40 from South Pacific Safaris Ltd two days after the tragedy, refunds of the camp fees. Izard and Tangiora say the cheques will never be cashed. Mrs Bunty Izard, whose son, David, died says, 'We are not being vindictive. We don't want the money. We only want to see something done that will stop this happening again.' Tunnel worker Tangiora still believes outdoor camps are a great idea. If he had another son, he would send him along, he says.

Crump feels like he's been hit by a logging truck. 'It's a tragedy. Some people feel the blame is mine. I loved those kids. The whole atmosphere generated in that camp was amazing. It got that way that the kids could talk freely about their problems and receive a sympathetic hearing from the others. We were achieving great things. It was an accident. It's dangerous in the bush. Accidents happen.'

Meanwhile, Reed still want a Crump book out every year and the effort planned for 1970 is making them a little happier than usual. It has been announced that Crump's soon-to-be-published next novel goes by the astonishing title of *A Good Keen Girl* and that it's about a young woman on a Bay of Plenty farm who takes astrology seriously. Crump, according to newspaper reports, is 'holed up in Te Teko doing full-time writing with an unlisted telephone'.

Reed have managed to shuffle Crump's newspaper saga, *No Reference Intended*, to the bottom of the pile. They don't like it much and want to delay it as long as possible, disturbed as they are by what they see as the continuing decline in his work. They do see a ray of hope in *A Good Keen Girl*, mainly because it raises memories of his extraordinary debut. But why, they want to know, won't he call it *A Good Keen Woman*? That way they'd have a perfect matching pair. They worry too about his continuing habit of denigrating any woman who steps into the pages of his books.

The big immediate problem with *A Good Keen Girl* is getting an unkeen Crump to come up with enough words so that they can even call it a book. Crump's books have always fallen well short of the number of words that most readers — and publishers — would feel made a novel. Larger-than-normal type, illustrations and the cunning placement of short and blank pages have long helped to beef up the number of pages between his covers. Even then, he's yet to hit 200.

The first version of *A Good Keen Girl* that lands in Reed's lap is barely 30,000 words. They ask him for another 10,000 and he manages a bare 4500 and that's that from the great wordsmith. So they split his 10 chapters into 14, bump the type size up another point or two and order more illustrations. There's even talk of dropping the cover price so they won't be accused of daylight robbery. Minus Tony Stones' line drawings and the cunningly placed blank pages, *A Good Keen Girl* would have added up to a little more than 100 pages.

But there's stronger-than-usual interest in the book, thanks to the familiar ring of the title and the novelty of Crump's female angle. There's little novelty in the book, though, which takes a slice out of the life of one Kersey Hooper, the rugged land-breaking owner of a rundown station who, halfway through the book, takes a wife, though he has little experience of such skittish and unpredictable livestock as women.

> She wasn't a bad looker, in a pale sort of way. Big round eyes the colour of a treated pine post and skin like a bucket of beastings. Didn't look as if she got much sun. Her hair was the same gingery colour as a new boot and she was fairly tall with long feet and hands but a bit herring-gutted on it. She never had much to say for herself.
>
> Their name was Chadwick. The old man was Alby, the old lady was Mrs Chadwick and the daughter's name was Faith.
>
> Alby opened another bottle of beer and then went into the kitchen to see how the tucker was getting on.
>
> The old lady was a tiger to talk. She told me all about how they'd had a little business of their own in Seaforth and sold it to build the motel. They'd only been in the place a few weeks and hadn't got it properly under way yet. She'd been married once before and had to divorce her first husband for deserting her. Left her alone and defenceless until Alby had turned up. The daughter had arrived about a year after they were married and the three of them had been a team ever since.
>
> But it didn't look to me as though there was much teamwork going on. Andy was hogging all the work.

'Now, tell us something about yourself, Mr Hooper,' said the old lady, grabbing at my arm. 'What line of business are you in?'

I told them a bit about how I'd taken over the Blackrange Station and then Alby came in to say the tucker was on the table and we went into the kitchen and got stuck into it. It was a pretty good feed, too. He'd roasted up a leg of mutton and slung a few spuds in with it. There was quite a bit of other stuff going but I settled for another lash at the mutton and spuds.

'I suppose you must get quite a lot of meat on your farm,' said the daughter.

'Too right,' I told her. My mate Bert and I have got onto a great lurk with the killer mutton. Guarantee the meat'll be as tender as you can get every time.'

'Really?' said the old lady. 'You'll have to let us in on your little secret, Mr Hooper. Some of the meat we get from our butcher is as tough as old boots.'

'Well, when you're going to kill a sheep for mutton,' I explained, 'you always want to shut it up in the yard with a few of its mates for a day or two, to let it settle down and get used to being handled, lets 'em empty out a bit too. If you run a sheep in off the hill and grab it and cut its throat while it's nervous and worked-up it's ten to one the meat'll be tough. And it's harder to make a clean job of it when they're kicking around, too.'

The old lady thanked me for the tip and reckoned she was going to pass it on to her butcher next time she saw him.

(from *A Good Keen Girl*, **1970)**

It's a strange book which even has Crump stumbling into something he's generally avoided in the past in his books, though not, of course, in life. Sex rears its awkward head as the book's hero stumbles into marriage without, apparently, even the most rudimentary knowledge of women.

'They're not like cows or anything, are they?' I asked.

'I wouldn't know anything about that,' said Bert quickly.

'I mean once a year or something,' I explained.

'Nothing as clear-cut as that,' said Bert. 'But there's times I begin to wonder.'

'What about dogs, every few months?'

'No, nothing like that. Just as well, too, come to think of it. It's bad enough as it is sometimes.'

'Well how the hell is it?' I asked him.

Bert paused to go over and get a billhook out of the corner and bring it back to lean on.

'Y'see, Kersey, women aren't the same as us. They're built different, for a starter.'

'In what way?'

Bert looked at me. 'You ought to have found that out by now,' he said.

a life in loose strides
·
116

He paused again, this time to get a hole started in my implement shed floor with the end of the billhook.

'Sex is funny stuff, Kersey. The more you get, the more you get. And the less you get, the less you get. It's a big thing when you look into it.'

(from *A Good Keen Girl*, **1970)**

A Good Keen Girl hits the bookshops and Crump travels to Auckland to help push out the book and to launch a recording career with the release of his first single, a laconic folksy grumble called *Bad Blue*. Crump has long fancied himself as a bit of a singer and a poet too. He's a useful enough guitarist, but that voice of his rides low and flat in the saddle. The song is no threat to The Rolling Stones.

At the launch of *A Good Keen Girl*, Crump lets it be known that 5000 copies have already pre-sold to booksellers and that he's turning his hand to writing a play. He's still in Te Teko, but he's looking for somewhere else to live 'away from the smoke, fumes and glitter of the city'. He tells a reporter that one of his forthcoming dramatic works is a television play based on a man who runs a 'bad news bureau — breaking bad news for those who haven't the guts to do it themselves' before asking the journo, 'Got a smoke on you, mate?' The blokes from the newspapers lap this sort of stuff up and run into print perpetuating the Crump character.

But not all his press is positive. Under the heading 'Mr Crump is a Little Bewildered', one reviewer of *A Good Keen Girl* notes that with the arrival of a major female character in a Crump book, 'the story fades away to a half-hearted conclusion. When a genuine female with genuine female foibles appears, our good keen author becomes a bit bewildered.' As in life.

Though Crump's not so bewildered that he doesn't know when it's time to move on. When visiting Waihi, the old mining town, he puts down a cheque for a $2000 advance that he bullied out of Reed as a deposit on a big old house. He's over the moon about it. Loves it.

'This place is truly magnificent. We play croquet on our own croquet lawn. It's a genuine old English country-house with grounds like a park. It's the best thing that's ever happened to me. I'm happy and it looks like staying this way. The only reason I've never tried to buy my own house before is because I never imagined it was possible.' He's so excited, he writes to Reed thanking everyone responsible for making it possible and inviting the whole of the office to come and stay.

Things are so much better that Crump and Vanda have decided to see if they can't get pregnant and have a baby and that comes to pass and Lyall, yet another son for Crump, arrives into an unpredictable life after the move to Waihi. Crump doesn't stay happy and excited for long. Boredom and bitterness and buggeration creep up on him, though he strives mightily to distract himself.

To a large extent, the Waihi pile is a party house, with Crump encouraging all and sundry to come and stay and leer up large. There are nude parties on the croquet lawn, Crump more than happy to flash his considerable equipment at the ladies, though it's ugly when he bends to concentrate on a croquet shot. It's all a bit outrageous for sleepy little Waihi, but what the hell.

News reaches him that he's been translated into Bulgarian for inclusion in a *World Anthology of Humour*.

§

13.

a tab of acid

1971

And here comes another book, just when the booksellers of New Zealand don't quite want another one from Crump. *A Good Keen Girl* has sold better than his previous few books, but there are still 10,000 copies of it crowding the shop shelves out there. But there's no stopping the next one and this time it's the book from a few years back that Crump reckoned was going to be a real beaut, something different from anything he's done before.

This is the book that Reed delayed for as long as possible. It's called *No Reference Intended* and it is different. It's serious. Sort of. It's Crump's take on the life of a newspaper reporter, Jeremy Cosgrove, a useless, unimaginative sort of journo who's as long on ambition as he is short on actual ability. These handicaps don't stand in his way on his rise from the bottom of the pond. It seems a bit like a concerted attempt by Crump to lift his intellectual profile.

He's bitter about those wankers, those writers and academics from years back who can't sell more than 100 copies of one of their earnest books and yet who are so rude about him. They sneered at his success to hide their jealousy. That prick Maurice Duggan called him an anecdotal ape. And he wasn't just jealous of Crump's popularity. He was pissed off about Crump marrying Fleur. The lovely Fleur, whom he had the hots for. So fuck him and the typewriter he rode in on.

With *No Reference Intended* Crump finds a new way to look at familiar themes, planting his newspaperman in rustic circumstances and using him as a guide. But he's a cynical rather than a laconic guide and Crump's attempt to make a big point about the untrustworthiness of newspapers comes emboldened by wordplay and long sentences, backed up with a lot less humour than usual.

He even pads out yet another too-short book by jamming in one of the yarns from *Warm Beer and Other Stories*, slightly adjusting the savage *Just Deserts* story to convert it into a tale within a tale, but it doesn't sit easily. The whole book doesn't sit easily, reading partly like a half-hearted attempt by Crump to raise his style and a personal vengeance on journalists.

> It was about this time that Cosgrove's career began to go a little haywire. After five more years, at twenty-nine, he was still battling on an insignificant country newspaper as a general reporter, with little prospect of a better, or even similar, position on a bigger paper — and he was becoming tired of fighting for recognition on papers that didn't seem to appreciate his efforts to raise their standards. He hadn't liked the country environment in the first place; now he hated it bitterly, and the people who inhabited it. The people who'd descended from those gallant pioneers who, according to Cosgrove's understanding of it, cheated and stole and plundered with such indomitable ingenuity for the land they handed down to us, and who, having got the bushland, proceeded to do to it exactly what they'd done to its native owners. Plundering their plunder with that unquenchable land-hungry spirit that lives on in those who bear their names to this day: the spirit that stripped our forests of the kauri, the totara and the rimu, and gave us instead the gorse, the blackberry, the barberry, and the naked eroding landscapes that can only be saved from silting into the sea at the cost of inestimable millions. How proud those trail-blazers would be if they could see their names emblazoned proudly on such solid symbols of today's agricultural prosperity as bank-overdraughts, bills of sale, mailboxes, television time-payment cards and perhaps even the door of the farm truck.
>
> Cosgrove's newspapers themselves were things that boosted his rising resentment and bitterness. An average of five extra copies for every local name you can work in.
>
> **(from** *No Reference Intended*, **1971)**

Under the heading 'Can This be the End of Crump?', one reviewer (Noel

Holmes in the *Auckland Star*) dismisses Crump's tenth book, 'a small newspaper saga called *No Reference Intended*', as flimsy. 'It is a little book. It's small to the heft — only 164 pages, despite large type. It is small in content, a poorish short story spun out to the point of absurdity. Is this the end of Crump? It doesn't have to be. He could go back into the world he knows and consult a few more bush blokes and forget those city slickers.... He is not the sort of writer who can make out by interviewing his typewriter.'

Crump doesn't care. He's holed up in Waihi working on his next book and partying harder and turning mean and unpredictable. Vanda is becoming seriously afraid again. Crump's answer to having nothing to do half of the time is to buy some booze and get drunk, or smoke some of the pot that's increasingly around the place. Or drop a tab of acid and say goodbye to most of the day. He goes down the pub, plays pool, brings strangers home and orders them to be fed.

One night he comes in late and pissed as a big nasty rat. Vanda's still up, watching TV, which for some unstated reason pisses him off. He lurches across the room, picks up the TV and smashes it to the floor, with a great blast as the tube explodes. One day when the washing machine's jumping round making too much noise for him and his hangover to cope with, he grabs a knife and cuts the live cord off at the wall.

Things are turning a shade violent in his dealings with his long-suffering publishers too. They've put out a collection called *The Best of Barry Crump* and are braced for what might come off his typewriter next in a pattern of what they see as seriously diminishing creative returns. As far as they're concerned, Crump is running out of fuel and they can't imagine that things are suddenly going to get better with whatever book he has coming next.

He's hassling them seriously for money again and now he's going to hassle them even more painfully with a new book that is just too awful for them to contemplate. It's called *Bastards I Have Met* and he knows they're not going to go for it. No way are they. 'It's not going to be even remotely acceptable to Reed. I've deliberately kept my other books free from bad language and references to such things as sex in the past, but only to suit Reed's requirements. They can live in the past if they want to, but I won't and now I'm going to use that sort of stuff in my work, mainly because of the change in public attitudes. Words and subjects that were unacceptable 10 years ago are now commonplace, except in the old firm. This new book is pretty ripe stuff and I don't even see any point in letting them read it.'

He writes to them wanting to know by return post whether they're interested in publishing a book called *Bastards I Have Met*, which he describes as an informal catalogue of bastard-types and the ungarnished accounts of the author's personal encounters with them.

In essence, it's a return to Crump's old string-of-yarns approach, cunningly disguised as something much more contemporary. This is Crump playing the outrageous bastard, a good role for a man with his outlook. He wears it well, but Reed aren't going to wear it at all. They send a letter to Crump's latest in an ongoing line of agents and representatives, advising him that *Bastards I Have Met* is not up to the usual standard of the Barry Crump they know and previously loved and therefore they are returning it forthwith and Crump and his agent can feel free to approach another publisher.

Reed hope that though this breaks the previously unbroken Reed-Crump publishing line, their decision is not seen as a permanent parting. But, after 11 fruitful years, it is permanent and Reed are just being polite. *No Reference Intended* was a flop as far as they're concerned. It's sold only a few thousand copies, a fraction of what they expected, and it even got bad reviews. Crump's market has moved on and grown up and Crump's too old-fashioned by far for the new generation, who probably think a good afternoon's fencing involves swords.

They have little faith that Crump will ever come up with a manuscript as good as his first two books again, and even if he did they'd be looking at a print run of only 5000. And a short print run puts costs up, so Crump's princely 15 percent royalty rate would have to drop to 10. And, of course, any advances would be smaller. They even go so far as to suggest to his agent that Barry might have to consider either writing short stories for magazines to re-establish his profile or start regarding writing as a part-time hobby and consider what full-time occupation might give him a living wage.

Crump is grumpy and announces that he's going it alone in the world of publishing. He's going to publish his next book through his own company, Crump Productions Ltd. He says the big publishers are terrible useless bastards who take as long as a year to get a book out. His company can do the job in only a few weeks, he tells a couple of reporters.

'And we can get more from it,' he says. The new book is *Bastards I Have Met*. 'It's a good book,' says Crump. 'It's mainly about the bastards you run into and things about them, experiences, that sort of thing.' And the book, featuring chapters on 26 sorts of blokey bastards from 'Actual' through to 'Zealous' — is duly released, published by Barry Crump Associates. Crump goes on maximum media offensive and gives his breakaway book his best shot, talking it up a storm. It's going to be a bastard of a success, Crump reckons, and it is.

It has its moments too, swinging between cynical and judgemental broadsides at 'Good' bastards, 'Intellectual' bastards and the awful 'Vain' bastards and the fond old bush tales of the 'Poor' bastards and 'Weak' bastards. It's Crump at his least soulful and most concertedly clever and though it will go on to outsell everything since *Hang on a Minute Mate*, it's a potboiler. And a preachy one at that.

I met a brilliant man once. You couldn't tell he was brilliant just by looking at him, but he was. Everybody said so. He was a brilliant lecturer or architect or something.

He wasn't what you'd call a handsome man, or a well-dressed one. Nor was he particularly charming, or witty, or interesting. As a matter of fact he was bloody rude. He interrupted conversations, ate with his mouth open and generally made everyone squirm by his sheer lack of consideration and common decency.

It didn't take me long to see that I'd run into a fully-fledged Intellectual Bastard (*Bastardus profoundus*). He was typical of them; he claimed to be an intellectual but he was really just a bastard. Half a dozen of the hundreds of obscure poems he'd written had been published in obscure literary magazines subsidised by the arts grants, so he called himself a poet.

He was a phoney and ignorant, and, like all Intellectual Bastards, he protected his ignorance by assuming an air of shaky superciliousness. His intellectualness was based on such things as throwing references to obscure subjects into the conversation and leaving you stumped for words. There's not a great deal you can say to such things as, 'Of course Domingo Faustino Sarmiento in *Defence of Freedom* claims that the press is a virtue, rather than a collection of type-face.' You either have to brave his scorn and confess that you've never heard of Domingo Faustino Sarmiento, or, agree with him. Either way there's an uneasy silence because he's interrupted the flow of the conversation and the atmosphere of the gathering and it always takes a while to get things going again after a thing like that happens. It's not worth trying to pin him down or prove him wrong because nearly everything he says is quoted from some musty book or other and the best you can hope for is to prove the book wrong, while he goes scot-free.

Few people speak so much and say so little as the Intellectual Bastard, and they're usually talking such ephemeral, arrant nonsense that nobody could be articulate about it, and they 'um' and 'ah' and croak and groan in between their words like somebody with a speech-impediment.

Most types of bastard are versatile enough to switch from one kind of bastardry to another, depending on the requirements of the situation, but the Intellectual Bastard is so busy maintaining his precarious perch above the rest of us that he can't let go for fear of falling in amongst us. Unthinkable! Everything he has an impulse to say must be carefully processed and worked-out before he says it because the Intellectual Bastard must be absolutely correct in all he says at all times.

The result of this is that he's rarely ever right, but since he can't see it he doesn't know about it, and because he doesn't know about it it doesn't matter, because he knows everything that does matter.

His humour is a kind of acerbitous wit that, boiled down, amounts to petty, catty, criticisms of other people. He can't fight and he can't work and he's a pacifist because he's frightened of losing his temper, and his view of that is as outrageously exaggerated as his self-importance — roughly proportionate to his actual importance.

As far as I'm concerned the Intellectual Bastard is a man with a great quantity of information and a great lack of knowledge. The poor bastard's the victim of the Great Academic Confidence Trick, usually worded something like, 'You'll get nowhere these days without a degree behind you'. And our student, hundreds if not thousands of times too often, interprets this as, 'I feel like I do because I haven't got a university degree. Once I get that everything is going to be all right. I won't feel anxious or inadequate any more. People will be nicer to me. I'll be offered jobs in high places at high salaries. Women will compete for my company. I'll be rich and famous and never have to worry about myself ever again.'

And so he embarks on his career of Intellectual Bastardry. And after many years of study he finally graduates, with the only experiences he's had during these prime years having been ones to do with studying for a university degree, and that's all the *knowledge* he can logically claim to have.

Unfortunately the only people qualified to either confirm or deny this state of affairs are those with university degrees, but by the time they've made it they're so thoroughly indoctrinated and personally committed that to explode the Academic Myth calls on them to acknowledge that their years of study and effort have been almost completely wasted. So they blindly go on supporting something that they know underneath isn't working for them. This causes them to become defensive and aggressive and anxious to prove how much more than us they know — how inferior we are to them.

Perhaps the most effective way of silencing an Intellectual Bastard would be to present him a ledger, with all he's ever *done* in one column, and the time it's taken him to do it in the other. Which goes to demonstrate that if there was any tangible way to assess the qualities of the Intellectual Bastard he wouldn't exist.

I haven't got a university degree and never had the opportunity to decide whether I wanted one or not, but I'm taking this opportunity, patient reader — Understanding Bastard (*Bastardus allknowingus*) — to tell you how pleased I am that you and I never turned out to be Intellectual Bastards.

(from *Bastards I Have Met,* **1971)**

The man in charge of letter-writing at Crump Productions Ltd, John Brown, now takes up the cudgel on behalf of Crump and starts persecuting Reed about the unbelievably small number of sales shown on their latest royalty statement and offering to sell the Crump back catalogue for them seeing as how they hardly seem capable. There is also a certain amount of open gloating about the success they're having with *Bastards I Have Met,* which, he tells them, has sold out its first printing of 12,000, with 50 percent of the forthcoming second printing ordered in advance.

They're planning a new Crump book later in 1972 and doubt whether Reed could make them any offer that would make them want to give up the independent publishing game, though they know they're new boys in an ancient and honorable business and they'll be in touch should they ever need any advice.

Reed, with customary corporate politeness, send Crump Productions an accounting of books in stock. There are nearly 10,000 copies of *A Good Keen Girl* unsold. They're mystified at the success of *Bastards*, but good luck in the unpredictable and heartbreaking world of publishing. *Bastards I Have Met* will go on to sell more than 100,000 copies.

Crump rolls up to Auckland and hangs around long enough to release the news that he intends to become a television producer and make a programme starring 'Kiwidom's mythical expert in all situations, Sam Cash'. He then promptly flees back to Waihi, after picking up his wife and two young sons and speeding off down the southern motorway. 'I can't stand the idea of more than one day at a time in Auckland,' he tells the *8 O'Clock* newspaper.

Wearing a slightly faded open-necked plaid shirt and a pair of well-worn grey strides, Crump puts on a faraway stare, rolls one cigarette after another and gives a rundown on the 1971–72 Crump, strongly pushing the angle that a mellowed Barry Crump, at 36, has found his natural niche.

According to Crump, the ideal situation for anybody to be in is to be as happy as it is possible to be. 'I achieve this by simply not doing anything I don't want to do.' He then goes on to fill up the reporter's pad with his thoughts on a variety of areas of modern life.

'I'll tell you what I think alright. Bloody politicians and unions are running round in the same circles all the time, going crook over the same problems without ever getting to the cause. And cities like this place, growing out of control, they're alright for some of the people in them, I suppose. But all that advertising and noise is not for me. Most of the city people I know also don't even like what they're doing, but they've been doing it so long that they've forgotten what they would really like anyway.

'And another lot I have problems with are protesters. They're against everything. They never see any good in anything — and there is a lot of good around. A lot of them talk about wanting a communal society. Put them in a commune and they'd go crook on that. But then when it comes to writing, for me, that's the easiest part. I make plenty of notes for books, priceless things. But when it comes to sitting down and writing, they're no good. I don't spend much time on a book. About a month — and *Gulf*, I wrote in five and a half days and nights. A lot of other authors are friends of mine, but I often think it only stays that way because we're separated by so many miles. I've got a feeling — I can't explain it — that when I'm 40 I'll write a really good significant book. But I'm not writing for posterity.

'The biggest con game in the country are the academics. That's the game that starts in the schools when they tell everyone that you can't be anything without a degree. The people who put this line out are academics. By the time the kids who go to university realise they've been conned, they've got degrees and they're part of the system, so they keep it going.'

Then Crump gets to hammering on about security and his feelings on the issue of home ownership. 'You're only as secure as you feel you are inside yourself. The best thing for encouraging insecurity is the very symbol of what most of society thinks represents security — a home of your own. I once bought a house. It made me more insecure than I've ever been. It's a stone around your neck. If you rent a place, the worst that can happen is not being able to pay the rent. So they sling you out. So what? All I've ever really owned is me car. And that's ideal.'

The truth behind this lie is that Crump's about to pull up stakes and get out of Waihi. Get out of New Zealand, in fact. Get out of the whole deal. Give it up and go away and find another way maybe. Find some bloody thing. Some bigger thing. Nothing's working really. He's sick of it all. These lines keep going through his head — something's broken, something's lost. The spell is broken. He's losing his self-belief, that self-belief he'd so carefully constructed with the aid of the blokeish media of New Zealand. He has to find something else to believe in.

In late November, the downmarket *Sunday News* announces it has secured serialisation rights to *Bastards I Have Met*. Crump tells the paper, 'I want to break out and get onto material I haven't been able to use in previous books. It's my 11th book and because it's something new I'm excited about the whole project. I'm publishing privately and everybody connected with it shows real enthusiasm.'

And as to why he didn't publish this book with his usual source, he says, 'I gave my publishers first refusal, but I already knew they wouldn't touch it. The word "bastard", even though we all use it or hear it, is still treated with awe in some circles.'

At this point, Crump and his interviewer are joined in the hotel bar by a bloke called George Johnston who, to the reporter, seems like a sort of Crump Mark ll. The standard of the interview degenerates rapidly and their conversation definitely isn't printable. Crump is stacking away beer as though prohibition is coming tomorrow.

In December, the NZBC refuses to allow Crump to be interviewed about *Bastards I Have Met*. Later that month, Crump claims he's made publishing history in New Zealand. He says he's the first author to print and distribute his own book, from a publishing company, Crump Productions Ltd, with John Brown of South Pacific Safaris, and go out and sell 12,000 copies of the book in two weeks. He says his manuscript for *Bastards I Have Met* was turned down by three major New Zealand publishers, convincing him to go it alone.

No one, including his old publisher, Reed, would handle a book with such a title, he claims.

From now on, he intends to be a 'publish yourself' author, he says from Waihi. His next book is well on the way and will be, says Crump, 'a whole lot of zany, crazy, entertaining nonsense'. According to the publishers who turned down the *Bastards* manuscript, says Crump, he was written out and on the downhill road after 10 novels. 'As my own publisher, I now earn a lot more money, but it's not material possessions I now seek.'

Crump hits Auckland again, gets up to a bit of business and a bit of mischief and, resplendent in burnt orange pants and a black embroidered shirt, he meets up with journalist Judy McGregor in the foyer of South Pacific Safaris about his forthcoming twelfth book following the 'sell-out' success of *Bastards I Have Met*.

'The new one is sort of utter nonsense ... more than any of the others,' he says. 'I'm not very clear in my mind about it all yet. But I've got the general atmosphere. It's not intended to make any sense on any level. It's got a working title called "You're Mad But We Love You Just the Same". But I could change it while I'm going along.'

Crump further says the new book will be funnier than the other 11. 'It'll be a scream. Hang on a minute, can you change that to riot? Scream isn't my word really. It'll be a riotous bloody idea.... How it'll turn out is another thing.

'I'm not very good about deadlines. I don't have them, but if I did I might bloody well keep them — perhaps.' When asked whether he needed a quiet place to write his books, Crump replies, 'Hell no. I can write them on the kitchen table with people feeding around me if I'm in the mood. Most people seem to think the material is the most important thing about writing a book. With me it isn't at all. Once there's the atmosphere you want you're right. The same material written by someone who's not in the mood is dreary. But if you're feeling bouyant and happy then it'll be good. If I'm floundering around a bit I sometimes go somewhere quiet.'

Crump has been having nightmares and now he's reading one in the newspapers. 'Mr Wally Crump (62), father of the outdoors author Barry Crump, has a mystery on his hands,' reports the *Auckland Star*. 'He runs a book exchange in Onehunga and, at Christmas, he locked the place up and went away. On January 5, however, police discovered it wide open, 10 people inside and the place doing a roaring trade. There was money on the counter, in the till and in ashtrays.

'Customers were ringing the shop bell and demanding somewhere to put their money, but no shop assistant was there to help and advise. The shop was officially open the next day. Neither Wally, nor his business partner, Mrs J. Collett, knows what had happened. "We're mystified," said Mr Crump. "We'd locked everything up, but at least people paid for what they got."'

Then comes the truth of what this awful bullshit is really about because it transpires that Wally Crump is, himself, a bit of an author. He tells the paper he wrote a book, *McDunnit Dunnit*, a while back and will have a follow-up, *McDunnit Wunnit*, out soon. Two weeks later the old man's back. Wally, who has parted from Lily and now lives with Mrs J. Collett, features in a more in-depth interview in the *Auckland Star*, plugging his forthcoming second book and talking about his life as a blacksmith, pig hunter, jockey, farmer, Onehunga bookshop proprietor and now, God help the world, 'novelist'.

Most of his life has been spent in South Auckland, he tells the paper. He raised his four sons — including outdoors author Barry — on a farm in Paparimu. Wally was born on a Bombay farm, where he learned to love freedom and the open air. He recalls 'stacks of pig hunting' on his own farm where, for eight years, he never bought any meat.

'I never had a boot on my feet in the bush. It was always bare feet, but I'm so soft now I'd have trouble walking across a carpet without boots on.' His feet were hardened walking from Drury to Pukekohe (nine miles) to work. And his father made him milk cows before work.

He talks sentimentally of the large blacksmith's business in Pukekohe, with four smiths, three coach-builders and a painter. When it was sold for a motor garage, Wally says he swore he would not shoe another horse. He talks about training horses at four in the morning at Mangere, winning some races, having a lot of fun and spending a bit of money.

Since he moved to the big smoke — 14 years ago at Otahuhu — Wally Crump has milked a few cows, but 'knocked any idea of going back farming'. He admits he was 'born lazy — or got lazy after I left the farm'.

Now there's no stopping Wally. He goes on a media offensive. And in an interview in the *Sunday News* he reveals that he wrote a 'hard case best seller' because his neighbour bet him five quid he wouldn't. 'Like father, like son?' asks the newspaper. 'Please yourself,' said Wally. 'Yeah, you could say that.'

Barry's dad is mellow and soft-spoken and, at 62, reckons he's had long enough to get used to the 'doubtful honour of being Barry's dad'. He likes most people except for politicians and 'nosey parkers'. 'After the pub', says Wally, 'the next best place for a yarn is a book. All you have to do to write a good yarn is do something then write something down about it,' he says. 'Inspiration is just another word for pencil and paper,' says Wally.

'Once Barry turned out some dreadful load of rubbish and had it published — it was a terrible bloody thing. My neighbour thought it was great. He thought I was just being a niggly old bastard and bet me five quid I couldn't turn out anything myself. Too damn right I could and I knew it,' says Wally, remembering the day he collected his £5 bet. 'I thought to myself that I could write an immortal classic if Barry could get this load of drivel to sell.'

Crump Productions Ltd are launching *Bastards I Have Met* in Australia and strike problems when the Australian Broadcasting Control Board views an advertisement for *Bastards I Have Met* after a Melbourne publishing firm asks the board if it will permit the use of the book cover in television commercials. The cover shows, besides the title, a vault-like door on which is printed: 'C and Z bank — B.I.G. Bastard Manager'.

The board decrees that it does not object to having the book cover seen on television between 9.30 and 11 a.m. and between 8.30 and 11 p.m. However, the board will not say whether the announcer reading the message that goes with the visual will be permitted to thunder *Bastards I Have Met* into Australian living rooms. When the board is told of the need for the spoken word, it rules: 'You may say it once.'

The *Sunday News* begins serialising some of Wally Crump's yarns. The first is entitled *Two Gallons of Red — and Mildred* and sets out: 'Every year towards the end of September, melancholia, or a close relative, impregnates me with general bitchiness. During these periods of depression I spend oodles of time, mostly the boss's, nutting out a decent Christmas vacation.

'But some flaming thing always puts me up a ladder with sandpaper, paint and volumes of carefully considered instructions. Mildred, my legally acquired wife, is very houseproud. In '69, a few days before the Auckland Cup was run, my old Humber poked a conrod, or some similar gadget, through the crankcase. The horse I sorted out to pay for the repairs couldn't get clear in time. I painted all the ruddy ceilings....'

It is announced there will be a new Barry Crump book out for Christmas. 'After his first and highly successful venture into publishing last year, the wild man of New Zealand literature is settling down to make another killing this year,' says the *Sunday Herald*. The new novel is called *Fred* and it's about a big city ad man who gives up the city in disgust and retreats to the West Coast. 'On the West Coast he finds, well, the West Coast.'

'*Fred*,' says Crump, 'is very much a return to *A Good Keen Man*.' The book is being printed in Japan — 'economics,' says Crump. Says the *Sunday Herald*, 'Now with a home in Waihi, a nice station wagon and a family — in fact all the mod cons of orthodox Kiwi living — Crump admits that he is doing very nicely, thank you. His whole life has changed, he says. "Never again will I work for anyone. I found out what there is in it with *Bastards* and am doing the same again with *Fred*. After that, who knows?"'

Crump's twelfth book emerges with a lot less trumpet-blowing than *Bastards* got. It's a slim volume, just scraping past 100 pages, even with the big typesize trick and some half-arsed amateur-looking illustrations. Crump doesn't have to leave the confines of his mind or his memory for this one. It's about a bloke who doesn't like the city much and feels like running away.

> If anyone up there was keeping a record of the number of jobs people went through they were probably getting a bit brassed-off with Fred by this time. He'd had over eighty changes of occupation in the past eleven years and the way he was feeling right then he was due for another one any old time.
>
> He'd been doing okay as an ideas-man for the advertising agency he was working for, but by this time doing okay in a place like that was the same to Fred as being a talented pencil sharpener. There were four sharply-dressed, finger-snapping executives at the agency and it took all four of them to reach a decision, or come to a conclusion, as though they had a quarter of a brain each.
>
> The week before, it had taken him most of an afternoon to convince them he was serious when he suggested that they print some of their immortal propaganda on rolls of toilet paper. And when they finally saw that he meant it they were deeply offended. They were still a bit chary of him in case he came up with any more ideas appropriate to the kind of products they represented.
>
> To be fair he had to admit he'd rather enjoyed the job at first, but the empty-headed jargoneering that was going on around the place was getting too much for him to stomach. He got such a fright when he caught himself starting to talk their lingo that he decided to take off at once for the South Island and try his luck down there. He'd been at the job for over five months by this time anyway.
>
> **(from** Fred, **1972)**

Crump plays his old hand of having his hapless but wily hero escape from the increasingly tight clutches of a woman — 'a good-looking hunk of work and he was quite fond of her in a way' — by abandoning her in a pub and climbing out the gents' window, tossing everything he needs in the back of his ute and driving south in search of the inevitable freedom and adventure.

It's just not a comic response to life's travails that strikes a common chord in the New Zealand of the early 1970s and *Fred*, slim as it is, slips right through the cracks, going on to sell only a few thousand copies. Crump's had it. He's about ready to run away from writing along with everything else. Everything's going to change.

In December, the *Sunday News* announces it will serialise *Fred* and 'keep you laughing right through Christmas'. And it sends reporter Anne Marie Nicholson to a pub to interview Crump — 'over a jug of beer and a double scotch'. Both were his.

'But the 37-year-old craggy-faced author is not really the regular New Zealand boozer. He says he goes to the pub "very rarely", unlike the characters in his 12 books. "And I enjoy a glass of red wine with me meal," he says.'

'An old, quality farmhouse out of Waihi has been his home for the past two years. He lives there with his wife and two children and when he's not working on his annual book, he's out hunting, travelling or "mucking around".' In an unconvincing attempt to impress Annie Marie, Crump sinks his whisky, cools his burning stomach with a gulp of beer and announces that he's keen on the 'liberating of women lark'.

'"A wife should be treated like a hunting mate," he says. "In a camp there's a certain amount of work that's got to be done, like the firewood, dishes and cooking. It's all measured out equally. This is what it should be like in the house. It's not fair the wife gets all the shitty jobs while the husband is out educating and enjoying himself."'

Asked what he thinks about men who go to the pub every night, he says, 'It's bloody sad. It would be cheaper and better if he did something with the wife and kids.'

He's working on book number 13 to come out next December. 'It's a bit mercenary really, getting them out for the Christmas market and all that. But I'm not rich. I just spend what I get. Living always comes first and writing second.'

The thirteenth book will turn out to be unlucky for Crump. It won't put in an appearance for another eight years.

§

14.

life is strange

1973

Crump's big-sales days are far behind him. His last book, *Fred*, fell far short of expectations. Whitcombe and Tombs, New Zealand's biggest movers of books, report they were expecting Christmas sales of 1000 copies of Crump's latest, but the total fell short of 500. They have returned some stock and are now ordering his books in small quantities and say that the Crump image is beginning to fade. Around the country, booksellers report they are holding plenty of Crump stock and that demand seems to have fallen right away.

'Who is Barry Crump? What makes him tick? Genius or fraud, artist or con man?' asks the *Sunday News* in May, atop the first in a series of in-depth interviews with Crump by journalist Ivan Agnew, who travels to Waihi to meet him and spend a week with him in his '1906, kauri-built, Victorian-style' house on a hill where he lives with wife Vanda and sons Alan (4) and Lyall (2).

The reporter arrives to find both boys are 'dressed in a pioneering style which would have befitted Daniel Boone's son, their Indian shirts indicative of what their parents hope they will become — independent and proud of their own individuality'. Crump doesn't bother introducing Vanda. He drives a late-model station wagon and swiftly whips Agnew off to the pub, telling him, 'I don't really drink as much as some people seem to think. I generally stay home, but it's a good day for drinking.' After several hours of drinking doubles and playing pool with the locals at the Rob Roy Hotel, they repair to the house where they polish off half a gallon of sherry and a meal of oxtail stew and next day Crump puts the townie to work splitting logs while he (Crump) fertilises the fields.

There will be no hunting. 'I'm sick of killing animals,' says Crump. 'There are better things for a man to do with his time.' He says the public have the wrong picture of him. 'They think I'm a great piss-head, but that's not true. They think I'm a rough and ready guy who swears and curses a lot and gets into a scrap every day of the week. That's not true either. I like people, so long as they accept me for myself. I'm happy to accept them for themselves. If they want to imagine I'm something else, well they can think that too. It doesn't bother me.'

Vanda tells the writer how she met Crump. 'It was in an Auckland pub, the old Vic. He just sauntered over to where I was seated and said in that commanding voice of his, "Stay there. I'll be back". With that, he returned from the bar with some drinks. It's crazy, I know, but I was madly in love with him from that moment.' She wasn't impressed with him as an author at the time. 'He was just a bushman to me. We lived together for a while, then we got married.' And she wasn't worried about the fact that he'd split with previous wives. 'I wanted him on any condition.'

He's not an easy man for a woman to live with, she says, but she is in tune with him and 'smart enough to give him his head'. She says that writing is only one of the things he's good at and talks of the many people who come to him seeking his help in overcoming their problems, the uncanny way he has of putting his finger on their hang-ups and swiftly finding the cause.

Crump is pulling interesting poses for his visitor. He sits in bed reading a book he says is about the 'revelations of an Indian saint and guru'. He is going through a slow, subtle change, says Crump. 'Everything I have done is leading to one thing. I don't know what it is, except God is trying to tell me something.'

The writer is impressed, thoroughly seduced by Crump and his over-sized charisma. He writes of the pilgrimages people make from throughout New Zealand to see Crump. 'I have seen them, girls of 17, men of 70, sitting on the floor of the Crumps' lounge asking this incredible man his views on writing, society, pollution, the bush, the environment, of the world's future, of death, of eternal life. While not handsome, Crump possesses a special charisma. Many women are attracted to him, this man with the appearance of a barbarian and the soul of an artist. The extent of his patience, understanding and sympathy is astounding. His over-riding virtue is his forthright honesty and great capacity for friendship. But paradoxically I have seen Crump drunk, ridiculing a woman who wanted to sleep with him, then reciting 60 verses of "Eskimo Nell".'

Reed receive a letter from Crump's old Latvian croc-shooting mentor Harry Blumenthals. 'Sorry to disturb your peace, but mine is gone the same way,' he informs them. 'Hardly I can concentrate on opal digging. It is about the English translated copy and photo negatives of "Latvian Crocodile Hunter in Australia". Many years are gone by since Mr B. Crump obtained these from me with intentions to publish with your publishing company. I would be very thankful to your help and willingness to locate them and get them back.' Reed have never seen the Blumenthals manuscript.

Down in Waihi, Crump's decided they're selling up and going away overseas. He's been reading about India and he wants to go there. Vanda's not about to argue. She's had it with Crump and thinks if she and the boys tag along to Europe with him, it'll be a great opportunity in a place so big to just disappear on him and get out of his ridiculous life. Recently, Crump got so bored he took up playing golf. He's so keen on it he's out at the golf course before dawn practising his drive and has to wait till the sun comes up and it's light enough to find the balls he's been belting.

A few weeks later, the *Sunday News* announces, 'He's Off to Find God' in huge headlines as if God may not exist unless Barry Crump can find him. 'I believe in God and I want to know Him better,' says Crump, shortly before leaving New Zealand by ship for the northern hemisphere.

'I'm going to India with my wife, Vanda, and my two boys to learn from the holy men and gurus,' he says. Crump doesn't know when he'll return to New Zealand. 'Maybe in a few years, maybe never,' he says. And he doesn't know whether he will continue to write. He says his plan is to simply make himself 'available' in the hope God will show him his true vocation. 'If anyone had told me a year ago that I would be talking like this I would have said they were mad. I know I am more of a sinner than a saint, but they say God works in strange ways. He must do if He wants me.

'I don't know why I became a successful writer. I was delighted when success first came my way, but to be really honest I never really worked hard at it. Not like some artists I know. Looking back, I know God has been good to me, although I don't know why He should pick on me because I can't think of a more ungodly person. God has touched me. I know He is there. I am just going to wait and cry out, "Take me God and use me" and I hope that He does.'

Before he leaves, he sells the Waihi house to an American couple, gives away his late-model tractor and many possessions to friends. He drives the tractor the seven-hour journey to a friend in a Coromandel commune and casually presents it to him. Crump rings the Reed office full of good cheer for everyone and full of the news that he's taking his family with him to London and wants two copies of each of his Reed books to take with him. The Reed gang are surprised he's got the cash to fund such an expedition and there are nervous jokes about expecting an urgent Crump telegram from Baden Baden or Pinsk demanding money immediately.

Crump and family board a passenger liner and sail to London, where he immediately looks up his old friend Kevin Ireland, who is amazed at the seeming change in his old friend. It seems absurd that after more than a decade of not seeing Crump, here he is coming in the front door talking about God. But Crump's still giving the version he dictated to the newspapers before he fled New Zealand. Down at the corner pub with Ireland in London, he's talking a little differently. Crump, after drinking a hell of a lot of Guinness, opens the door to his secret self a crack and seems to let Ireland look in. Crump is almost incoherent with grief and anger — about the foolish marriage to Fleur and how the literary set turned their thin, judgemental backs on him and about those boys drowning in that lake and how many people thought he was callous and indifferent because he didn't run round talking about it. And what the hell could he say? It was an accident. Accidents happen in the bush.

They don't understand. And he doesn't understand either, this light that seems to come out of him when all he can feel inside is darkness. Ireland reaches for comforting words, but Crump's not listening. He's too busy closing the door to his personal horrors.

Next day Crump starts to warm to the idea of being somewhere no one knows him. He goes down to Carnaby Street and outfits himself with all the latest hippie gear, flared jeans, a big felt hat and a shirt with a big bright sunflower on the front. He's wandering the streets feeling every inch the groover, when a passing New Zealand rugby team spots him and sends him skittering nervously into a public toilet to change back into his usual get-up.

He visits the Russian Embassy, inquiring about the royalties on the hundred thousand translated copies that were supposedly published there. They tell him he's welcome to visit their country and may have his royalties, so long as he spends them there. They even offer to prepare an itinerary for him, but trips to Russia aren't on Crump's agenda.

He looks up a surprised Fleur in London and spends an evening in her sitting room talking about everything, including the old days. He even starts pondering on what might have happened if they'd stayed together. Fleur's blood runs cold.

He announces to Ireland that he's taking Vanda and the boys to Germany where he's going to catch up with a mate who runs a golf course for the American army and that he's going to buy a BMW motorbike and ride it to India, where the family will join him on his great spiritual quest. Once in Germany, they play a bit of golf and buy a converted bread van, which they tour around Europe a bit in, but once Crump gets bored with being a tourist, Vanda takes the van and the kids back to London to stay with Ireland, while Crump plays a bit more golf and hangs round in bars drinking and spinning outrageous yarns to Yanks.

Then he buys himself a 750 cc BMW motorbike, a beauty that he intends to ship back to New Zealand when this adventure's over, and wobbles off in the winter snows in the general direction of India. In Austria, while he sleeps in a camping-ground, someone slits a hole in his tent and lifts his wallet and the 300 American dollars inside it. In Bulgaria, he tries to look up the bloke who included him in that anthology of humour, probably thinking to hit him up for some cash, but fails to find the bugger and rolls on.

In Istanbul, a taxi driver advises Crump to look approaching drivers in the eyes 'or he might crash into you'. He goes on to survive several crashes, Afghani bandits and even an offer of sex with a woman some rough-looking jokers shove into his tent after he takes a meal with them.

'And then Amritsar. I've made it. I get through the border and ride my battered BMW into India feeling pretty good about life. And lucky. Lucky to have got here, but luckier still to have done it. It has taken two months. I've ridden from Germany to India in less time than it took Jean and me to drive from Auckland to Wellington in the '34 Chev.

'The bike's now worth about half what I paid for it. The tank and exhaust pipes are scraped and dented. The headlight is a broken poultice of wire, no indicators, flasher, lights or horn. Half the front mudguard is broken off and the crashbar is torn off one side and the footrest bent back against the muffler. The clutch-lever and rear-vision mirrors are back in Turkey somewhere. The handlebars are twisted. Half the fins are broken off one tappet-cover and the front forks are bent and almost rigid. And she's still running like a dream.'

He heads for Kashmir where he puts the BMW in storage and lives as a boarder with a family on a houseboat on a lake. Crump visits a yogi or two, listens to readings from holy books, grows strangely close to the family's nine-year-old boy 'Sheffy'.

> 'I'm be your Chella,' said Sheffy.
> 'What's that?' I said.
> 'I fill your firepot, wash clothes of you, paddle shikara. Look after you.'
> 'You do that already,' I said. 'What am I supposed to do in return?'
> 'You think to God for both of us.'
> 'Is that all there is to it?'

'Sure, okay?'

'Okay,' I shrugged.

But there was more to it than that. A hell of a lot more. I didn't know what I was letting myself in for. There was great excitement in the household that night when Sheffy told his family he was my Chella. Ramani squeezed my arm and made a speech about how I'd honoured his family, and his father's family and his father's-father's-father's families as well. He speeched again in Kashmiri for his wife and Gulam's because they didn't know English talk....

It kept getting deeper. The responsibilities of having a Chella became more than I'd ever had with my own kids, or whole family for that matter. His name became Chella and I never heard anyone else in the community call him Sheffy again, except me, once, by accident. I got a hurt look and no other reply.

He had to have a new coat. He left school, that was my job. His parents and brothers relinquished all authority over him, and he began to order them around, especially his mother, something disgraceful. The situation would have been completely ruined by any other nine-year-old I knew, but Chella had an air of responsibility about him that was more than his new freedom and authority could undermine.

We had to eat out of the same bowl. He slept curled up against me. When I went to the lavatory at one end of our island he waited outside. When he wanted to go to the lavatory he'd touch the very spot on the ground where I was to stand and say, 'Here you wait!'

If I'd kept my side of the bargain as conscientiously as Chella was keeping his, I'm sure we would have given God spiritual indigestion. I'd been loved by some good women but I'd never been attended to so constantly and energetically as this young bloke was laying on me. If he was a dog I'd have had to shoot him.

(from *The Life and Times of a Good Keen Man*, **1992)**

Crump decides to send for Vanda and the boys to join him in his blissful new life, but when he rings London, he learns that they've taken off. Vanda has seized her opportunity and she's off with another bloke, in the Canary Islands or somewhere. Crump's had his fill of India. He's running out of money and the only way he knows how to raise any is to write and he can't write here. Anyway, he's starting to get a bit too tangled up here and he's getting so skinny, if he stays much longer there'll be none of him left.

At which point he discovers that if he wants to take his battered BMW motorbike with him, as planned, he has to pay the bike's value to the Custom Department, or have it confiscated. He duly delivers the bike to the Custom's compound where there are acres and acres of VWs, Ford Transits and dozens of every possible motorbike. Crump then has to throw himself upon the mercy of the

New Zealand embassy for a bit of help getting home.

Money is borrowed and forwarded and Crump flies to Auckland via Bangkok, and Sydney, landing in a very strange frame of mind, barely remembering who he was when he left and what exactly he is now. He seems to have lost a wife and a couple of kids in the midst of all this. Life is strange.

§

15.

the nearest pub

1974

Crump is back in New Zealand, skinny and weird and a bit fucked up and empty-feeling. In Auckland, he reconnects with Lenna Rainger and her family who are living in Parnell. Lenna is a Baha'i now and her happiness with her new belief impresses Crump, who's feeling hacked off he didn't find the answer he announced he was going to find in India. Lenna won't let him live with her, so he stays in a van he's got parked over the hill down in Judges Bay.

Crump gets a call from London that Vanda and the kids need help and he flies back to London and pays their airfares back to New Zealand. He settles them in a flat and seems to accept that it's over, though every time he turns up in the years ahead, Vanda's stomach gives a little lurch. She never stops being afraid of him. Feels like she never will till he's dead and in the ground.

Crump tells the *Sunday News* that he has embraced the Baha'i faith, which had its foundations in Persia in the nineteenth century, with the advent of a god-man his disciples recognise as 'the return of Christ'.

'I don't know all the answers about Baha'i, but I do find that it relates to me and I'm so serious about it that I've pledged to stay off the grog. Our faith condemns alcohol and illicit sex.' And there will be no further books written in the old Crump tradition. 'I'm past all that now,' he says. 'I don't know whether I will ever write another book again. If I do, then it won't be about the things I have written about in the past.' Crump says this with such sincerity he almost believes himself. It's uncanny.

Crump takes to some public preaching. In April, he writes an article for the *Sunday News*, explaining his search and his conversion.

'For a good few years now, I've been blessed with the freedom from having to spend a large part of each day working at a regular job. This has given me the ability to pursue whatever I liked, and that's what I've done. It didn't take me long to discover that the things we enjoy in our leisure become boring almost as soon as we start doing them full-time. I tried everything I could get into, and that was plenty. I tried being poor and I tried being rich.

'At one stage I had everything we're taught we need to make us happy — a nice home in the country, a few acres, the animals, the orchard, the garden, the workshop to work in on rainy days, the open fire, self-propelled lawnmower, no money worries and a few weeks' work each year that could be done whenever or wherever I felt like doing it. But I was worse off than ever. There was either something wrong with me or something wrong with the ideals of society. I kept looking.

'During the past two or three years I've been intrigued by the quickening spiritual atmosphere that caused me to gradually become aware of the reality of the existence of God. There's religious groups and general spiritual revival springing up all over the place. Almost everyone I spoke to had some strange spiritual experience recently. Where was it coming from?

'I studied yoga, psychology, Christianity, Buddha, Krishna, Muhammed and anything and everything else. And they all seemed to claim that anyone who didn't subscribe to and practise their beliefs was lost, which left me more lost than ever. Here it was again. Either I was mad or there was something inadequate about the very religions of the God I was becoming more aware of every day. And I was more aware than ever that there was something very spiritual afoot amongst us.

'I left New Zealand and travelled around in Europe for a few months. I saw only that the more material stuff people have the more they want and the less of it they're willing to part with. A very depressing spiritual situation. Then I set off alone on a motorbike to ride from Germany to India, in search of some access to God that would either make sense to me or establish my insanity once and for all. After many adventures, I made it to India and lived for two and a half months in Kashmir.

'There are some very God-aware and enlightened people in those regions and I learned a great deal from them and made some very wonderful friends. But shortage of money and one or two other influences caused me to return to New Zealand, where I was promptly told about the Baha'i faith by a friend. By this time I was getting pretty chary about religious sects. I decided to look into this one only until I found the discrepancies. Then it could be shelved away with all the others.

'I'm still looking into it, and in the process I've already discovered a world-embracing knowledge of God that welcomes and enlightens all of mankind whatever their religious beliefs are. It is a faith that answers all the questions of anyone who genuinely wants to ask, regardless of what his intelligence quotient has been measured at. It's a faith that proclaims and guarantees that Kingdom of God on earth. A faith dedicated to the promotion of the oneness of mankind, the whole earth, one country, and mankind, its citizens.

'I was so captivated by the sheer power and beauty of the writings of this faith that when I read only a couple of the hundreds of Baha'i books, I went to the friend who'd introduced me to this wonderful knowledge and said: "I'm a Baha'i. What do I have to do to join up?" Baha'u'llah writes: "To merit the madness of love, man must abound in sanity." I'm still not too sure whether I'm mad or not, but if I am, I'm more happily mad than I could ever have imagined was possible. And there are more of us going mad every day.

'All-U-Abba.'

It's Crump's most ingenious disguise yet.

Late in 1976, Crump reappears on New Zealand's television screens, as an interview subject on *The Edwards Show*, giving off a distinctly serene ambience to host Brian Edwards and telling him he is alcohol, sex and worry-free these days. An attractive woman sits nearby nodding agreement. They are beyond sex, they tell a bemused Edwards. Crump, with a large, lopsided grin on his face, says he felt discomfort with his past fame. One TV critic, reviewing the performance, says, 'Ah well, there's always Fred Dagg.'

Crump is living in Oratia, in West Auckland, since dropping out of the limelight in the early 1970s. According to *Herald* writer Robyn Langwell, the 'dinkum Kiwi writer is living happily in a home-made whare in the middle of the bush, cooking over an open fire and spreading the word of Baha'u'llah among friends and anyone else he bumps into'.

The man 'once described as the meanest bastard of them all has found God and his last five years have been spent quietly but happily getting into the Baha'i religion'. But 'Crump is still Crump, rolling his own, spitting tobacco and talking about "chicks".' He has been in town during the week getting together with other Baha'i at an international teaching conference at the Auckland Town Hall.

He doesn't work except for the occasional odd job to pay the bills, though the 'one-time animal hunter, bush guide, best-selling author and New Zealand identity has had a bit of trouble convincing some people that he is "for real".'

'But I'd never put anyone crook on a thing like this,' he says. 'If it didn't stand up to any scrutiny and any questions I just wouldn't even mention it. It's dinkum mate, dinkum — we're all going to be Baha'i sooner or later. It's spreading fast. It's going to be global, absolutely global, mate. My attitudes may be a bit outrageous and some people seem to get annoyed with me, but it's just because the ideas are a bit ahead of them. But the number of people who have said, "Thank God you came along" makes me know, if I ever needed to know, that this is the right thing to be doing.

'It unlocked me, dear. It will unlock anyone. There's nothing like it anywhere in the world.... People seem to think that I'm a changed person since I got religious, but I'm still the same old me. I'm still on the same old trip, I've just changed buses and we're heading in a new direction.'

Crump, now aged 42, says he'll try and sum up his life story in a sentence — 'but it may be a long one'. 'When I was young, everyone said, "Learn a trade, you have to learn a trade". But I just could not. I went ahead and lived my life as it made sense to me. I just could not see how a man could fulfill himself working eight hours a day at a job he didn't like. And so with the freedom my lifestyle gave me, I found the thing I was looking for in the writing of Baha'u'llah. And that's where it's at — there's just nothing else like it in the world.'

Crump says the deaths of the five boys at his bushcraft camp in Te Teko changed his life: 'that was a hell of a knockback. I had to change. I still think about the parents of those kids. That experience made me a lot more humble — and that's always worth a few points.'

As for writing … it 'was terribly important for me and still is, but I've got to be in the mood. I wrote 12 books in 10 years, but I could only do it when the feeling took me. I haven't had that feeling for a while. It doesn't worry me. I'd be terribly happy to write again, but I'll just sit and wait for it to happen. I realise and treasure my talent as a writer and I must preserve it. I would only be mistreating it if I sat down and tried to force it.'

But he says if he ever does write another book, there will be a change of style. 'There'll be no more backbiting and criticism. That was pretty ignorant of me. I don't feel guilty anymore about anything I've done. I just didn't know enough in the earlier days. Sin is simply ignorance and I know better now. I was always a bit unhappy, a bit unsettled and lonely, but all the Crump books and boloney had a meaning. They led to an end. I'm still the old Crump at heart, just filled with a lot more love these days.'

News reaches Crump that as sales of *A Good Keen Man* have ground to a standstill, he may have first option on the remaining 2000 copies for 65 cents each.

Crump gets hold of a 1930 Model A Ford, a car cut down to a small truck with a canvas canopy on the back. He hits the road, going south and to a place he finds solace in. Or something like solace anyway.

He turns up on the West Coast, in Greymouth, where he's running low on funds and he pauses for a bit and attends some Baha'i meetings. One of them is a celebration of the twenty-first birthday of a woman called Robin. 'I'd noticed this fascinating looking girl at Baha'i gatherings and we'd never seen enough of one another. I ran into one of the Baha'is in the street in Greymouth and she told me that they were having a birthday party for Robin at their house that night.'

He turns up and points all of his wicked old charm at her. He seems to command a certain respect, she notices. He's very entertaining and she finds him fascinating, even though he's more than twice as old as she is and not very appealing to her physically. But he seems exciting and full of promise. Overflowing really. And next thing she knows, Robin is loading her trailbike on the back of his truck that very night and heading off into the unknown with an unknown quantity everyone seems to have heard of.

They land up living in an old farmhouse outside Hokitika which they furnish from the local tip. 'It's always amazed me what people chuck out. Good stuff with years of use left in it, thrown on the dump to make way for a newer model.' After the high life in Waihi, Crump is going back to basics with a vengeance.

Robin picks the furthest bedroom away from Crump to sleep in. She feels uneasy about him. She's nervous when he takes the truck and her bike with him to get the truck repaired at the garage. She doesn't like to lose her escape route. But they settle down into living like a couple, sort of. Crump doesn't seem very interested in sex. They live like flatmates really. Robin thinks maybe that's what happens when men get past 40. It's more like she's his mate. And she is too.

They buy some used possum traps and move on working the roadsides and swamps to make some money, because they have next to none. They whitebait. They live rough, sleeping in the Model A and cooking over an open fire. Robin picks up fast on Crump's bush skills, loves the life in lots of ways, though finds it harder to love the man. They stick around the West Coast, but people know how to track him down. Once he's sent air tickets to go to Christchurch for a television interview with the Canon Bob Lowe. On instruction, Robin follows him over on her little motorbike, meets up with him at the hotel he'd been booked into and drives him round the city on it.

Then, when it's over, they drive back over the treacherous Arthur's Pass, big hefty Crump wobbling round on the back behind little Robin on her 175 cc bike. Crump orders her to stop, wanting to boil a billy. He's always wanting to boil a billy. She doesn't understand this constant need for tea till she realises it's some sort of ritual. 'Go get some wood,' he tells her. She doesn't know anything about fires and fuel and brings back a bundle of damp wood. Crump goes apeshit, throwing an almighty tantrum and calling her a dozy bitch who can't light a fire like his other chicks. He's foaming with rage at her uselessness.

She's shocked, but she'll see more of his rages. He says rage is the only emotion worth having. And she's surprised and a bit bored too by Crump's fondness for pubs and sitting endlessly in bars with other blokes, playing pool and getting skulled. He drinks a lot of whisky, she notices. Being Baha'i hasn't stopped that. But she doesn't drink herself, knows nothing about drinking, so doesn't know what it means, whether it's bad, or just what men his age do. She does notice from fairly early on that it takes seven double whiskies to get him to a certain stage of drunkenness, where he's slurring and starting to lose perspective. By the end of it, four doubles will do the job.

Robin asks him why he drinks so much and he tells her, 'I'm doing it for the pain — for the effect. I don't really like the taste, but it dulls the pain.' And when she pesters him about the pain, he romanticises and says, 'Oh the pain of the material world and having to deal with all these messed up people in a world full of wankers.'

There's a pattern to his life as they drift around. When he gets to a new town, he marks out a pub as his, a bit like an animal marks its territory, though he stops short of barking at the barman and peeing against the bar. The pubs are always dead keen to have him as a customer and make sure they've got the Johnny Walker Black Label whisky he favours. And if Crump becomes a customer, then other new customers follow, often from rival pubs.

After a while, he can start to affect the society of a small town. Blokes start spending even more time than they used to at the pub, people who hardly ever darkened the door of the place start going. He has a lot of power, especially among older people who sometimes seem in awe of him. And he can be sweet and amusing, entrancing and outrageous and funny with his bottomless bag of yarns. He even has his own sort of language. But he's been through this scene so many times, he sees it with another eye. 'See that guy over there? And that guy over there. I'll bet that within a week they'll be trying to talk like me, calling every joker "matey patata".' It amuses him. The power and the pointlessness of it.

People send him mail to pubs. Crump doesn't like letting any sort of address out, so if someone wants to make contact and they know roughly where he's living or where he's heading, they point their letters and bills at the nearest pub, thinking Crump will visit it sooner or later.

Booze and tobacco are the major drugs of choice for Crump. He smokes a bit of marijuana too, though usually when young people are around. He is fond of that more solitary big hit, acid, one night waking Robin up and begging her to stay awake and be with him while he's taking this trip. It's not her thing at all, really.

Not much of Crump and his chauvinism is, but she's powerfully drawn to him, though she sometimes wonders what she sees in this old man whose idea of an exciting time is to sit up in bed drinking billy tea and telling old hunting stories.

Sometimes, at home, he lets other sorts of stories out, about how his father used to treat his mother and how he and his brother would beg her to leave him, but she wouldn't. He talks once of how his father dunked his head in a water trough three times and only took it out twice, holding his head under so long he thought he was going to drown. How his sister was running round the farm for days with her arm broken by the old man.

But Crump lays down a sort of challenge to Robin to stick it out in a lopsided life with him through his challenges that his 'other chicks could never keep up'. She decides she's going to be the one to keep up. And soon she does. Next to his increasingly solid six feet of manhood, she's a wisp. But she comes with some skills. Robin's dad had been a tree-felling contractor and she'd learned how to use a chainsaw, tie ropes, secure loads, climb trees and rig up shelters. Soon she's outpacing him on possum lines.

At the end of the whitebait season, they get married. In accordance with Baha'i law, Crump even seeks out Wally and gets his permission to wed. Lily, Barry's mother, is dead some years now. Barry didn't make it to the funeral. Couldn't handle it. He and Robin buy another motorbike and go roaming round the North Island. Then they return to the coast, pick up the Model A and drift south, across the Haast Pass to Otago, where Crump wants to try his hand at gold-panning. In Queenstown they buy some equipment and ask for directions to the nearest gold, ending up camping on a river-flat in the Moke Valley, living on toast and tea and roasted rabbits and stewed possum.

They're starting to pick up a bit of gold, but winter bites to the bone in these parts and they're not looking forward to it getting any colder, when they run into Alex and Lorna King and their kids, up from Gore for their regular holiday visit to the area. They get invited to a party, meet the owners of the spread they've been parked on and take up the offer of moving into one of the buildings in Seffertown, the old goldmining ghost town perched high on the hill above the river.

They move in and set themselves up nicely, well out of sight of most of the human race. They live off the land, hunt possums, keep horses, grow hay, upgrade their gold gear and in the end of it are picking up as much as an ounce of it a week, in flakes and small nuggets. This means nothing to Crump, who is as inclined to give it away as hoard it up. Down panning at the river one day, a bloke walks past. Crumps tells him gidday and the bloke says, 'I know you. You're Barry Crump and you're a Baha'i.' And Crump says yeah and the bloke says, 'Well, I'm a Christian' and Crump says, 'What say we go up to the hut and I'll put a brew on. We'll have a talk about it.'

the nearest pub
•
145

'I wouldn't drink tea with you,' says the bloke. And Crump, who's slow to anger in these situations, says, 'Isn't it funny? We're both going in the same direction, but it looks as though we're on different buses' and the bloke tramps off.

They stay two years, knocking along together alright, seemingly, though they're as different as oil and water, Robin so sober and serious and contained, Crump so big and spilling over everywhere. Then they pull out and drift north, looking for somewhere else to be.

The newspapers report that filming has started on a pilot television programme based on Crump's *Hang on a Minute Mate*, part of an ambitious $400,000 13-part series. Producer Alan Lindsay tells the *Christchurch Star* the aim is to sell the programme overseas. 'It would be good to sell it in New Zealand too, but it is aimed at the international market because New Zealand television just cannot offer the money to make it viable.'

§

16.

shoot-through time

1980

'New Zealand's original good keen man, itinerant author Barry Crump, has emerged from seven long years of seclusion — with a deep Rarotongan suntan and his first book for nearly a decade,' announces the *Auckland Star* in October. Both are the results of several months he has just spent with his wife Robin as self-described Baha'i missionaries on a two-hectare rock named Tapuaetahi, off Aitutaki in the Cook Islands. The 45-year-old author says the new book started out as an article for a golf magazine and 'grew and grew'. He says whenever he mentions it, people think it will be about religion 'and I can't blame them — that's all they've got from me for years.

'But it's back to the old *Good Keen Man* style', except that it's about golf rather than deer-culling. 'It's very funny.' says Crump. 'It just flew out of the end of the pen.' The book is called *Shorty* and Crump will publish it himself, though he says publishers have been queuing up to get their hands on the manuscript.

But their best offer is 10 percent and they say it's impossible to get it in the shops before Christmas. I don't believe that, so I'm going alone on it. It's at the printer's already and I've only been back from Rarotonga for two days.

'I suppose my personal attitudes to life have changed since I gave it all away seven years ago,' he says. 'I've been off the treadmill for a long time now and I can see some pretty sad things in our society, especially the materialistic side of it. Things have become so much more important than people and that's terribly sad in itself. They say we should produce more, while I reckon we should need less. I suppose I'm lucky — I don't have a beef with anyone and I don't believe in criticism. I reckon anyone can do whatever he wants — it doesn't bother me.'

A Good Keen Man, which he wrote at 22, 'just went mad', he says. 'It's had 20-odd editions and sold hundreds of thousands of copies. I still get royalties from it, but they're not much these days. But money you get for nothing is no use to you at all. You have to put something in before you can take it out and I wasn't doing that. Besides, while you're sitting there on your pile of money all your friends are working and the ones who are the same as you don't want to know. They're not interested in bushmen. They sure didn't want to know me.'

When Crump found religion and 'dropped out', he moved to the Waitakeres — 'just living' and helping his brother Bill with his solar-panel manufacturing business. 'A lot of people said I'd gone loony, but there was nothing I could do or say about that.'

From there, he moved to the West Coast, trapping possums, catching whitebait and cooking over an open fire. 'And Robin loves it. She likes the outdoors even better than I do — she's a real good bushman.'

In 1977, the Crumps moved to the rugged mountainous country behind Lake Wakatipu, settling at the long-deserted gold-mining settlement of Seffertown. 'Gold was one of the few things I hadn't had a bash at and we did alright. At least, we made enough money for our needs by working fairly hard. It was a beautiful spot — just the two of us in this old ghost town with some chooks and horses. It was good there.

'We met a lot of nice people in the district and were happy — but I figure it's always good to leave before they find out what sort of ratbag you are.' The Crumps had three bitter Otago winters and chose their Cook Islands retreat for tropical sun.

Now back in Auckland, the Crumps have found a temporary home in Henderson as a base until *Shorty* comes out. 'If I make a bit of money out of it, we'll relax and go out on the road again in the van and think about writing another book next year. I am a Baha'i and I always will be. I can't imagine not being one. But right now, well, I'm getting on with the business of living.'

Crump has offered the *Shorty* manuscript to several publishers, including

Reed, who are most surprised to receive a Crump story out of the blue and that it's so much in the old Crump style. They're interested. It's simple, it's funny, it's a bit on the short side and the beginning is very thin. But Reed feel that after such a long silence from Crump, they could make a lot out of 'the return of Barry Crump' or, 'Look who's back'. Hardback, they think they could do maybe six or seven thousand, paperback maybe 15,000. Not the numbers of the old glory days, but decent enough numbers. Sales of Crump's back list, including the once-golden *Good Keen Man*, have pretty much ground to a halt.

But, in the end, Crump's not about to get back into bed with Reed and in November *Shorty* is published, with much made of the fact that the book is Crump's first in eight years and that it is self-published and distributed. According to reviewers, while not a literary tour de force or a patch on *A Good Keen Man* or *Hang on a Minute Mate*, it is entertaining.

It is in fact another potboiler, only 90-something pages long (including illustrations) and concerned with a golf-obsessed cow cocky, inspired by Crump's personal fondness for the game. Crump's thirteenth book is an inauspicious return after so long and sells as poorly as the last book, also named after a bloke, *Fred*, back in 1972.

After all those years with his back turned firmly against the whole idea of ever writing another book, Crump, about to turn 47, is about to release the second new book since the big silence and he's making big promises about many more to come. 'My attitude to writing has changed. After *A Good Keen Man* and the other big sellers of the 1960s, I became too big in the public eye for what I really wanted. I was going round being interviewed on television, addressing clubs and attending functions, but that wasn't me. It was something that just happened. Now I really want to get into it — just make enough to keep us going.'

Shorty has sold 80 percent of its print run, he tells everyone, though no one asks what its print run was. The new book will be called *Puha Road*. 'My wife Robin gave me the idea for this one,' says Crump. 'She doesn't worry about things much, doesn't see much difference between being wealthy or broke — I do. *Puha Road* is about materialism and luck, about two guys who start a rubbish dump in Herne Bay and … well, read the book.'

The Crumps are living the nomadic existence. Home is their 1964 Volkswagen Kombi van, now parked 'somewhere in the Waitakeres'. He reckons he wrote *Puha Road* in 19 days — sitting in the van at the bottom of a quarry in Opononi because the story ends in a quarry in the Hokianga and he wanted the right atmosphere. Crump and Robin will soon pack the van and head 'somewhere up north' to write the next book which, like the last two, Crump will publish himself.

The reason Crump camped in a quarry was because he was up north making an unexpected appearance at eldest son Ivan's wedding, which took place on a cold day in a church with corrugated iron flapping in the window frames. Second son Martin is there, now fully grown but in awe of his famous father. He's had encounters with him over the years, often not very successful ones. When he was 14 and working in a car parts place in Parnell, Barry walks in one day looking for something for one of his vehicles.

Martin isn't entirely sure that this guy is who he suspects he is, but he looks so like the father he knows better from photos than from flesh that Martin can't help himself and stares at him. 'You've got a lot of nerve to look an adult in the eye,' Crump tells him. 'What is it you want?' Martin asks, 'Is your name Barry?' 'Yeah.' 'Well, I'm your son Martin. How are you doing?' They shake hands awkwardly and Barry comes over all flustered, trying to say the right thing. He tries sporadically, for a day or so, to build some sort of bridge to his teenage son, but in the end gives up and disappears again.

This night in the quarry, though, freezing cold and eating pumpkin, which he hated, cooked on a camp oven, Martin sits enthralled, almost afraid to move in case he breaks the spell of his father's company as Crump spins the yarns after a day in the bosom of his abandoned family.

Crump and Robin have been spending time camping on the edge of a golf course in West Auckland, wondering what the hell to do next. The options are running short, along with the cash, and Crump's always likely to get edgy in the big city and want to shoot through.

But sometimes the city's streets are paved with gold. Driving through Henderson one day past the car-sales yards, a flash new Toyota Hilux four-wheel-drive ute catches his eye. On a whim, he stops, checks the shiny set of wheels over and goes into the office where he suggests to the joker there he should give head office a ring. Crump gets on the blower and rumbles to the suit on the other end that he's Barry Crump and he does a fair bit of travelling round and that if they'll give him one of those Hiluxes, he'll advertise it for them.

As it happens, Toyota are looking for interesting new ways to get Kiwis into four-wheel-drives and a character like Barry Crump seems a perfect pitch. They throw the idea at their agency and the agency catches it with glee. A month or two later, the word comes back that Crump's got his deal. Better than that, they'll give him the free use of a new ute, replace it with a new model each year the deal continues and give him $2000.

In August, Crump arrives in a Rolls-Royce to start work at his new job — hosting a talk show on Radio Pacific. 'We're gonna call it *The Crump Hour* and it's part of the change from less talk to more entertainment,' he says of his first venture into broadcasting. 'It ought to be a bit of fun. If it isn't it's not worth doing, is it?' He then picks up a chainsaw and cuts his carefully staged way into the studio for the television cameras.

Crump's hunting strange bush again and insists that Robin comes as part of the deal. He's too insecure about the strange science of radio to go it alone, so she tags along and learns to flick switches and answer phones and keep the tea coming as the new radio star points his personality at a microphone. After a stint sharing the breakfast show with announcer Paddy O'Donnell, Crump wangles his way into an early-morning slot and swiftly builds a following among the insomniacs and taxi drivers with his show, *The Bush Telegraph*. They talk about any old thing, from the unpredictability of life to the breeding habits of the domestic chook.

Crump hams things up in the studio with a sound-effects dog called Scum and people ring in about his dog and tell him about their own dogs and next thing there's a full-on mongrel dog show been inspired and being staged at Auckland's Western Springs Park. Another listener rings in with a poem he's written and next thing there's a flood of poems, which they edit down into a 56-page collection and publish. Crump's having more fun than he imagined he would.

'We thought it might work out and the money has certainly been useful. And I decided if it started to get to either of us we could just bugger off, but actually we've turned out to really like it. It's better than TV because you don't have to worry about putting your teeth in. You sit there at the microphone and it's like a lot of people floating around in the dark. Just disembodied voices. We never bother working out anything before we start.... Just make it a rule that there won't be no smut, religion, politics or rubbishing anyone. It's gotten to where a beautiful spirit has been generated. We practise loving the people.'

But any thrill is bound to wear thin eventually and Crump starts to feel like he's tied to some sort of treadmill. Even worse, it's a treadmill located in the middle of a city and he's getting sick of the city life again. 'The station keeps changing management and I didn't listen to any of them. When we have time, we'll go out and get a few trout and give them to the Radio Pacific people who seem to like us least. Actually, we've had difficulty finding anyone in that category.'

Crump cuts the first in what will be a 14-year string of ads for Toyota in some rough bush north of Wellington. They match him up with a slim, small actor called Lloyd Scott, playing Scotty, the salesman who sells Crump the ute. They will go on to grow older together on television. This ad will become a soap opera and it will make Crump an older, gnarlier sort of national icon, tapping into that laconic, do-anything-for-a-laugh charisma that he's been polishing all these years. On TV, it shines as he casually drives his ute up sheer cliffs and off mountain edges, throwing away a carefully polished line as he goes.

Back at Radio Pacific, Crump's decided it's shoot-through time. He's had fun, but it's fading. 'All we're leaving with is a set of wheels, but that's OK. I've never gone for this bloody public stuff. I've never liked it. Well, I haven't minded it so much. Doors do open and you're allowed to make mistakes on a bigger scale. This Radio Pacific thing was the first real job for both of us. We took it seriously, but we didn't get to settle down to it. If we had to get to the station at five in the morning, then we'd get up at three. We never failed to turn up.

'Now it's spring and time to get on the road. We're already knee-deep in material stuff, yet all you need for a home are a few sheets of corrugated and a big wrap of polythene. That's what we reckon anyway. Anyway, if I hang around cities too long I start to get in the shit. I've found there's something funny about me. I affect people and I start to get notorious.

'The talkback radio thing has been quite fulfilling, once you get everyone's hearts in the right place. If people start to be concerned about the good, then all the bad in their lives seems to somehow slide off. The biggest problem has been telling listeners we're going. I reckon we've become family to people whose families aren't there.'

Crump tells whoever's listening that his 14 months with the station has been one of the great adventures of his life. He is ever-grateful to Paddy O'Donnell for introducing him to the microphone and encouraging his progress against all odds. 'Paddy got me by the throat and tried to make something of me. It was a hard job. I was a clumsy oaf, right off the turnips. He could have put me down and had a load of laughs at my expense, but he never did and I respect him for that. He introduced me to a kind of radio that was very brash, forward and extroverted.'

In a sudden outburst of emotion, he tells the *Herald* that fourth wife Robin is 'the best person I have met' and that a large part of his current contentment with life is because of his Baha'i faith and 'meeting the right chick'. The couple are shaping a future uncluttered by the whims of publishers, producers or bank managers. The new Crump, says the old Crump, is interested only in doing what he and his wife decide, not what is dictated by his primary dislike — 'future commitments'. He has written a couple of television plays but when he was offered 'pathetic money' for them, he put them on the shelf.

An Australian company had made him a generous offer for another idea, but he didn't feel like working there. 'I'm not interested in money,' he says. 'At the moment, we're living in a flat, which we have never done before, and we find that living in a flat in Auckland is quite an adventure. But if it starts to go wrong, we will move on.'

Crump says he doesn't sit in shops autographing his books. He says he doesn't 'care a fig' if they don't sell.

He has recently done a guest spot on the *Hudson and Halls* television cooking show and talking about a five-part TV series based on *Hang on a Minute Mate*, due to be screened later in the year. He doesn't care how his Sam Cash character is portrayed. 'I expect my stuff to be changed and I am never worried about it. I have seen it hacked to pieces, completely misrepresented, but it doesn't worry me,' he says. 'I am not competitive or ambitious. I don't seem to be able to get uptight about that sort of thing.'

He's thinking about his next book and says his recent books have been 'a bit more literary' than his 1960s works and that he has been experimenting with writing techniques. The next book — an 'if and when' project — will be a collection of snippets and anecdotes. 'It will be entirely like the ones when I first started writing, so I'm heading back to the full circle.

'I will be just writing about everyday life, but this time I won't get sick of the whole deal like I did back in the early 1970s. I've settled down now and my head is right. Nothing can worry you once you get your head right.'

Crump's head's never entirely right, though. For a start there's no getting away from the old man. Wally's been ringing Barry on air during the radio show. It's hard for Barry to cope with, but he does, as he always does with the old man. No rancour, no vengeance. It's hard for him to stomach after what the bastard did to him when he was a boy, but he does. Crump can be a bastard about all sorts of things, but he can't seem to get too interested in looking back in anger. It's a fight you can't win. There's no defeating the past, though of course it can be rewritten. After all, there's what did happen, there's what could have happened and there's what *should* have happened.

The 70-minute television movie, *Hang on a Minute Mate*, adapted, directed and produced by Alan Lindsay, is now out. The TV version stars Alan Jervis as Cash and *Goodbye Pork Pie* star Kelly Johnson as his mate Jack and was completed a year ago. Although *Hang on a Minute Mate* has yet to be screened on television, video cassette sales have been good, says Lindsay. Auckland company Vidcom has been producing 250 cassettes at a time and is onto about the fourth run.

The film is also to be released in Australia, where the distributors expect to sell between 3000 and 4000 copies before Christmas. Negotiations are also underway for distribution in Britain and America.

Crump's fourteenth book, *Puha Road*, is released to a flutter of interest and lackadaisical sales. This one marks a return to some of his old form. It's a sprawling yarn, twice as long as the aptly titled *Shorty*, filled with better quality illustrations, some of which have the look of *Hang on a Minute Mate* about them. That's hardly surprising. Crump's recycled and had adjusted some of the Dennis Turner line drawings from *One of Us*. There's no credit for Turner or anyone else. But this book, finally, is Crump with a bit of his old crunch back. And some of his old themes, and some newer more personal ones.

When I was twenty I ... took up newspaper reporting, which I was pretty good at. Then I got married to a girl I'd known vaguely at school and we settled into paying off a house we had built at Pakuranga.

I didn't get on any better at marriage than I had at school. My wife was always pushing me to 'make something of myself' and I was always finding it hard enough to stick at the reporting jobs I got as it was. She claimed I drank too much and I happened to know it was barely enough.

Eventually we found ourselves the constantly-bickering parents of a four-year-old daughter. We couldn't talk to one another without it becoming an argument. It wasn't doing our daughter any more good than it was doing us. I left one morning in April, by mutual agreement, and never went back there.

I heard a few weeks later that my wife had moved into a flat and put the house up for sale, but I was busy with other things by this time and didn't care what she did. I'd given up trying to make it to the top, I was staying at the bottom where it wasn't such a hassle.

Some of my friends tried to persuade me to pull my socks up, but I liked my socks the way they were, and set about catching up on all the good times I'd missed out on while I was married.

There'd be plenty of time for the pulling up of any socks that needed it later on, I reckoned.

Three years later I was a wreck. An alcoholic, they claimed, and finally I was forced to agree that they could be right. I couldn't get work any more because I couldn't be relied on to meet a deadline. With thousands unemployed nobody had to put up with a slack journalist. I had two choices — go into an institution or pull up those socks they'd been warning me about. I decided to have a go at the sock one.

(from *Puha Road*, **1982)**

Once again, Crump's painting the city as a terrible place where the women trap men like possums and hang them out to dry on the nine-to-five line. All a real man can do is find a good mate and a half-decent set of wheels and hit the back road to freedom. Crump livens things up this time round with another familiar trick, matching his hero, who wears the unlikely name of Gavin Midwinter, with a good, keen but utterly hopeless and accident-prone cobber called Eric 'Muxy' Muxworthy. It's not exactly a ripping yarn, but it does tear along, following the two losers as they become winners, after scoring a vast amount of money for being the five-millionth car to cross the Auckland Harbour Bridge.

This brings them back to town with a vengeance which involves them buying a chunk of land in one of the toniest suburbs in Auckland, turning it into a rubbish tip and giving away most of their wealth. It's Crump jousting with authority and the straight life, but apart from the occasional contemporary detail, it could as easily have been written in the 1950s as the 1980s. Crump's love of and feel for land and landscape hasn't deserted him. He seems reconnected.

> There was something about the north that attracted both of us. Muxy liked the easy pace and unhassled attitudes of the people. It made him less flustered and accident-prone. There was something about the hills and the harbour that attracted me. I'd always had a love for the sea, but this was different. There was something about the way the reaches of the Hokianga harbour stretched themselves out among the hills like a flat grey sheet of pewter, with chunky dark dots of islands scattered here and there like thrown dice along the miles and miles of sparsely settled shoreline, and across the headland you could quite often hear the roar of the surf out on the coast. Mounting back from the shore of the harbour the gentle crumple of manuka-spreading ridges rose higher and higher to join the heaping tumble of heavily bushed ranges back there against the sky.
>
> **(from** *Puha Road*, **1982)**

Then *Hang on a Minute Mate* finally hits the TV screens and, to mark the occasion, *Listener* writer Tony Reid sets out to track down the suddenly elusive Crump for an interview. Reid rings Radio Pacific to be told that Crump is leaving town. When he finally corners Crump and asks for an interview, Crump responds, 'I'll give you a tip, mate. I'm not worth it.'

Reid finds Crump and Robin in their house surrounded with possessions which Crump then offers to Reid and his photographer — anything that won't fit in the Toyota. 'Tomorrow we're off to the scrub. I don't know where and that's the exciting part. I think we might spend a bit of time in the Urewera. Just camp somewhere by a stream where I can do a bit of trout fishing and Robin can keep a few chooks.

'Last time we were away, we were down near Queenstown working a gold-mining claim two and a half hours of horse-riding from the road. It was a great adventure and we moved on before we started to feel jaded. We left when the price of gold was at its highest.'

Crump's suddenly sounding older and maybe even wiser, at least to the journalist. But he's not listening to himself. Not believing. Just giving the mythology another whirl round his tongue like mouth wash.

'I was 22 when I wrote *A Good Keen Man*. Actually, I was living under a false name and hiding from the cops. Life went mad and so did I. I still groan to think about it. There I was — successful, sought after, churning out books. Scrawling them out in handwriting like the tracks of a drunken fowl.

'For all I knew it might be alright to have lots of money, an OK sort of thing. But in fact I was worse off. I wasn't where I was meant to be and I was kidding myself. For quite a while everything seemed exciting and good. I was up to a lot of mischief — all the things I had missed by spending my youth in the bush. Women, boozing and dancing. Oh I was living high. I was rough on the chicks.

'The 1950s and '60s were pretty good in New Zealand, you have to admit that. You could safely leave your keys in your car from the time you got it to the time it was repossessed. Go into a pub, drink all day and pour everyone into the old Model A. As long as the tyres lasted, you wouldn't hit anyone. I was bunging it all on. But I couldn't keep the pace up. I was never really the same as the image. I was never really like that. I could feel OK drinking piss and shagging sheilas. Still I was already bored. I'd tell myself it was a problem finding chicks to keep up with me. Bloody phoney, mate. At the end, I suppose I just grew up. Praise the Lord.

'So I shot through to Aussie and spent three years shooting crocs. I'd never have left there except that I got shipwrecked, stuck in New Guinea and repatriated. When I got back there's all this publicity and I think, "What the hell" and I believe I wrote another book to prove that I could do it. Immediately plunged back in the shit. I forget what I did in the following years. I was never scared of going broke. I never saved money and I never did anything that was personally productive. But around 1971–72, I owned a home. Only time in my life. Well, there I was sitting on the croquet lawn and hitting the piss. I got talking to this Seventh Day Adventist.

'These blokes had their lives transformed by a spiritual thing. "Why not God?" this Seventh Day bloke said. I told him, "God's not for me. I don't rubbish him, but if you're trying to get me baptised, sorry mate". However, I was lost and world weary. Later, I went out into the night. I could feel an awareness. I knew there was a God and I knew everything I had done was a total balls-up. I thought, "What do I do? How do I start? How can God show me what to do?" I went overseas and searched through the East. The newspaper headlines said, "Crump Goes To Seek God". Now here's the remarkable bit. It wasn't long before the headlines said, "Crump Finds God".

'I was a Baha'i and I told people about it. It was like saying, "Here I am with my head stuck out". Soon they were asking me on various TV shows for a natter about things. There I was running around and saying, "This is the answer". But all those interviewers have never been able to come up with anything wrong with my beliefs. They can't. Nowadays I want nothing more than to be remembered for finding Baha'i. It is the most benevolent faith anyone could think of. It's not against anything. Well, it's not too strong on the drink. I've always had a bit of a weakness there. Dates from my deer-culling days.

'It's a yardstick to live by, both reassuring and hard to live up to. It means there are no more excuses for Crump. I would say I only get unhappy when I drift away from prayer or Robin is miserable. She has the same belief. In fact, when we first sprung each other, I'd given up any idea of finding the right woman. I'd reached the bottom of the barrel in that department.

'When Baha'is marry, they have to get permission from all living parents. That was tough, but we managed. Now, I don't need anyone else but Robin. I never knew I could be that happy and, after six years, we are still seldom apart for more than a few hours. I know that some people think Baha'i has affected my writing. Well, they don't understand that my stuff has always had odd aspects to it. I admit I've never been able to talk much sense about it. Here's something that has nothing to do with Baha'i. Now, I wouldn't say that I'm foul-mouthed. Not really, but it's true that I'll say "bloody" in front of a lady. Still, there's never been any swearing in my books and I don't know why. I'd have thought there would be.

'My publisher once said my typescript was immaculate. But have a look at the state of this room. Doesn't make sense. At the moment, I'd like to do a book about dogs. I've known some hard-case dogs and I've been wanting to write about them for a while. Perhaps I will. I never go anywhere without a pen and paper. Just to scratch down lines of dialogue. And you get some beauts. There was a time when I had a van and lugged the wife and kids around Europe. We stopped at a pass in Switzerland and there was this amazing glacier. Mist, clouds and this colossal glacier jutting out for about a mile. It was an overwhelming view of sheer rock and ice.

'This car pulls up and these Kiwi farmers get out. One bloke stands next to me, cranes his neck and lets his mouth hang open. "My God," he mutters. "She'd be a bastard to muster." But I don't use stuff like that. It's just for myself. Actually the very best writing I've done is in old 4000 to 5000-word letters to friends. When I crash, someone will run out with them and make a bundle.

'I suppose my writing does represent a sort of nostalgia. I'd like to leave my bones here and, when I'm overseas, I love every bastard in the whole place. But, in particular, I admire my generation — jokers like Ed Hillary. You don't see men of that standard in the newer generations. We've become a nation of cheats. We dodge on deals. We're furtive. I've become a bit cautious about people wanting to rip old Crump off. I feel like apologising for saying that, but it's the truth. I'm 47 and getting harder on people who insist I am an unfortunate fool from the turnips. I don't let youngsters be cheeky. It's bad for them.

'Anyway, we'll load that Toyota up in about 10 minutes. Moving on is no sweat. It's easy to put in 24 hours a day because it is another, better adventure. And Robin loves washing by hand. It's a joy to her. Lucky for me, eh?

'I'm happiest when we're together in the truck, blapping down the road, watching that white line and having a yarn. In the back, all our gear — the .22, books and paper to write on. If you're not going back you save petrol — it's only half the mileage. I tell you, it's an incredible country out there, and we are two of

shoot-through time

157

the free-est people we've ever met.'

Martin's mother had always warned him to watch out for his dad, because he had a bad habit of hurting and disappointing people. Not that Martin or Ivan or Harry or Lyall or the other lost boys Crump left behind ever had to watch out for him. Mostly they'd have to seek him out. Martin spends quite a bit of time with his father during the talkback radio adventure. They play golf, go to the pub, smoke a bit of dope and shoot a lot of breeze. But they never get much into the deep stuff. Crump isn't the sort of sorcerer who likes to share his secrets.

Crump and Robin have moved into a flat in Remuera and Martin's been talking to his father about buying a car off him. They've been seeing each other three or four times a week to play golf and, Martin thinks, getting on really well. He's having a wonderful time, feeling like he's really getting to know him at last. Martin rings and tells his dad he still wants to buy the car and that he's saved up the money for it. Crumps tells him, 'Oh we're looking for quite a bit more money for it now'. Martin says no problem and that he'll be round at the weekend to do the business and catch up.

Martin pops round to the flat on Sunday morning and they're gone. No car, no furniture, no goodbye note on the door. Nothing. From having seen Barry three or four times a week for a year, Martin's left facing the blank where his father used to be. He's devastated, thinking maybe something went wrong, they were evicted or there's been an emergency that took them off without warning. But the days and then the weeks pass without a phone call.

Then, a few months later, Martin's in town and he spots Robin in Newmarket and as he greets her and gives her a hug, across her shoulder he sees Crump, in a doorway three shops down the street, hiding from him. He can't believe it.

§

17.

stretch nylon slacks

1983

rump and Robin have found a new place to call home, a bit of a shack, quite a bit of a drive up the river behind Opotiki, in a dark valley on a dead-end road. It feels like about as far away from everywhere as he can get. And that's just where he feels like getting. He makes it a base and they drift off when they feel the urge.

Crump's always been a bit keen on writing poetry and during a return to his beloved West Coast puts pen to paper himself with an epic poem for children, 'Mrs Windyflax and the Pungapeople', which won't be published properly for years. It has a sweet, simple charm, inspired by Crump's discovery one day, walking a track near Punakaiki, of a pair of tiny shoes stuck in the mud. Rather than see them for what they are — children's shoes — Crump reinvents them as the lost footwear of a member of the fabulous Pungapeople, Westland's answer to the leprechauns of Ireland, and writes his poem.

He sends it off to Radio Pacific and one of their announcers, Jim Henderson, reads it out on air. The station is inundated with requests and tells listeners who want a copy to send in a stamped self-addressed envelope and $2. Hundreds come in and are forwarded to Crump who, with Robin doing the donkey work, struggles to satisfy the sudden demand.

One of the Toyota television ads starring wise-cracking, hard-driving Crump and goofy, nervous Lloyd Scott wins two awards in Australia. The ad has also won an Axis award for the best New Zealand commercial — despite some criticism about dangerous driving. A spokesman says the judges in Australia viewed the Crump commercial as a clear winner and were impressed with Crump's performance and the script. They were tickled pink with throwaway lines like when Crump, bouncing madly around in his seat, says to his passenger: 'You're not married are you?'

In December, Crump comes down from the hills and puts his feet up at Auckland's poshest 'poncey palace', the $40 million Sheraton Hotel. He's come to tinkle glasses with car dealers and make another television commercial for Toyota. 'It took me 10 minutes to tie me tie,' he says. 'It's the best dressed up you're going to see me for quite a while.' It is Crump and Robin's first time back in the city since he gave up his yarnspinning show in Radio Pacific. They live in a three by four-metre A-framed whare they built in the Motu River area of the Urewera. 'It's a bit of a contrast with this place,' says Crump.

'My mate lives over the river. He's got 11 dogs and we catch live deer with them. I can't afford a chopper. When we run out of bread, we also do some possum trapping.' And Crump is using his 'old dunger' of a typewriter to write another book. He hasn't decided on a title yet, but reckons he may call it *The Scavengers*. 'It's about a couple of guys who see how long they can hold out in the Ureweras. It's like a boys' adventure story, really. One of the characters is only 13 when he goes in there.'

The new book isn't in the humorous style of earlier efforts like *The Odd Spot of Bother*. 'I've put everything into this,' says Crump. 'It's my best shot. It's a proper novel. It's longer and I've rewritten it all. I've really done my best with it. With the others, I just dashed them off and as soon as they looked good I published them.' He's not sure when he'll publish the new book because he wants it made into a film first. 'Some movie makers are real interested. It's just a matter of raising the money.'

The Crumps live on $40 a week and keep their income below $11,000 a year 'so there's no trouble with the tax department. We have no possessions. We don't need them.'

And is Crump, now 'getting on for 49', planning a family? asks a reporter. 'If it happens, it happens. I can't grow older. There's something wrong with me ...

A different sort of middle-aged swinger — the golf years.

New Zealand Magazines Archive

With Robin at their place up the river, at the end of the road out the
back of Opotiki.

Graeme Brown, Kokako Studios

Crump, designed and posed to look like Crump. Someone else killed the pig.

Graeme Brown, Kokako Studios

Crump puts a smile on a bad situation — with Wally at the *Wild Pork and Watercress* launch party.

With Lloyd 'Scotty' Scott on an ad shoot for Toyota.

Crump, the all-meat diet starting to show, pauses to pose with the Queen while picking up his medal at Government House.

The New Zealand Herald

Crump and son Martin share a smile and a smoke.

Lighting another of his
eternal cigarettes.

Crump, looking a little wasted, but still scribbling in his notebook in 1992.

New Zealand
Death Certificate

National Number
1996/527/16103

DECEASED

First/given name(s)	**Barry John**
Surname/family name	**Crump**
(If different First/given name(s) at birth	**-**
from above) Surname/family name at birth	**-**
Date of death	**3 July 1996**
Place of death	**Public Hospital Tauranga**
Cause or causes of death	**Ruptured Aortic aneurysm - 2 days**
(as specified in doctor's certificate or coroner's order)	**Peripheral Vascular Disease - years**
Name of certifying doctor	**D D Archibald**
Date last seen alive by certifying doctor	**3 July 1935**
Sex	**M**
Age and date of birth	**61 16 May 1935**
Place of birth	**Papatoetoe**
If not born in New Zealand number of years lived here	**-**
Usual home address	**157 Kaitemako Road South**
	Welcome Bay Tauranga
Usual occupation, profession or job	**Writer / Novelist**
Date of burial or cremation	**8 July 1996**
Place of burial or cremation	**Pyes Pa Cemetery Tauranga**
Age of each daughter	**-**
Age of each son	**Not Recorded**

PARENTS

MOTHER: First or given name(s)	**Lilly Valley**
Surname or family name	**Crump**
(If different First/given name(s) at birth	**-**
from above) Surname/family name at birth	**Hendrey**
Occupation, profession or job	**Sewing Teacher**
FATHER: First or given name(s)	**Walter William**
Surname or family name	**Crump**
(If different First/given name(s) at birth	**-**
from above) Surname/family name at birth	**-**
Occupation, profession or job	**Dairy Farmer / Farrier**

MARITAL DETAILS

Marital status	**Married**	**Four more marriages**
Age at marriage	**58**	**Details Not Recorded**
Place of marriage	**Alexandra**	
To whom married: First or given name(s)	**Margaret Louise**	
To whom married: Surname or family name	**Nicholson**	
Age of spouse or former spouse	**44**	

Certified to be a true copy of the above particulars included in an entry recorded in this office.

Issued under the seal of the Registrar at **Lower Hutt**
this **3 day of April 1998**

Proof of departure — Crump's death certificate, mistake and all.

Crump shoots through for the last time — the funeral.

I'm pretty fit I find. I'm just waiting for the next door to open, whereupon we'll immediately enter in the spirit of the adventure.'

Early in 1984, Toyota has to remake one of its ads starring Crump being taken on a hair-raising ride through Wellington streets by city slicker friend Scotty. Toyota ad agency Colenso don't need Crump for the remake, which is just as well. He comes down from his self-built whare only about once a fortnight to pick up mail from Opotiki.

Then the *Dominion* finds Crump and wife Robin living in Collingwood, 135 km north-west of Nelson. They've moved there, they say, to fill a temporary post for the Baha'i faith which is now their lifeblood. Crump is now 49. The couple have no children. 'If any turn up we wouldn't object,' says Crump.

The couple's total material possessions amount to Robin's bike. 'People don't believe our lack of interest in material possessions,' says Crump. 'They can't believe we're not milking the television advertisement for a few bucks. Our deal is that we make an ad and they lend us a ute. That's our basic thing with them.

Crump disagrees that the ad could encourage reckless driving. 'I drive a lot more sedately now. I used to drive with a bit of flair, but I don't now, so people can't say there's that mad coot doing what he does on television. I've been writing some good stuff lately — some far out poetry and I've written a really beaut novel about two blokes and how long they can hold out in Urewera National Park.'

He doesn't see any conflict between the *Good Keen Man* image and being a committed Baha'i. 'The good keen bloke image was imposed on me, but it must have some substance. But it was not what I would have thought I looked like.' Now he says, 'I'm probably one of the best men I have met. I'm honest and straight and I have to be discreet about how I handle things and people for that reason.'

Crump and Robin travel across to Golden Bay to look after brother Bill's place while he and his wife Sigrid take a six-month trip to Europe. The local Baha'i community need some support, he says. Barry's still there when Bill returns and they spend a few days together. Bill is shocked at the level of harassment his little brother has to put up with because of his books. Barry's constantly apologising for the interruptions. Then he and Robin shoot through.

Crump stars, with actor Peter Bland, in a video explaining the intricacies of the new Goods and Services Tax to the public. He and Robin take up an offer from the people who own the land their rented shack is on out the back of Opotiki and buy 11 acres of rough land. He's a landowner again, though he's keen to suggest that he's never done this sort of thing before. He also finds himself a keen young man who seems interested in handling his tattered financial, business and publishing affairs. He's the bloke who runs the pub Crump favours in Opotiki. His name is Craig Howan, a hard-case entrepreneurial sort of bloke 20 years younger than Crump.

Howan's strong, silent, unexcitable character appeals to Crump. Maybe he sees something in him of his younger, more carefree self. Maybe he's just in sore need of a mate and a piss-it-up-and-shoot-through compadre, someone to organise what to him often seems unorganisable. But whatever it is, they get to know each other a little better during Crump's sporadic visits to the pub and a deal, untainted by anything as untrusting as ink on paper, is struck.

It's a load off Crump's mind, but it's going to be quite a load on Howan's.

Crump, now 50 and calling himself a goat farmer, is pushing his forthcoming book which he's still saying is about two blokes who go bush in the Urewera. He also travels to the West Coast to take part in a celebrity debate on the subject of whether West Coasters can do anything. Writer Keri Hulme will be taking the negative side. Crump won't. He loves the coast. Howan tags along and the two of them have a fine old time, living life the way Crump loves it. Rough and ready for anything, and anything often comes along.

This deal with Toyota is working out real well, especially now that Howan's helped screw some serious money out of them. It's raising Crump's profile no end too, people suddenly pestering him all over the place again. And not just the older people now. The kids are onto him now, thanks to the television. Turning that somehow into book sales would be magic.

Crump's taken over Howan's fancy Japanese automatic camera and he's getting very keen on photography, swiftly focusing on things that interest him. These pictures almost never involve living things of any description. Crump likes ancient inanimate objects. Fenceposts, falling-down forgotten farm sheds and long-drops, letterboxes, rusting abandoned farming equipment. He also does dead trees and is often excited by interesting cloud formations.

In March, Crump is flown by charter plane from Opotiki to Whakatane and on to Auckland to make an appearance on the American television programme *Lifestyles of the Rich and Famous*. Crump reckons he must fall into the famous rather than the rich section of the show. The truth is that he's richer than he used to be.

In May, he makes an appearance singing one line in a TV commercial featuring New Zealand entertainers performing an America's Cup song. His line is, 'One people on the land'. It's his first time singing in public since he released that non-hit record in 1970 featuring the ballad 'Bad Blue' which sold 250 copies.

Crump says he now confines his vocal talents to parties. 'I've never seriously thought of going into singing. I'm a bushman.' Crump owns two dogs, Dan and That. 'The only word he seems to respond to is "that".'

'Our life,' Crump dramatically tells a reporter from the *New Zealand Woman's Weekly*, 'is like a bloody fairytale. Ten years ago, we were driving up the road and our van was clapped out and we saw one of these Hilux things and rang up the company and said we'd advertise them if they gave us one. If I'm going to endorse something I'd rather it was that than a lot of other things.

'We're not rich. It would only embarrass us if we were. Too many of us have got too greedy and it's causing a lot of trouble. There's plenty of money around this land. Miles of it. I know people who are wasting the stuff. I haven't ever thought of a thing I wanted that I haven't got. We bought a bit of rough ground up a river on the edge of the Urewera country. Real rough. A cottage sort of thing. We're knocking that into shape. It's a pretty good-looking spot. Doing fencing and getting into breeding angora goats on a helluva small scale. Highly dubious if we'll ever make a crust out of it.

'If Robin hadn't been one of those who loved living on the road, she'd have got left behind. It just turned out she loves it more than I do. It's helluva hard. A few times trundling through a strange town at night, just about out of gas and money … it's hard to handle. It was the same with all the women till I met Robin.

'They're reprinting some of my books and that's bringing in a bit of money. They used to be a bit disjointed and lazily written. I wrote *Gulf* in five days and nights. The essence was there but … I want to make a craft of it now. Nothing left to prove really. I only write if I'm feeling good. If it's painful to write, then it's going to be painful to read, eh? I just write like I'm writing to someone I love. It might be a bloke I want to tell this yarn to. I've got very little to say to other writers. Most writers are pretty serious about it. It's only a very small part of my life.

'If I was ever going to be remembered for something, it would be that I'd found the Baha'i faith. Not written books or done award-winning television commercials. That's a bloody big game. The Baha'i faith is the most important thing on earth. I've been telling journos that for 10 years and the buggers won't listen. But we're forbidden to proselytise — it's regarded as bad manners and I quite agree. Most people I run into would prefer it if I wasn't religious. They'd love me to be boozy and raucous and … it's an image. I'm fitted with it. I can't knock off from it.'

Ha ha, thinks Crump, having delivered another great load of bull into the undiscerning mouth of the media. It amazes him how they swallow it. And in the retelling of his myth he retools it till it's running sweet as a newly tuned motor.

Soon after, the *Herald* reports that Crump is working on his 'most serious book yet'. It's called *Wild Pork and Watercress* and that it'll be in the shops by Christmas. Living in the Urewera, he rises every morning at three o'clock to work on it, he says. 'It's a full-length novel.'

He's writing it on an electric typewriter which — given that he has no electricity — he hooks up to a makeshift powerplant in the river below his shanty. Everything goes sweetly until there's a bout of heaver-than-usual rain and a flood rages down the river, dismembering the power plant and silencing Crump's DIY technology.

When told of the disaster, his Auckland publisher arranges for a manual typewriter to be swiftly dispatched to Opotiki by Road Services bus and the book is now into its last stretch.

The idea of a major novel has been with Crump for two years. He has rewritten the beginning three or four times and polished and constantly reworked other passages. 'This book's a brute of a thing with a mind of its own. It even gets me up in the middle of the night just to change a comma.'

Jack Lasenby finds himself passing through Opotiki, having been fishing some of his old favourite waters back in the hills, and rings Crump to catch up. 'Come on up,' says Crump. 'I'm easy to find. Just drive up the road beside the creek. After a bit, you'll see an old pig with a litter on the side of the road. Keep going and when you're about 10 or 12 miles up the road, you'll find a burnt-out bus. Keep driving and then look across the creek and you'll see our place. Give a beep on your horn and I'll come across and get you.'

So Jack takes it easy and gets there eventually, past the pigs and the burnt-out bus, and toots his horn. Crump comes out, gets in his Toyota, revs it up in a manly manner and roars down into the stream like a hero, sending a huge wave right up and over the cab, and then nips up the bank to Jack, spins the ute round in the gravel and shouts out like John Wayne, 'Hop in.' Then they're down and back across the creek in the same parting-of-the-Red-Sea manner. All very dramatic. Jack's suitably impressed. Then they set in for a marvellous night, having a hell of a lot of catching up to do.

About sundown, Robin announces she's off to a Baha'i meeting and starts getting out her trail bike. 'Here, take the Toyota,' shouts Crump, tossing her the keys. She hops in the cab, turns over the motor quietly, tick, tick, tick, and drives down quietly into the stream and slips across so gently the eels probably don't even notice and then tidily up the other side and off. Crump grins awkwardly at Jack. 'Course, there are two ways of crossing the river, right?'

Crump's been working with Auckland publisher Beckett. They put out a collection of Crump's old stories, *The Adventures of Sam Cash*, last year, matching up *Hang on a Minute Mate* and *There and Back* and it sold pretty well. The TV exposure is making a difference. Crump's got a good feeling about this new book, really reckons this is the best one ever.

In September, Crump announces he has completed *Wild Pork and Watercress* and gone back to his goats. He pronounces it the only thing he has written that he likes better than *A Good Keen Man*. The book will be launched at Te Waiti, near Opotiki, in a couple of months. Crump's new publisher, Cliff Josephs, announces that *Wild Pork and Watercress* will be launched deep — and unreachable except by chopper or four-wheel-drive — in the Urewera because it closely resembles the author's natural habitat. Guests will be fed with copious quantities of wild pork, trout, venison and watercress. Survivors of the eight-hour bash will be transported back to the relative comforts of Opotiki by four-wheel-drive vehicles.

Craig Howan has been working on Crump about sprucing up his image. 'You've got to look more like the sort of Barry Crump that people expect,' he's being told with such regularity that he almost starts believing it himself. It's almost unsettling. He's put into jeans to look a bit more with-it and he wears them, but he's not happy in them. 'They're the most uncomfortablest things on the planet, but someone took my old pants away and I think they've burnt them.' He reckons jeans restrict him. He usually wears revolting-looking things he picks up in op shops around the place. He's particularly fond of stretch nylon slacks. He is and will always remain a fashion-free zone. The hat arrived when the hair started leaving. Otherwise he wears things till they're worn out.

There seems to be serious interest in his book this time round. To coincide with publication, the *Auckland Star* runs an excerpt from the book, while down in the deepest, darkest Urewera, the star of the show arrives half an-hour late to the launch of *Wild Pork and Watercress* — ard then the helicopter that flies him into the site of the function lands, pointing Crump the wrong way round for his expectant audience.

'Land again, Barry,' a member of one of the assembled TV crews and photographers scream out. But Crump lopes around the back of the chopper's whirling blades, followed by a Maori boy he describes as 'a family friend Lyle Mato'. 'With the kid, Barry,' a photographer calls out, but Crump strides on, climbs a bank by the clearing alongside the Te Waiti Stream and greets the assembled assorted media and mates, 'Gidday, taken your bloody time, haven't you?'

Crump strides on into a tented area, a bandstand blasting out reggae music and a huge icebox full of cans of beer and accepts from Cliff Josephs a copy of *Wild Pork and Watercress* bound in pigskin. There is one as well for actor Lloyd Scott, who plays Crump's sidekick 'Scotty' in the now-famous Toyota television ads. At the end of the speeches, Crump orders everyone, 'Get into the sludge' and retires to loll on a grassy slope where he is immediately surrounded by people with microphones, tape recorders and cameras. As he rolls himself a cigarette, Crump dispenses some of the usual wit and wisdom.

And 'no', *Wild Pork*, which tells the story of a young Maori kid who dodges the attentions of Social Welfare, had no hidden message. And 'no', the novel's runaway, Ricky, definitely isn't modelled on his little mate with him. All the boy manages is a shy 'Gidday' for the big, scary and increasingly drunk crowd. Robin takes over the talking from him. She says the boy is a special cobber of Barry's. He's been teaching him the basics of bushcraft. Together they've been doing a spot of small-game shooting.

Crump is presented with a letter from the poet Sam Hunt who has written to the *Auckland Star* asking them to tell Crump how much he enjoyed their extract of *Wild Pork and Watercress*. Crump smiles from under his greying moustache and tells the reporter, 'Say a great big ta back, because I can see that he's been there. I don't really know Sam, our paths have hardly crossed, but he knows what it's about.'

This isn't turning out to be as good a day for Crump as he's furiously making out. Out of the blue, his father has turned up with his new woman, Joyce, in tow. Now it seems like Wally can't get enough of his now-famous second son. Barry's squirming inside, but he makes out that they're his VIP guests for the day and Wally and 'step-mum Joyce' aren't coy about lapping up all the attention that's on offer. Wally reminds everyone he too once knocked out a book. Full of bullshit, he claims the book was on the best-seller list for six months in the mid-1960s. He wrote it, he reckons, because Barry had bet him five dollars he couldn't.

And there'd been another book from his pen, about parliamentarians, but a newspaper lost the manuscript and he hadn't bothered to try writing again. Instead he concentrates on reading his son's offerings. Some he's found to be very good. Wally especially likes the ones he got for free. Barry tries to make the best of a loathsome situation.

Wild Pork and Watercress is being well received. The *Auckland Star* declares it 'an almost unbelievable tale made believable by its raw earthiness as Crump displays his bush lore'. Whether Crump's stars have collided in the heavens, or the incredibly popular Toyota ads or just the fact that *Wild Pork and Watercress* is perhaps Crump's most powerful and best-crafted full-length story, the book is a bit of a best seller just like the old days.

It is Crump's masterpiece. He's finally realised that all his writing life he's been banging out the same story. 'There's only one story. Everyone's only got one yarn really, but you can put so many slants and angles on it.' *Wild Pork* picks up on the theme developing at the end of *Puha Road* where the storyteller is developing a teacher/pupil relationship with a boy. But the new book has a gritty realism and a dark edge to it that Crump has only previously found in some of his short stories.

It even alludes to the damage wrought by men who walk out, leaving their women and kids behind. Even more remarkably, the tale is told from the point of view of one of those boys.

> My proper name's Richard Morehu Baker but they always call me Ricky. My mother was quarter-Maori and I was born in 1974, years later and a lot darker-skinned than my brother and sister, and don't let anyone tell you that doesn't make a difference. I always had trouble fitting in. People were always getting a surprise to find out I actually belonged in our family. I was also a bit overweight and not much good at sports and stuff like that.

By the time I'd been at school for a few years I could read miles better than most of the other kids but I wasn't much good at anything else, and they decided I was a slow learner. They shifted me around from class to class, trying to work out where fat Maori boys who can't play rugby or learn simple stuff fitted in. I knew they had me all wrong, but there wasn't much I could do about it.

I've always been able to remember just about anything I want to and it's easy for me to learn things. Too easy. I was worried about all the stuff that was going into my head, and they were shoving more in all the time. The wrong sort of stuff, too. I couldn't forget a lot of it. I used to be scared my head was going to fill up till it couldn't take any more and I'd suddenly go mad, or burst or something. So I took time off school, which I usually had to pay for with more trouble. But heads are only so big.

Anyway, while all this was going on my parents got divorced and my mother took custody of me, mainly because nobody seemed to know exactly where my father was living. He was never allowed in the house when he'd been drinking, and he just did more and more drinking till he didn't come home at all. Things got worse at home and school until in the end my mother couldn't handle me....

(from *Wild Pork and Watercress*, **1986)**

The boy is sent off to the country to be raised by his Maori auntie and Pakeha uncle — the former sweet, caring and constantly serving up great grub, the latter a crusty old kid-hating grouch, fighting to scratch a life out of their overgrown farm. Uncle Hec warms to the boy and starts to serve up great advice on the ways of the farm and the bush. Then the auntie dies, the Social Welfare threaten to come and take away the boy and he and his uncle go bush, which is where the adventure begins.

This book's no string of yarns. It's a simple but cleverly shaded novel that builds its intensity and ends with a surprise and a question mark. Crump writes compellingly about the beauty and pain of life in the bush and keeps clear of the cynicism and smart-arsery that has marked so much of his past work. With its epic bush adventure and its mysterious ending, *Wild Pork and Watercress* is reminiscent of John Mulgan's classic *Man Alone*, but the characters and the detail are all Crump's.

It's taken me nearly all winter to unravel Ricky's handwriting and get his story written down more or less how he meant it. One of his books has been wet and one whole passage is indecipherable. I could tell, though, from a few phrases I was able to follow, that Hec and Ricky planned to buy this station and present it to me in return for my having helped them. Another piece I was able to pick out was Ricky saying to Hec, 'Maori skin isn't so brown on thin people as fat ones. True. I tell you!'

One or two other things he's left out of his story, such as the scene I remember in the kitchen here when Ricky discovered that Hec was illiterate. And later the touching little scene when Hec told Ricky he could have the .22 on his fifteenth birthday.

I must say here that everything I knew about in Ricky's story was consistent with what they'd both told me. As for the huia, I don't know, but Ricky's description of them tallies in all respects with every reference I can find to them. If I had to guess, I'd say that those huia still exist, and that Hec and Ricky found them.

Owen Mallory, who was here last summer with his team, practising for one of his Himalayan expeditions, described any attempt to tackle those Huiarau bluffs without proper equipment and experience in rock-climbing as 'extremely foolhardy'.

And that's what I think must have happened to them. Hec and Ricky must have dropped off one more ridge in a tricky place — too tricky. I do believe they're still out there in the Urewera bush, two ragged skeletons lying at the bottom of some bluffs, somewhere along the Huiarau Range. Kokako Bluffs.

And yet if I walked outside right now and saw that wisp of smoke I always look for up on Cave Camp Bluffs — but no, it's been too long now.

That's all I have to tell, except that whenever I notice their old rifle there in the corner I think of Hec and Ricky, and I recall those last few words of Ricky's story:

'We've got a few hassles coming up, but we can handle them. We're okay now.'

I'm not a particularly religious man, but if there's any justice in this life Ricky and his Uncle Hec are okay. Still sticking it out together and handling their own hassles in their own way. I hope so.

(from *Wild Pork and Watercress*, **1986)**

Robin has agreed to be interviewed and sits in a pub in Opotiki, sipping a very large glass of lemonade. 'How do I describe myself?' she ponders. 'I'm a hard person to get on with, a realistic type of person and an infuriating type of person too. I'm very forthright and not very guarded in my speech. That could be construed as a know-it-all.'

For more than 10 years, the resulting article goes, Robin Crump has been the quiet strength by Barry Crump's side. She has kept slightly out of the way of the publicity her husband has attracted, but that publicity does not bother her. 'It's life, isn't it, if you are married to someone who writes books? If you are a plumber, you have to come in contact with a lot of people who want their drains dug.'

But where the Crump household in the Urewera is concerned, privacy is maintained to the full. Even at the recent book launch for *Wild Pork and Watercress*, the reception was kept away from the house. Robin proudly mentions the tubs where she hand washes clothes and the television set run on power from a generator rigged up by Barry. It's a simple life, running their feral goat farm which they hope will become viable in about two years.

In winter they go possum trapping to earn some cash. 'We like what we're doing now,' says Robin. 'Barry and I get on really well and we like doing the same sort of things. We understand each other. We have very few problems and if we do we talk about them.' She often makes the 30-minute journey to Opotiki and invariably calls in at the library. She also likes to sew.

'I can make my own clothes, but I make a terrible job. I get all excited because I want to make something, and then halfway through I realise I haven't sat down and thought about it. Then I get fed up with it and don't finish it properly. So the finishing is not so good.' Robin says she enjoys children and teaches a pre-school group at Opotiki every Monday. This leads to the question of whether there will ever be the pitter-patter of tiny Crump feet. 'Children?' she asks. 'That's in the future.'

So what is in store for Robin, aged 30, and Barry Crump, aged 51, asks the reporter. 'We don't really make plans,' says Robin, 'although I suppose my plan would be to do a bit of everything in my life. I've done a fair bit already.'

Up at the end of that rough river road, the pitter-patter of little feet has been considered. In a bid to fulfill Robin's desire for children, Crump has an earlier vasectomy reversed. But he still seems to be firing blanks, though he's hardly really firing at all. Robin's starting to get restless and less happy about her confinement in the back of beyond with an old bloke whose ideas of a good time are to talk to the goats, go and get drunk as a skunk in Opotiki every week or two and upset the neighbours by driving too fast down the river road. He's starting to act a little crazy too. And he amuses himself with the wicked torment of women sometimes. Or that's how it seems to Robin.

A middle-aged guy comes to visit and he drinks with Crump and when the guy gets up to leave, Crump tells him, 'When you get home, wake your missus and get her to cook you a decent feed. There's nothing a sheila likes more than to look after her man'. The next day Robin runs into the bloke's wife and she comes up to her and says, 'Robin, you know I can't understand what's got into him. He came home and woke me up at two o'clock in the morning and asked me to cook him a meal. And I've got to go out to work in the morning.'

It's a rare man that Crump doesn't manage to manipulate.

§

18.

a loaded rifle

1987

In January, a *Sunday Times* reporter is allowed into the confines of the Crump homestead where the famous writer is discovered singing the praises of nature round his way. 'Everything's in harmony. You've got it all here. There's the mineral kingdom doing its thing, undisturbed. There's the vegetable kingdom — nothing so beautiful as a valley full of manuka between spring showers. Absolutely exquisite. No one could deny it. It's like a beautiful Japanese garden. And there's the animal kingdom, birds and things. Then there's us, the human lot. It's all here.'

Crumps says his current challenge involves tidying up his act. 'You know, getting me own character and personality tidied up a bit.' He neglects to explain what he means by this and, taking a drag on his limp roll-your-own, complains quietly that the Crump image has never been accurate. He can remember going to 13 or 14 primary schools. 'My father was a blacksmith who got into sharemilking. Swore I'd never milk another cow when I left home. I did once give a guy a hand to milk a herd once, but that's another story.'

So he headed south 'and the further south I got the better I felt. I was attracted to them low, bush-covered hills and I always have been. It's never gone away. Bush-covered hills. There's just something there. I just like looking at 'em. Spent most of my life groovin' around the roads, living in huts and vans. Got to know New Zealand,' he says, rolling another fag and topping up his tea with condensed milk.

It's the possums that have kept him and Robin going, he says. 'I've always had a bag of possum traps. Years ago, we lived in a Model A that I sort of re-built. We'd pull up in rest areas, because y'know there's actually more possums in rest areas than any other stretch of the country. There's lots of bits of paper and people chuck stuff. Possums are nosey little buggers and they like a bit of clear grass too.

'You could tack a trap to the corner of the truck so every possum would wake you up when it got caught.' They'd get three or four a night, skin them and put the skins on the spare tyre of the Model A to dry. 'It's all we had to do to make a living. The rest of the time we just kept going. And by keeping me head down, not advertising too much and resisting the commercial side of it, I managed to live like that until I was about 50.'

They bought the place at the end of 20 km of twisting road from Opotiki with money from television commercials. 'More than you could really squander, but not enough to buy anything really good.' Totally uneconomic, he says, but something to work at.

'I've stuck a few posts in, fenced off a paddock and caught some goats. Got an angora off me brother at mate's rates and now we're breeding. Magical animal, the goat. They've started clearing all the scrub. I'm getting more done now than I have in me life. And living in the country, you don't have to get up and go jogging every bloody morning. You keep reasonably fit, living round here.'

He gets away for a few days every now and then, he says. Otherwise he'd be like most of the guys he knows who live out in the bush — 'all introverted and inclined to be a bit broody with other people.' Crump produces a fancy Yashica camera and announces, 'And I'll tell you another thing I'm doing. I'm taking pictures of old sheep yards, broken-down buildings and stuff. I want to do a study on old fence posts before they disappear. Got TV and video too. Yep, we make use of every modern device we can lay our hands on. You can live both ways, you know. I think you have to be able to in this world.'

Crump says he's working on a book about a man and a dog. 'I'm not doing any more till I've been down south to refresh myself on some of those sheep stations — till I've smelt the tussock and been kicked by a horse. For a while there, I was writing one book a year, whacking them out like a weight of throbbing spaghetti on a plate. It was easy. It was fun.

'But now I'd like to rewrite me last book. I learned doing that book that you have to put in the graft. I've been pushing them out too fast. I'd like to go back and do that one properly. I'm really getting into writing proper novels and it's quite a craft. As you get older, you lose the vigour of the writing of your youth, but you gain the craft. You look back and you see where you went wrong. And you know there's only one story. Everyone's only got one yarn really, but you can put so many slants and angles on it.'

He's been practising some of this stuff so long, he hardly needs to think while he's saying it. And if he is thinking he's wondering what the hell's going wrong now. He can feel Robin pulling, trying to get away from him. The black clouds are coming down on him and all he can do is get away every now and then. Just bugger off in the ute.

But when he comes home, it's the same old shit. She writes him a letter, telling him how she feels and what she thinks they need in their relationship and asking him to talk to her about it, but he just rips it into four pieces and throws it in the fire unread. He's starting to frighten her. He never hits her, but he throws things at her. A crowbar. Cups of hot tea. It's a kind of contemptuous violence. One time, he grabs her by her lapels and spits straight in her face. Once or twice, she sleeps the night in the paddock because he's inside with a loaded rifle. Sometimes he makes out he's going to drive them off the road.

One night, he suddenly kicks her out of bed shouting, 'Ring the police. Tell them your husband's about to bash you.' They've only just got the phone on, but the police are 20 km away. Robin opts to spend the rest of the night talking him out of his madness. She's becoming increasingly convinced that the day might not be far off when he actually does her in. The most peace she gets is when he's writing. He seems almost obsessed then, at it day and night, writing first in longhand and then onto the typewriter.

Crump's black, raging moods are starting to affect everything. Even Dan, Crump's dog, is turning strange. Crump takes Dan with him when he roars off to the pub and leaves him locked in the cab of the ute for hours and hours on end. Then, all the way back, Crump talks to the dog, like it's his mate or his child. He makes Dan do tricks. Shouts, 'Speak up Dan' and Dan barks and makes him jump fences on command for visitors. But Dan becomes frightened of Crump and doesn't always bark when spoken to and cowers when Crump shouts at him to jump the fence.

One day Crump's at the table with Robin, talking about something that's pissing him off, getting angrier, when suddenly he lifts his gun, leans across the table and shoots the dog dead. And as Dan lies there, eyes glazing, Crump turns to Robin, 'Honey, make me another cup of tea. A man needs another cup of tea when he's just lost his best mate.' Dan isn't the first dog Crump's shot. And not the last.

Young Davey Hill was as keen on dogs as a starving tapeworm. He often had two or three hidden in the scrub along the big swamp and up the gully behind his father's homestead. Mongrels of all sizes and description that were surreptitiously fed from Davey's plate and late-night milkings of the house cow when he couldn't get scraps for them anywhere else. On an average of about once a month his father would hear Davey's dogs barking at night or catch him sneaking down to feed them, and another batch of stray mongrels would be released with a boot in the ribs and shouted and stoned off the place — on to somebody else's. Even Davey couldn't say where all these dogs came from. They just turned up and, in time, were turned out again.

Outbreaks of sheep-worrying were so prevalent that the farmers in the district took their rifles from porch corners almost as often as they put their old felt hats on. Old man Hill waited in apprehension for the phone to ring every time he heard a shot fired on a neighbouring property. Mr Hill was a very tolerant man, but when Davey turned 15 and expressed a desire to leave school and home, he found it impossible to discourage the boy beyond pointing out the usual things about education and learning a trade. The Ringatu Rabbit Board won easily.

So two weeks and two phonecalls after leaving high school Davey Hill left home with five dogs his father had never seen before and a shotgun that his father was never going to see again. He also had a lot of embarrassing last-minute advice and a bacon-and-egg pie from his wistful mother. His father drove him to the railway station in silence and there was more embarrassment while they waited for the train. Even the dogs were embarrassed.

The Ringatu Rabbit Board Inspector met Davey at the station and helped him load his dogs and gear into a Land Rover. He was a big easygoing bloke with a grin and a pipe. It was the first time Davey had ever been treated like a man; had someone bowl up to him, stick out a paw and say 'Pleased to meet you, Dave, I'm Joe Scott. How did your dogs take the trip?'

As they drove madly along a road down the side of a gorge, talking about grown-up things like rainfall and erosion, Dave felt better about having left home.

'It's all dog and gun work out here,' explained Joe. 'We gave up the poison a couple of years ago. It's only a matter of keeping the old bunny down to where we've got him, now. We'll never get the last one or two, but we can't let them breed up on us again. There'll be a Maori bloke in the hut up there with you. He's a bit rough on his dogs, old Kingi, but he's a bloody good rabbiter for all that. One of the best I've had yet. You'll find him okay to get along with.'

The road left the bushed gorge and wound around into a valley that had been brought into pasture and divided into farms by the Government. You could still see patches of rank grass among the manuka and fern. The road from here on was strictly for Land Rovers.

a loaded rifle
173

'There's a couple of dairy farms at the head of the valley,' said Joe. 'They take all their stuff in and out the other way. This is only a short cut. All this country's going back. Bushsick as hell.'

Dave didn't give a flax basket of kumaras whether the place was bushsick, lonesick, homesick or seasick. It looked pretty good to him.

Night and rain fell together as they arrived at the end of the clay track that led to Kingi Cooper's hut. He opened the door and stood like a lumpy statue against the light from a Tilley lamp on the ceiling behind him. Joe and Dave climbed out of the 'Rover, slammed the doors and went up onto the verandah of the hut.

'How's things, Kingi?' said Joe, following him inside.

'Been raining on and off all day. I worked some of the flats this morning and knocked off.'

'That's the idea. There's no need to work in the rain — this is Dave Hill, he'll be giving you a hand up here for a while. Kingi — Dave.'

Dave shook Kingi's big, engulfing hand and said hello.

Kingi was casually friendly. He was also the fairest-skinned Maori Dave had ever seen. In fact, he looked more like a slightly-curried European than a fair Maori. He gave Dave a hand to tie up his dogs while Joe unloaded the 'Rover.

'Where's your dogs, Kingi?' asked Dave as they walked toward the hut in the rain.

'Got 'em tied up all over the place,' replied Kingi. 'You'll see enough of 'em in the morning.'

Something about the place puzzled Dave. Something that wasn't quite right. It was only when he was lying in his bunk that night and Kingi and Joe were asleep that he realised what that something was. Dogs always kick up a hell of a racket when someone arrives, especially at night. There hadn't been a sound from Kingi's pack. And he was supposed to have 14 of them.

Joe left them in the morning, which was fine, telling Kingi to ring him from a neighbouring farmer's place if they needed anything before he came again to pay them, in about two weeks' time.

Kingi and Dave set out to work on a strip of country along a river beyond the hut. Dave's dogs were all over the place as soon as he let them off the chain, but not one of Kingi's left his heels before he told them to. He had everything from big scarred lurchers — all chest and legs — to pocket-sized burrow dogs. Terriers, spaniels and even a sheepdog. And not a pure-bred among them. Dave's dogs looked pretty much the same, but there the similarity ended. Kingi's pack was as highly trained as rabbit dogs can get. When he put them into a patch of cover the fast dogs spread out around it at places they instinctively knew were strategic, while the small hunting dogs dived into the fern or scrub and worked methodically through it. When a rabbit was driven out into the open it had little chance of getting far. The odd one or two that escaped into a burrow were guarded until Kingi got there and threw a handful of granulated Cyanogas into the hole and dug in the entrance to seal the gas in. Dave shot a rabbit that doubled back past him and didn't let on how surprised he was to have hit it. He could see by this time why Kingi didn't bother carrying a shotgun. With his dogs he didn't need to.

Dave was a bit ashamed of his dogs, which were getting in the way all the time, but Kingi didn't say anything, so Dave decided he didn't mind.

Dave didn't want to knock off when it was time for them to work their way back towards the hut. They got eight rabbits for the day, which Kingi said was fairly average.

They fed the dogs from the carcass of a ram that was hanging in Kingi's dog-tucker tree with a piece of fencing-wire round its neck. That was how Kingi killed his dog-tucker rams.

The following afternoon when the dogs were chasing a rabbit round the side of a hill one of them started barking on the trail and Kingi seemed to be more interested in the dog than the rabbit.

'Poor old Wally. Never thought he'd go that way,' he said, shaking his head sadly.

'Lots of dogs do that,' said Dave.

'Not mine,' said Kingi, and Dave remembered Joe's remark about Kingi being a bit rough on his dogs.

The dogs caught the rabbit and came struggling over to where the two men were leaning on a fence, one of them bringing the dead rabbit in its mouth. Kingi turned casually away from the fence and called Wally in.

'Here, Wally. Here, boy. There's a good dog now.'

He began to pat the dog roughly on the ribs and then grabbed it by the muzzle with one hand and took out his sheath-knife with the other.

'Never thought you'd go that way,' he said to the cringing dog as he doubled its head back, cut its throat and swung it into a clump of fern, almost in one movement. He wiped the knife on the thigh of his denims and stuck it back into its sheath.

Dave had turned away, his face as white as a cigarette paper and his ears roaring like surf. A silent circle of dogs stood 20 yards out from the fence. Dave led the way towards the next gully so Kingi wouldn't see his face. Kingi behaved as though nothing out of the ordinary had happened, which it hadn't; but Dave wasn't to know that. Kingi told a joke about a bullock-driver, but he had to do all the laughing himself. Dave had just noticed that the band of blood on Kingi's trousers where he'd wiped the knife wasn't the only one.

A few days later they drove to a farm in Kingi's old truck to get a dog-tucker cow the farmer had left a note in their hut about. The cocky was in the middle of his milking when they arrived at the cowshed.

'I've got the old girl in the yard here,' he said, leading the way past cud-chewing, muddy-legged cows to the back of the yard, where the sick cow drooped near the rails.

'The vet says she's a gonner. Been going down in condition for a couple of weeks. Not much left on her, but she might be worth a feed or two for your dogs. We'll put her out into the yard so you can shoot her and....'

'This'll do,' interrupted Kingi, running one hand along the cow's bony spine. Then he had his knife out and her throat cut before the farmer or Dave realised what he was doing. While they watched in silence Kingi held the cow against the rail until she sank to her knees and rolled over, kicking feebly. Then he stooped to wipe his knife on the quivering rump.

The other cows began to stir around the yard, bellowing and snorting at the scent of blood. Cows stirred and stamped in the bails. A set of cups fell off and lay sucking noisily on the wet concrete. One by one the other three sets of cups fell and were trampled by restless feet. Dave and the farmer looked a little wild-eyed at each other and then at Kingi, who was steeling his knife to begin skinning.

'I think you've lost a lot of cups mate,' he said, glancing at the cocky. 'Give us a hand to roll her over, Dave.'

Dave went over and pulled weakly at a hind leg. The cocky shut off the vacuum in the pipes and began to let the rest of his cows out through the shed. He had as much show of getting milk from bulls, the state his cows were in. He went up to the house without another word to the two rabbiters.

As they drove away with the quarters of meat glowing on the back of the truck, Kingi said: 'I think he's a bit annoyed with us for upsetting his cows. How the hell were we to know they'd go that way?'

In the two weeks that followed, Dave managed to get away on his own most of the time and work blocks of country that were too small and patchy for it to be worth two men doing. His dogs were getting good at the work and he didn't miss many rabbits. Though not having any fast dogs, he had to rely on his shotgun a fair bit. Occasionally Kingi would come back to camp with one less dog than he left with and sadly explain that Biddy or Whisky or Nigger had 'gone that way'. Dave was so uncomfortable in his presence that it was a relief to get out on the job in the mornings, where he could forget about Kingi in the enjoyment of the work and watching his dogs improving.

Joe came, paid them and went.

Then there was the horse. An old station packhorse that they were to shoot for the dogs with a .303 rifle Joe had left with them for the job. They pulled up at the gate of the paddock with all the dog-tucker gear on the back of Kingi's truck. Sacks, rope, shovel, steel hooks, gambels and axes. The horse had seen them coming and came over and hung its tired old head over the fence to see if there was anything to do or to eat or only to watch. Dave sat in the truck and said to Kingi: 'You shoot him. I'm not much good with a three-O.'

'She's right,' said Kingi. 'I think I'll be able to catch him.'

'No,' said Dave, getting quickly out and grabbing for the rifle. 'I'll shoot it.'

But Kingi was already walking towards the horse. Dave watched as he stroked the nuzzling head and ran a hand down the horse's neck. Then he climbed up on the fence and over onto its back, speaking quietly to it. The horse turned and began to walk along the fence to the gate, with Kingi sitting on its back steeling his knife. From where he was sitting, it took him four slashes to get its throat properly cut. Dave could hear the blood pouring onto the ground as the horse wandered in an aimless little circle. When it went down, Kingi stepped off and deftly wiped his knife on the hide as the horse rolled over to kick out the last of its life in the mud it had made from walking up and down the fence, waiting in case it was needed.

It was then Dave began to really hate Kingi.

The next day one of Dave's dogs barked on the trail when Kingi was there.

'That Ruff of yours barking on the trail, eh?'

'Yeah.'

'Never thought he'd go that way.'

'No.'

'Got your knife on you?'

'No, I haven't.'

'I'll fix him for you. Here, Ruff. Here boy. There's a good dog....'

Dave just watched.

Joe came, paid them and left.

Three more dogs, a horse, two rams and a cow.

Joe came, paid them and left. They caught the Rabbit Board's old packhorse that had been turned out for the winter in a cocky's back paddock and loaded him up for a trip to a hut in the hills beyond the river. It was an area that had to be given a rake-over every three months or so. They crossed the river and let the creaking horse lead the way up a side valley to a slab hut in the tussock, four hours from the base hut.

They worked all their country in eight days. Every morning Dave shifted the packhorse to a new stake-out and occasionally cut a bit of extra grass for him. Kingi cut another dog's throat for coming into the hut after it had been chased out. Dave was getting so good with his shotgun that Kingi, who was against their use, admitted that it was handy to have sometimes. He had only seven dogs left and Dave had four.

They were loading their stuff into pack-boxes for the trip back to the base hut when two of the dogs started fighting outside. One of Dave's and one of Kingi's. Dave ran out and grabbed a hind leg but Kingi didn't need his help. He stuck his boot on one of the dog's neck and grabbed the other by the muzzle. While the two dogs struggled and squirmed he took out his knife with his free hand and tested the edge with his thumb. Then he doubled back the head of the dog in his hand....

Blood sprayed up his sleeve and across the back of his coat. Then he bent to wipe his knife, on the ribs of Dave's dog under his foot, before giving it a few casual rubs on the steel. Then he took the dog by the muzzle. Dave turned away.

They headed for the base and it was getting late by the time they reached the river. Kingi caught up the packhorse and climbed on top of the load to save getting his feet wet on the river crossing. Dave stood on the bank and watched the horse stagger to its overloaded knees among the boulders in the river. One of Kingi's feet, which he'd tucked into the pack-straps, went right through as he came off. The horse plunged through the water and on to the rocks across the river and stood snorting at the blood on Kingi's coat. His foot was still wedged between the pack-strap and the load. He reached up to free himself, talking quietly to the horse. Dave couldn't hear what he was saying, but he knew well enough. Never thought you'd go that way....

Dave raised his shotgun and quietly cocked the hammer behind the choke barrel. He knew exactly where to aim. At that range it was easy. The number four pattern burnt the horse neatly across the rump. It only took the terrified animal a few seconds to reach a bend in the river and stumble and plunge around the corner out of sight. Kingi looked like a rag man, bouncing along among the boulders and hooves.

It was too late to go for help that night. First thing in the morning he'd do all the things you're supposed to do when there's an accident in the back country.

At 10 o'clock that night Dave threw the dregs of his tea into the sizzling fireplace and went out to have a yarn with the dogs; to tell them everything was okay now. When the cold had drawn all the heat from the fire out of his clothes he gave the dogs a last pat each and went inside for another mug of tea.

Kingi was standing there. With all his weight on one leg and his back to the fire. He seemed somehow to be all out of shape. Something had happened to his nose and forehead. He opened his mouth to grin but it didn't look very funny.

'Didn't think you'd go that way, boy.'

(from 'That Way' **in** *Warm Beer and Other Stories*, **1969)**

Robin leaves him. Comes back once, leaves again and stays away. She's been with Crump 11 years. But they're friendly enough when the divorce comes through to take each other's photographs outside the courthouse with their papers as souvenirs.

§

19.

ill-considered remarks

1 9 8 9

There are plans to make a movie version of the best-selling *Wild Pork and Watercress* blowing in the wind. But it's an unpredictable wind and the plans aren't going to come to anything. Crump's never happy with various attempts at adapting a screenplay from his book. Usually there have been attempts to introduce sex and violence and bad language into the story. The absence of these items from most of his work has become a matter of pride to him.

'Crump's Place' (as Robin always answered the phone there) is now a bachelor pad. With the sort of money that's coming in from Toyota, thanks to an exclusivity deal that Craig Howan has helped Crump strike, and *Wild Pork and Watercress*, Crump buys the chunk of land next to his. He now owns 11 hectares, including an old kauri homestead, circa 1906. The walls are too far apart from each other in the house for Crump. He stays holed up in the shack out the back with its open fire. He likes the comfort of small spaces.

When he's sober enough, he's writing for as long as 14 hours at a stretch. His latest effort is *Bedtime Yarns*, a solid compilation of bits and pieces, short stories, extracts and poems, including *Mrs Windyflax and the Pungapeople*. That should hold the line till he can get this next book finished.

Crump and Howan like to get away together when they can, just drifting off round the North Island, but more often south and across Cook Strait. Crump's either got some research he needs to do for his next book or there's some other good excuse for jumping in the ute and chasing the white line. They convince themselves they can make their own documentaries and buy a fancy video camera and the two of them head off looking for great yarns and characters to tell them. They find their colourful characters soon enough in various pubs, but as soon as they point their camera at them, the colourful characters go all colourless on them.

So they forget about that and Crump concentrates on taking photos and jotting down notes and pointing out places to stop. Howan and Crump have become close, despite the 20-odd years between them. There's an air of *Hang on a Minute Mate* about them, with Howan young Jack Lilburn to Crump's craggy, yarn-filled Sam Cash. The younger man, for all that he's a hard man on his own ground, is dazzled by Crump. Crump has chosen to shine that powerful light that comes out of him on Howan. They call each other 'brother'.

On one of their trips south they land up at Barrytown on the West Coast, now the home of Mike Bennett, Crump's old mate from deer-culling days and from the croc-shooting adventure. Crump's knocking the booze back pretty heavily and steadily and looking pretty out of shape. Bennett fixes him up with a place to stay and Crump hits the Barrytown pub most days, putting away the best part of a bottle of the Black Label they get in especially for him and a bucket or two of beer as well. He doesn't cook, just opens cans of Irish stew. He drives everywhere, won't even go for a walk on the beach with Bennett. But he's writing. That never seems to quite stop now.

Howan helps Crump put together a dozen of his rustic photos for a calendar called *Barry Crump's Humble Abodes* and they sell the lot. Crump's keeping his head down these days. He's not that interested in walking the walk and talking the talk, but if a reporter ever does corner him, he feeds out some of the familiar defence lines. God's his major prop these days. In the old days, he and drink were 'firm friends'. Now almost his only indulgence is a couple of packets of tobacco a week for his roll-your-owns. 'I suppose I'm a difficult bloke to live with. I'm beginning to think that. I don't perform to what's expected of me. My philosophy for enjoying life is don't do anything to any other bastard you wouldn't want done to you.'

His sixteenth novel is on its way. It's called *Bullock Creek* and Crump's pretty happy with it. 'It's a proper novel and I reckon it's pretty good.' He has just finished putting up a new fence at his hideaway near Opotiki and is breaking in more land. Negotiations are still underway between Crump and film-makers over the rights to *Wild Pork and Watercress*, his hit novel from 1987 which, to date, has sold more than 50,000 copies.

Bullock Creek turns out to be a classic old country Crump, vivid and ringing with detail and the sure pulse of reality.

> A morning as cold as a crowbar tells The Doughmaster it's time to get ready for the winter. He sharpens the chainsaw and cuts a heap of blocks off the dead macrocarpa that's leaning against the end of the woolshed and fills the woodshed up at the house. Last year when the water-supply to the homestead froze Lorna carried her water up from the river in plastic buckets. The usual water-supply comes from a spring up the hill through an alkathene pipe lying along the top of the ground, probably one of the first things on the place to freeze up. So he gets on the roof and fixes up some of the sagging spouting and gets rainwater running into the tank for the first time in years. He butchers five big Mangatane wethers he's been saving and Lorna packs all the meat in the freezer.
>
> **(from** *Bullock Creek*, **1989)**

Crump has had the call from the ad agency to make a new set of Toyota TV ads — real hair-raising ones, these, more hair-raising than the 1984 ad featuring some wild driving round the streets (and traffic tunnels) of Wellington which was withdrawn after one screening following a complaint from the Accident Compensation Corporation, who said it 'didn't set a good road safety example'.

'Nothing's fair,' says Crump. 'It's just what you get away with that counts.'

In the middle of 1990 it is announced that Crump will star as the subject of one of the *Magic Kiwis* television series — not that Crump will be able to see the programme when it screens. 'The man from those Toyota ads cannot get TV where he lives by the Pakihi River, at the back of Opotiki,' the *Sunday Times* reports. *Magic Kiwis* director John Harris describes Crump as 'a wonderful person to interview. He could read from the phone book and make it sound interesting.' It was necessary to cross the river to get to Crump's place. 'He drives through it the way he does in the ad,' says Harris.

Crump doesn't get many visitors. 'They find the road a bit rough.' Asked what stunts Toyota has up its sleeve for future ads, Crump says, 'I'm anxious to find out. The last one gave me a fright.' It featured Lloyd Scott and Crump flying off a mountain in a ute.

Crump has also been making appearances at Toyota conferences and vehicle launches throughout the country, work he says he doesn't enjoy but is glad to do. 'It makes you grow up a bit. It's like jumping into the water in the middle of winter.' Crump has also just finished making a video with All Black Buck Shelford aimed at offering inspiration to young business people.

Crump tells a reporter he's preparing himself for the star role in a feature film based on his best-selling *Wild Pork and Watercress*, which he claims has now sold 100,000 copies. 'It'll be fun to have a go at being an actor,' he says. The shooting is to get underway in 1991 and the producers 'have the money together', though the exact budget is a secret. Craig Howan confirms that it will be between three and six million dollars. Says Crump, 'At the moment, we are just doing the very early part of the script. And I'm going to take the leading role.'

Crump is working on a new book. 'I can't believe it. I'm writing an autobiography, a book about my life. I never thought I'd do one. I've said so more than once too. I plan to have it out next year. I didn't plan on doing it. I sort of flopped into it really. I started by writing down a few facts. Before I knew it I was on my way with enough to start the book. I didn't muck around with writing. Like always I just got stuck in and got the bloody book done, even though it's about me. Well, as much as I'm prepared to tell about me.'

Howan talked him into it, somehow convinced him that maybe the best story he had left to tell was his life. And Crump just sat down and wrote shit for a while until something started happening. As he was always telling Robin, he's not a man for hanging out dirty washing in public and he's certainly keeping his strides on in the telling of his life story.

There are things in life he regrets. Ill-considered remarks mostly. But there are three things you can't get back — the speeding arrow, the spoken word and the lost opportunity. He's going to call his autobiography *A Strand of the Rope*.

The *Magic Kiwis* Crump special screens, with Crump admitting on camera that he's putting on his 'customary act for the media'. He also claims his appetite for adventure stories was sparked when his mother gave him a copy of *Coral Island* 'by Robert Louis Stevenson' (though that book was written by R.M. Ballantyne). He also says he never took any pleasure in shooting animals. 'I don't enjoy it — never did.' That apart, he's laying out the usual legendary bullshit.

Crump's going through a high-profile period. A couple of weeks later he appears in *Sunday* magazine listing his favourite things. Under the heading of 'Films/Shows', he says, 'The last show I went to was the Moody Blues in Munich in 1971. It scared the hell out of me. It was also the first show I went to. I've seen some good films. Steven Spielberg's stuff is quite fascinating, isn't it? But I'm getting weary of those films where the craggy-featured idiot and the absurdly dressed girl blow all the other actors and most of the scenery and props to bits and end up sucking at each other's mouths. Ho hum.'

On books, 'I write more novels than I read these days. My average week's fiction-reading is the clues in the *Listener* crossword.' Music, 'My having-a-bath record is Beethoven's "Emperor Concerto" fifth piano. Other than that I like some country music and good guitar playing.' Places, 'New Zealand. It's one of the best parts of the earth. I reckon that Fred and the Trevs Dagg dribbled a bibful when they so charmingly pointed out we don't know how lucky we are, mate.'

Pastimes, 'My favourite pastime has always been writing — mucking around with words. I also like to ride the valleys and ridges in the moonlight on Shiraz, my gutsy little Arab stallion with my two dogs sniffing the territory ahead of us and a silly bit of a song running through my head.' People, 'I haven't met anyone I couldn't like. I couldn't be bothered being anyone's enemy. Of all the people I've met, I think that Tibetans are my favourites. I have a remote and cordial relationship with them.'

Crump heads back to his remote river valley and out of nowhere, like she does every year or decade or when the spirit moves her, Tina rings him and says, 'I've got to see you' with her old drama and the voice that still excites him even after all these endless years. 'Come right now,' he tells her. She drives down to Opotiki and beyond to Crump's lonely patch. He throws out the woman he's had come and live in and Tina moves in for a few days. She still loves the feel and the way of him, the familiarity of his hip against hers as they walk, an arm tight around each other. It's like being kids again. She wants him to make the Model A and the galloping noises he used to make her laugh with back in the 1950s. 'Oh no,' he groans with a big silly smile.

'I never wished you any harm,' she tells him. 'I wanted to kill you every now and then, but that's quite understandable and only for a short time. I know I haven't been able to count on you for many things, but I've always counted you as a friend.' He just smiles his big silly smile, though it's a sadder big silly smile than Tina remembers it.

Another, more timid, visitor turns up at the end of Crump's road in the shape of Andrew Campbell, Fleur's son, the little boy who, 30 years before, looked at Crump's shotgun on the wall and fantasised about pulling it down and using it to save his mother from this terrible man.

Now Campbell is in the book business himself, managing editor at Reed, Crump's old publisher, and he has become curious about the man who strode across the path of his childhood. Campbell still feels the bruise of the experience. He hears stories about Crump from publishing mates, tracks Crump down and arranges to visit him.

Crump picks Andrew up at the river and drives him across into a scene with intense rural-Gothic overtones. There's a decapitated cow in the middle of the paddock in front of the rough little shearer's hut Crump's living in. Back up the hill there's a substantial old farmhouse, but Crump says he only goes up there to cook.

Crump has just butchered the cow and there are plastic bags full of its various bloody bits everywhere. The freezer is chokker apparently and the left-overs are going to the dogs. There are goats wandering everywhere.

Inside the hut there's a woman Crump doesn't bother introducing staring at a tiny portable television set which has such bad reception it looks like a snowstorm and sounds like white noise. She must be seeing and hearing something in it no one else does.

To Andrew's surprise, Crump rambles on about publishing and literature and books he's read, surprising the younger man with his serious interest in writing. He enlivens the conversation further by sprinkling it with impromptu renditions of corny country songs and an especially impressive reading of the Lee Marvin hit, 'I Was Born Under a Wand'rin' Star'.

§

20.

there's a chill

1992

Crump's given up on Opotiki. Couldn't stand it any longer up there with goats and the occasional needy human for company. That adventure's over. There's a chill coming into the edges of Crump's life he hasn't felt before. Like snow coming down from the high country. He packs up what he needs and and pulls out. He gives a neighbour the $20,000 tractor with the front-end loader that Craig Howan had bought him and he boots the ute across the river for the last time. No looking back.

In June, Crump briefly becomes a pop star when his duet with Lloyd 'Scotty' Scott, 'Side By Side', peaks in the national charts at number two. The song's from the latest Toyota ad.

In July, Crump's autobiography, now called *The Life and Times of a Good Keen Man* is published. Tina had told him to leave her out of it. 'You'll only get it all wrong,' she said. Crump is holed up, living in Auckland in a warehouse in

Airedale Street, owned by Howan. 'He's a good lad,' says Crump. 'He's the only agent in the world who only has one client. Me.'

Crump's happy enough camping in Airedale Street, a big-city cul-de-sac off Queen Street, opposite the Auckland Town Hall. He's drinking at the Queen's Head pub round the corner. And one weekday lunchtime, he drifts in and some cheeky woman at a table with a bunch of her woman friends pipes up and shouts out something really original at him. 'Where's Scotty?' All her friends laugh, and Crump mumbles something out the side of his mouth where the fag's not. He's heading out the back and then he changes his mind and turns back and she — the cheeky one — pulls out a chair and invites him to join them.

Her name is Maggie. She's a woman in transition, a working solo mother who has recently swapped her job at the Housing Corporation for a redundancy package. She was lining up a job in Saudi Arabia, then found out she couldn't take her five-year-old son Anton with her.

Crump doesn't even know why the hell he's sitting down. This isn't what he normally wants to do, but he does it anyway and they all have a wonderful afternoon, drinking and letting Crump enchant them with his well-oiled wit and wisdom. In the midst of all the impromptu socialising, Crump inquires, 'You don't know anyone who could do some typing for me, do you?' and the good-looking one called Maggie pipes up, 'You're looking at the best there is'.

She's been slightly bowled over by his 20-foot-high personality. He's rolled out one story after another and has them all in stitches. What a neat guy, she thinks, never having previously thought too much about Barry Crump at all, other than knowing who he was.

She reports for duty at the warehouse next day and starts typing up a manuscript for a book Crump is calling *Gold and Greenstone* and it's only then she realises who and what she's stumbled into and starts feeling a little awed by the strange reality of working with a famous author. What has she got herself into? But she puts her tail up and her head down and gets on with the job. Maybe that's what gets Crump's attention, because on the second day at the warehouse, he asks her out to lunch. This flusters her. 'If I'm there, I'm there and if I'm not I'm not,' she tells him, but Crump doesn't hear it that way and comes back three hours later shouting at her for standing him up.

Maggie goes off thinking she doesn't need this, even from a famous old author. So, by the third day things are a bit rocky between them, but by the end of the week when Maggie's almost finished typing the manuscript, relations are warmer again and they do go out to lunch and Crump tells her the only reason he wanted to have lunch with her in the first place was to talk about the book and make sure it was being 'typed with feeling'. With *Gold and Greenstone* typed and gone, Crump finds further employment for Maggie typing up a book by Sigrid Crump, wife of big brother Bill, and during that time they start dating, if that's the word. But after three months, Crump starts getting unhappy about being in the city and wants to shoot through.

By this time, Maggie is temping, not quite knowing which way to try and point her life next and starting to experience strong feelings for Crump. Her only immediate responsibility is her little boy, so when Crump says to her one day, 'I'm going, are you coming?', she packs up her belongings and jumps in the Hilux with Crump and Anton. What the hell, she thinks. And what the hell it is.

She feels she has nothing to lose and if it doesn't work out following an uncertain trail with this unpredictable man then she can always go back. Her friends all told her she was mad running off with a man she'd only known three months. And what sort of man was he anyway, this Barry Crump? But she doesn't care. She tunes into her own wild streak and off they go.

And of course it's Maggie and little Anton who are fitting into Crump's life rather than the other way round. There was never much potential for that. There's no way Crump could have moved in with her in suburbia in Auckland's Hillsborough. So it's Maggie and her boy who do all the adjusting. And sometimes that's an adventure and sometimes it's hard. Crump finds it hard taking on a five year old — especially one he regards as a spoilt little so-and-so. 'Children of solo parents are always spoilt little so-and-so's if they're brought up by women,' he says like he knows something about the subject and he takes little Anton in tow and sets about disciplining him. And it's all made much harder by the fact that Anton's jealous anyway of the relationship that has sprung up between Crump and his mother.

They head south and down to the South Island and the West Coast where they live rougher than Maggie thought possible. There's a magic in this life, but it's a rough one and she can feel her softness being rubbed off. That house in Hillsborough might be the last comfortable place she'll ever live in. It's hard too, adjusting to being round the legendary Barry Crump and suddenly feeling invisible as all eyes turn to him.

Whenever they're out around other people, she sees them wanting to talk to him, touch him, listen to his old engine tick over, smile at the treacly rumble of his voice. And he puts up with their intrusions, mostly. He barks occasionally.

They fall out of the bottom of the Coast and into Central Otago and to Wanaka, a town on a lake. Anton is feeding a duck and a man walks by and trips over the duck. Introduced by accident, they all get talking and it turns out the man who tripped over the duck owns a big station and there's an old farmhouse down on the flat that's up for rent. So they take it. A step up from camping with the Hilux, thinks Maggie.

But it's a plain little farmhouse and it's a hard little life compared to

Hillsborough. Maggie has more time on her hands than she's used to. It hangs heavy sometimes. Her 16-year-old son Simon arrives to live with them and goes to the local school. A pattern sets itself on their life. Crump gets up and potters around. They go down to the pub late morning. He drinks his Black Label whiskies and Elephant Beers and she sips white wine.

Later, they drive back home and after dinner, around 10 or 11 at night, he'll go off and write till three or four in the morning, have a few hours' sleep and get up and start pottering around. He's working on a book called *Arty and the Fox*, a story about good times and laughter, he says. Good times means old times. Increasingly, Crump seems to lean to the past. The good old days when every horizon hid a new adventure. Sometimes they just drive round the back roads real slow in the Hilux and Crump takes photos of things that catch his eye. Usually old abandoned things, rusty antique farm machinery and old fence posts.

Sometimes he doesn't talk at all. He can be morose, just withdraw into some black cave. It's a kind of depression and it's not something he wants to talk about. Maggie just leaves him alone. Sometimes he drives off alone just to be alone. Other times he seems to almost need to be around people. And sometimes he opens right up. Once he tells her about the accident with the boys at the camp. Tells her what he says is the whole story. Then he never talks of it again.

A few months later, Crump dismisses any suggestion that being made a Member of the British Empire signals a move to join the establishment. 'I am the establishment, mate. The bushman establishment. It's bloody good, to tell the truth. It's nice to be recognised as being a damn good bloke. It's a bit confusing, though. I don't really understand what an MBE means, though I reckon it might be good to hang one of them on a Swanndri.'

The casual front is carefully constructed. Crump is very taken with the honour. If he could have gotten away with wearing his medal on on his Swannie, he would have. He'll keep it in a drawer, for easy reference. Crump is still in Wanaka with Maggie and the boys, 'having a go at being a householder', he tells the media, breaking horses, helping a farmer friend and working on a book. 'I tell them I'm sort of keeping my head down and my strides on and trying to stay out of all the trouble you tend to get these days.

But Crump's still a bomb waiting to go off. The poet Sam Hunt comes to Wanaka in the midst of a 300-plus show tour he's doing to pay off the Inland Revenue Department. Hunt and Crump barely know each other. 'We've met on three roundabouts and five forecourts of petrol stations.' But Crump recognises a fellow spirit, another bloke who walks the lonely path and decides to catch Hunt's show.

First they spend a lively afternoon in Hunt's campervan, parked behind the pub. At one point, Crump looks across at Hunt and says, 'We're like a couple of wanted men in here, aren't we?' Then Crump wobbles off and turns up later at

Hunt's performance in the pub that night, so pissed by the end of it they have to carry him out afterwards. As the legend is being assisted from the crowded bar, a young joker comes up to him. 'Gee Barry, I love your hat, where'd you get it from?' Crump, with a droopy drunk smile, reaches up, takes his hat off and plants it on the fan's excited head, slurring at him, 'She's yours cobber.'

Unfortunately, this fan has a particularly small head and the hat slips down over his eyes, mercifully denying him the sight of his hero being carted, rubber-kneed, out the door.

Gold and Greenstone makes it 18 proper books. It's set in Crump's favourite part of the country, the West Coast, and concerns the adventures of a country girl called Sally who hooks up with an older bloke called Quin after her dog bites him. Crump's writing about a life, his life, and a place that he loves and it shows.

> Down the Buller Gorge to the coast, through the scrubby hills of old Charleston to the windblown flaxy coastline of Punakaiki, the air milky with spray from the Tasman rollers marching in to explode against the broken rocky coast.
>
> More hot sausages and bread in a flaxy clearing on a dusky bluff. The dog ate one of Quin's sausages off the bonnet of the ute when he wasn't looking.
>
> 'Garn, you bloody thing!' he said, aiming a kick at it, which the dog just avoided.
>
> 'It beats me why you cart the bloody dog around with you. It's no use for anything.'
>
> 'Yes he is. He looks after the ute and my stuff. He's for protection.'
>
> 'You need protectin' from the dog, if y' ask me, the thievin' bastard.'
>
> 'You can't blame him really, he's hungry. He hasn't had anything to eat all day.'
>
> 'The bloody thing's not worth feedin',' said Quin, throwing it a crust of bread.
>
> A bit further down the road he got Sally to pull up while he skinned a run-over possum almost one-handed, with an old pocket knife he carried, and threw it on the back for the dog. Then he washed his hands in a creek there and got back in. His arm was hurting him.
>
> 'That'll keep him quiet for a bit.'
>
> 'Thanks Quin.'
>
> **(from** *Gold and Greenstone*, **1993)**

Crump's less inclined to shoot through these days, but after a couple of years, things start to sour in Wanaka. He's not as user-friendly a local legend as he might seem. His lifestyle doesn't sit right with some people. The cops get in on the act too, lurk down the road from the pub waiting to apprehend Crump on his way home.

In mid-April, 1994, it is reported that Crump is to appear in court charged with resisting police after being stopped near Wanaka earlier in the month for suspected drinking and driving. He also faces a charge of refusing to supply a blood specimen.

A Toyota spokesman says he is not aware of the charges and declines to comment on whether they will affect future plans for Crump's popular TV commercials in which he drives. On 20 April, Crump appears in Alexandra District Court and is remanded without plea to 25 May. Crump is becoming disillusioned with life in these parts. He starts muttering about Tall Poppy Syndrome and how maybe it's time to move on again. They've been too long in one place.

On 20 May, he squeezes his now corpulent frame into a dark suit and visits Government House in Wellington to collect his MBE. Crump is one of several dozen recipients honoured at the investiture ceremony, but attracts the most craning of necks from the guests when it's his turn to be bestowed with his medal by the Governor-General, Dame Catherine Tizard.

Asked afterwards what he'll do with the MBE, he says, 'I'll stick it in a drawer. I can't think of what else to do with it. You couldn't really wear it with anything.' With his medal pinned to his suit and sipping a glass of wine, he seems at home in the lavish surroundings of Government House.

'Quite a motley-looking bunch, aren't we?' he grins, looking around his fellow recipients. He has been awarded the MBE for services to literature and says he considers himself first and foremost a writer, but would always be a bushman as well.

He's not sure why his books have sold so well, but is glad to have proved you don't need 'sex, violence and foul language' to make them sell.

Crump reckons the country's falling to pieces. The average New Zealander is bewildered by the pace of change and by the loss of rock-solid mainstays of life such as job security. 'There is a spirit of anxiety out there. Things which have been reliable for years have fallen apart. People can't even trust their livelihood any more. Joe Average today is far more uncertain and unhappy than he was 10 or 20 years ago. No longer as carefree or open. We have become hungrier and more anxious, less inclined to give. There's a general anxiety which pervades the whole outfit.'

He blames it all on the old enemy, materialism. 'In the old days we were never thieves, but many people these days are thieves, both legally and illegally. We're caught up in a materialistic vortex. The air is filled with exploding theories of one government after another. People are cynical of the government now, the system is the cause of its own destruction. Our present system is lamentably deficient. They can't get it together and they never will. I sincerely hope things will change soon.'

Things are lamentably deficient in Wanaka too. Some people resent Crump, don't understand his lifestyle and that being creative can involve sitting in the pub boozing it up when decent people are working. They don't know he works at night and anyway who does he think he is driving home from the pub in his bloody free Toyota Hilux, pissed as a rat. A menace and only getting away with it because he's famous.

The cops set him up and that's why Crump takes a swing at them. It's time to get out of Dodge again and go somewhere quiet where they hardly know him at all. If such a place could possibly exist. Maybe something involving a boat. He hasn't done that for a long time. He decides on the Marlborough Sounds because, he says, it's one of the last parts of the country he's still to explore properly. And, of course, the only way to explore the Marlborough Sounds is by boat.

Crump and Maggie just happen to run into some people in a pub in Picton who just happen to have a 55-foot fishing boat for sale and Crump, who's a hasty shopper, buys it straight off. But it's an old boat, not in the least designed for comfortable living, never mind having a couple and an eight-year-old child on board. It doesn't really work out. In January 1995, the *Evening Post* tracks Crump down in Havelock. 'We were going to live on a boat, but it didn't work out,' he says.

Crump says he is as at home on the water as in the bush. 'I spent a few years on the Barrier Reef in Australia, had a boat up there. I also had a fishing boat operating out of Auckland. A good Kiwi bushman can handle bloody well near anything.' He still has a Toyota for land travel and will be shooting another commercial later in the month with his old mate Scotty (Lloyd Scott). 'I believe it's singing together as far as what I can gather from what the sheila said on the phone.'

Of *A Good Keen Man*, he says, 'I knew I could write about what it was like and I did.' He feels nostalgic for the old days. 'The '50s and '60s in this country were the best. We didn't know that then, but we certainly know that now. It has degenerated. The farmers nowadays lock their gates and put a sign up and say keep out. In our days, they would give us deer-cullers a pack horse and give us mutton. People were trustworthy, nobody pinched anything, your property was safe.'

As to the plans to make a feature film of *Wild Pork and Watercress*, Crump has suggested *Once Were Warriors* director Lee Tamahori to direct it, but isn't sure of his commitments.

Crump runs into a man from the old deer-culling days in the pub at Havelock. Selwyn Bucknell was a government hunter in the 1950s like Crump and though they didn't meet till the mid-1960s, Bucknell knew all about Crumpie. Knew who he pinched some of the stories in his famous early books from.

Crump comes up behind him in the pub and growls a big 'Gidday' and they have a few drinks and Crump hits Bucknell up for a letter to help him get a gun licence. Bucknell thinks it's a bit odd having to give the famous hunter Barry Crump a letter so he can get a gun licence. The two see a bit of each other over the year or so Crump stays in the area, usually at the pub rather than each other's places. They talk about the old days, the extraordinary experience they shared, what it felt like not to come out of the bush for five months, and most of that by themselves.

A couple of times, Crump puts his arm round Bucknell's shoulders and says, 'Buck, they don't know do they?' And Bucknell nods. They just don't know. How could they?

Arty and the Fox is Crump's nineteenth and a good-hearted, throwaway, elongated yarn about a hardcase joker just trying to make a quid.

> The world turned around. As the part of it we're interested in rolled into the sunlight the snowy peaks along the Turnbull Range were tinted pink. For a few moments Pyke's Peak looked like a huge ice-cream in a black cone. As the light spread down across the bushed mountainsides, it gradually lit up the roofs and roads of a small country town called Matea (pop. 1675), on the banks of the Turnbull River, until the sun struck diamonds on the dewdrops in the spider-webs on the fence outside Arty Brown's place on the edge of town, and lit up the splendid array of junk along Arty's fences and around the sides and back of his big shed. We won't show you what's inside that shed just yet, some things take a bit of leading up to.
>
> **(from** *Arty and the Fox*, **1994)**

Crump rings sister Shirley right out of the blue. 'Why am I thinking of you?' he asks her. 'Are you alright?' She's OK. She's just fine, up in Auckland with her husband. This sudden call, though, sets Shirley thinking that maybe it's Barry who mightn't be alright. He's rarely ever let her see inside, though once, on a visit to her, he opened the door to his soul just a crack. Sat there on the lounge floor as the two of them reminisced, though there were no happy childhood memories to share. Just darkness and fear.

'You know,' he told her, 'it's taken me half my life to realise I'm not Dopey. That I can do things.' And he talked about his nightmares. 'Even to this day I can smell the rubber of the old man's gumboot as he kicks me in the head.' And he cried. The tears poured down his face. These were their reminiscences.

So Shirley rings him back a month or two later, worrying. But he says he's OK, that he's thinking of moving to Tauranga. At least he'll be closer, she thinks. At least she'll know where he is. It hasn't been easy keeping in touch with Barry over the years, as he raised unreliability to a fine art. She'd long since learned not to rely on him to stick to any timetable, even when he gave the impression he was trying to keep to one.

It wasn't his style. If something bigger or better got in the way, he'd be off chasing that. But he'd ring now and then to say he was in the city and that he'd be out to see her and they waited for him to arrive. And they were still waiting five years later.

But she forgave him because she felt she understood him. Shirley even forgave him not turning up to their mother's funeral in the 1970s. She never knew if it was just that something else got in the way, or that he didn't want to appear vulnerable. But it didn't matter.

Down in Alexandra, justice grinds on at the District Court, where a charge of driving while disqualified against Crump is found proved. The court is cleared briefly at the request of Crump's counsel, Mr Stephen O'Driscoll, while he addresses Judge John Macdonald on a matter he says he does not want to become public. When the public is readmitted to the court, the judge says he has found sufficient 'special reasons' to discharge Crump without conviction.

Toyota says it's sticking by its TV ad frontman despite his recent court appearances. Toyota spokesman Andy Cumings says, 'He's been discharged without conviction, so that in itself is not something to make any changes about.'

Crump bungs out another book, *Forty Yarns and a Song*, a collection of bits and pieces dedicated 'to life in New Zealand in the fifties and sixties. Those great days!' The 'song' of the title is 'Song of a Drifter', where Crump puts a rhyme to his self-mythology as the ultimate loner.

> And if we meet some other place
> A stranger you will be,
> I can't remember name or face,
> They're all the same to me.
>
> I'll greet you like a brother,
> I'll make you laugh somehow,
> And then one day I'll drift away,
> Just like I'm doin' now.

(from *Forty Yarns and a Song*, **1996)**

§

21.

last white line

1996

C rump, wife Maggie and her eight-year-old son Anton have moved to
Welcome Bay, in the Bay of Plenty. 'My wife has relatives in this part of
the country,' he says. 'The climate is a bit warmer than Wanaka and the digging is
easy.' The couple are developing a native tree nursery in the hills on their property
overlooking Tauranga and plan to grow plants for sale for people wanting
'something bigger than potplants' for garden landscaping.

The business is being run primarily by his wife as Crump works on a new
book featuring one of his best-known characters — Sam Cash. He is reluctant to
talk about the book 'in case my publisher finds out'. He's excited about this one
and reckons it'll be his best ever. But then, he always reckons that. He's going to
call it *The Return of Sam Cash*....

Sam Cash looked at the nearly bald bloke behind the desk without seeing him, and heard what he was saying without listening. Beyond the bloke, whose name Sam could never remember, he could see through the window the neat row of pensioner units. Maisy Burke was cutting some dahlias with a pair of scissors outside her unit, and old Pete Prendergast was sitting hunched on a kitchen chair in his doorway, both hands and his chin resting on his walking stick. Nick went past on the mower.

'This simply isn't good enough, Mr Cash,' said the nearly bald bloke. 'This business of the piano, now. You had no authority to move the piano in the first place, and Mrs Harcourt tells me that some of the songs you encouraged them to sing were — rather bawdy, to say the least. It simply isn't good enough, you were employed as a gardener, not an entertainment officer — are you listening to me, Mr Cash?'

'Eh?' Sam ran his hands through his greying hair and tried to pay attention.

'I say this business of the piano. It isn't good enough.'

'It was Rosy Dewar's birthday,' said Sam.

'Well it's not good enough,' repeated the bloke. 'You can't go shifting pianos around without authority. I'm afraid you've been something of a distruptive influence ever since you've been here Mr Cash.'

'What do you keep the bloody piano for?' said Sam, bringing his attention back from wherever it had wandered. He found it hard to concentrate in these situations.

'The piano is provided for the use of our tenants on social occasions and such,' said the bloke primly. 'You can't just go shifting it around willy-nilly like that. It's just not...'

'Hang on a minute,' said Sam....

(from The Return of Sam Cash, **unpublished)**

Being in Welcome Bay puts Crump back in contact with his old mate George Johnston, who lives down the coast apiece. This isn't quite the Crump George remembers. He seems spent. That's the word they used for trout and deer. Spent. But that's hardly surprising, for God's sake. He's lived at least three of any normal person's lives. And he looks it. His skin hangs on him. That faraway look in his eyes is even further away than it used to be.

Crump and Johnston take fishing trips on Johnston's boat, sometimes not leaving the wharf, but just opening a bottle of whisky, Crump talking about how he's going to spend the rest of his days enjoying the things he knew well without having to burst himself. In the old days they'd have blasted their way to the bottom of three bottles of whisky, plus beer and an endless supply of pies. Crump loves pies.

Once, in the old days, Crump and Johnston found themselves out at Auckland Airport and hungry enough to eat their way through several horses. Instead, they have to settle for the airport canteen and a warmer full of mince pies. George puts a couple on his tray. Crump glances across and loads four, five, six pies onto his tray. George makes his three. Christ, six is ridiculous. Crump'll kill himself with those pies.

It's a long, slow queue, and Crump eats a pie. Then another, and by the time he fronts up to the glazed girl behind the till, he's holding a tray covered in crumbs which a sparrow is tucking into. 'There were six,' he tells her.

People from Crump's past start turning up. Simone Rainger, Lenna's girl, comes to visit and he seems to love seeing her. She stays the night and in the misty morning when she leaves, Crump's outside digging drainage ditches, his face grey with strain. He looks frightening.

In May, Crump is hassling new publisher Hodder Moa Beckett for some up-front cash if they're serious about wanting his new Sam Cash book. They're promising 10 grand and Crump wants that pronto. He's all out of cash again.

Up in Auckland, sister Shirley is still being niggled by this feeling about Barry — that all isn't well. She knows he probably wouldn't tell her the truth anyway, but she has to make contact and another telephone conversation isn't enough. She has to see him. She drives to Welcome Bay and what she finds there shocks her.

He has a home. A proper home. She's never seen him in such surroundings. There are freshly baked muffins on the table, curtains on the windows. There's care in the air. And he's busy putting up his fences, proud to show Shirley the native trees he and Maggie are raising. 'You know,' he tells her, waving his arm towards their little home on the hill, 'it's really only a packing shed done up... Pretty nice, though, eh?'

It's almost like he's found a home for the first time. But there's another shock in Shirley's heart. The cold, cold feeling that her big brother is dying. He looks terrible. Defeated. Finished up. She puts her arms around him and whispers, 'Barry, are you well?' knowing he won't tell her the truth.

'I'm OK,' he rumbles at her. Shirley doesn't believe him, but she goes for a little walk with Maggie, comes back and asks him again. 'I want you to know I'm OK,' he says. And in his way, he is. And he goes back to his fences.

Crump spends a lot of time sitting on the hill up behind the house, staring out at nothing in particular.

Just a few days later, on 1 July, Crump is rushed to Tauranga Hospital after suffering a suspected aortic aneurism. The doctors say his arteries are so clogged he must have been suffering angina and severe pain for years. He's been treating that with a bottle of whisky a day and as many cigarettes as he felt like rolling. He's aged so fast.

In hospital it quickly becomes evident there's nothing the professionals can do for Crump. He's shooting through and he's in no condition to talk about it. Martin is there with Ivan. On 3 July, brother Colin phones Shirley on his mobile for the decision to turn off the life-support machines. She says goodbye and

Crump's off chasing his last white line.

Colin goes to tell Wally, now in his 80s, that Barry is dead at 61. The old bastard seems to take it quite well, mumbles some platitude like, 'Oh well, he had a good life'.

On 18 July, 15 days after Barry, the old man dies. At the funeral, a picture of Barry is displayed on his coffin.

§

bibliography

A Good Keen Man (1960)
Hang on a Minute Mate (1961)
Two in One (1962 compilation)
One of Us (1962)
There and Back (1963)
Gulf (1964) — now titled *Crocodile Country*
Scrapwaggon (1965)
The Odd Spot of Bother (1967)
Warm Beer and Other Stories (1969)
The Best of Barry Crump (1970 compilation)
A Good Keen Girl (1970)
No Reference Intended (1971)
Bastards I Have Met (1971)
Fred (1972)
Shorty (1980)
Puha Road (1982)
The Adventures of Sam Cash (1985 compilation)
Wild Pork and Watercress (1986)
Crump Collection (1987 compilation)
Barry Crump's Bedtime Yarns (1988 compilation)
Bullock Creek (1989)
The Life and Times of a Good Keen Man (1992)
Gold and Greenstone (1993)
Arty and the Fox (1994)
Forty Yarns and a Song (1995)
Mrs Windyflax and the Pungapeople (1995)
Crumpy's Fireside Companion (1996)
As the Saying Goes (1996)

Posthumous publications:
Song of a Drifter and Other Ballads (1996)
Back Down the Track (1998)
The Pungapeople of Ninety Mile Beach (1999)

index